P9-EEM-215

POINT LOMA NAZARENE UNIVERSITY
RYAN LIBRARY
3900 LOMALAND DRIVE
SAN DIEGO, CALIFORNIA 92106-2899

The Brave New Service Strategy

658.812
G983b
1/01

The Brave New Service Strategy

Aligning Customer Relationships, Market Strategies, and Business Structures

Barbara A. Gutek and Theresa Welsh

LOMA NAZARENE UNIVERSITY
WITHDRAWN
RYAN LIBRARY

AMACOM
American Management Association

New York • Atlanta • Boston • Chicago • Kansas City • San Francisco • Washington, D. C.
Brussels • Mexico City • Tokyo • Toronto

Special discounts on bulk quantities of AMACOM books are available to corporations, professional associations, and other organizations. For details, contact Special Sales Department, AMACOM, a division of American Management Association, 1601 Broadway, New York, NY 10019.
Tel.: 212-903-8316   Fax: 212-903-8083

This publication is designed to provide accurate and authoritative information in regard to the subject matter covered. It is sold with the understanding that the publisher is not engaged in rendering legal, accounting, or other professional service. If legal advice or other expert assistance is required, the services of a competent professional person should be sought.

Library of Congress Cataloging-in-Publication Data

Gutek, Barbara A.
   The brave new service strategy : aligning customer relationships, market strategies, and business structures / Barbara A. Gutek and Theresa Welsh.
      p.   cm.
   Includes bibliographical references and index.
   ISBN 0-8144-0527-4
   1. Customer services.   I. Welsh, Theresa M.
HF5415.5.G78   2000
658.8'12—dc21   99-054932

© 2000 Barbara A. Gutek and Theresa Welsh.
All rights reserved.
Printed in the United States of America.

This publication may not be reproduced,
stored in a retrieval system,
or transmitted in whole or in part,
in any form or by any means, electronic,
mechanical, photocopying, recording, or otherwise,
without the prior written permission of AMACOM,
a division of American Management Association,
1601 Broadway, New York, NY 10019.

Printing number

10   9   8   7   6   5   4   3   2   1

Contents

Preface

Why This Book?

There are many books available on service businesses that tell you how to find and retain customers, and many of them have valuable information and advice. But we wrote this book to address what we think is a serious omission from the current literature. We believe executives, along with the consultants and academics who advise them, have overlooked an important distinction in the delivery of services—one that affects all aspects of operating a service business—and is the message of this book.

What makes *The Brave New Service Strategy* unique?

- This book was written primarily for *people who operate a business.* The concepts are of benefit to anyone involved in service businesses, including executives, operations managers, professionals, consultants, and anyone who structures or oversees service delivery.
- Other books discuss how to give excellent service, but using a unique business model we call C-O-P (Customer-Organization-Provider), we tell you how to structure your business to have tight or loose links between any two components (C-O, O-P, C-P), so excellent service results naturally.
- This book is based on a solid idea backed by research. It goes beyond anecdotal evidence or standard precepts (such as "be polite when you talk to a customer"). In-

stead, it examines what happens in service interactions and shows how the business structure affects the success or failure of a business.

- This book explains the underlying reasons why service businesses do not satisfy customers. Books intended for service workers provide techniques for dealing with angry customers or explaining unpleasant facts to customers, and this kind of help is useful to service workers, but it does not help the business executive or operations manager understand the underlying problems. This book does.

The Concept: Encounter vs. Relationship

In her work as a management professor, the first author, Dr. Barbara Gutek, developed a unique insight into how service is delivered in modern America. The essence of the concept is that there are two basic ways customers and providers interact:

1. In encounters, the customer may know the organization (McDonald's, Gateway Computers, Charles Schwab Discount Brokers, for example) but receives the service from whoever is available
2. In relationships, the customer and provider know each other and have continuing contact with one another (you and your personal lawyer or accountant, for example)

Each of these is fundamentally different and has different consequences for having and keeping satisfied customers.

These two modes of service reflect the two ways a business can be organized:

1. An encounter business is organized so the customer deals with the organization, not with a specific person. Customers interact with a counter clerk or call a help line, for example. New customers come from advertising or contractual arrangements.

2. A relationship business is one in which a specific customer and provider engage in repeated transactions together. The customer comes back because he knows he will see the same service person each time. Consultants and stockbrokers generally have relationships with their customers, and new customers usually come from word of mouth.

There are consequences for customers, employers, employees, and stockholders in each of these ways of delivering service:

1. For *customers,* going to someone they know for service creates a bond that is absent when they get service from an organization where they see whoever is available. In a relationship, the customer is tightly linked with her service provider, but in an encounter, customers do not know the actual provider, although they may know the organization. This simple difference, which managers and business owners do not often fully appreciate, makes a huge difference to customers.

2. For *employees,* there is more satisfaction in having relationships with customers (whom they get to know) than in interacting with strangers all day. Such relationships can be personally and financially rewarding, but for the provider, managing these relationships and keeping their personal and professional life separate, can also be difficult. Workers in encounter style jobs such as call centers which offer few opportunities for career development must adjust to a workplace that is fast-paced and stressful. They may perceive the one-time customer in terms of negative stereotypes, making it difficult to meet the customer's needs.

3. For *employers,* designing encounter systems can be challenging and creative and can result in fast, uniform and efficient service for customers. But because the front-line employees have little reason to care about the customer, managing them is not easy and turnover rates are high. Operating a firm delivering service in relationships is easier and typically requires little management

oversight. In many industries, however, such independent firms have had a difficult time competing with well-managed encounter-style operations. Technology is increasingly important for employers of both kinds of service firms.

4. For *stockholders,* encounter businesses may be profitable, but they could be made even more profitable by using the concepts presented here rather than offering what they cannot deliver. Encounter businesses can be duplicated or franchised, while relationship businesses cannot. In a relationship business, the business may be privately owned or operated as a partnership.

Service business owners usually understand that customers value "personal service," and relationships are inherently "personal." But service encounters are not—and cannot be—personal. What customers get is not a relationship; it only looks like one. In some encounter businesses, customers are given some of the trappings of a relationship—a smiling grocery store cashier who addresses them by name, an airline counter clerk who knows where they like to sit. While these features are fine, they are a weak strategy for achieving customer satisfaction. These business owners should concentrate on the strengths of the encounter strategy. Customers like encounters because well-structured encounter businesses are fast, convenient, inexpensive, and reliable. Loyalty to a company offering service in encounters is based on these features, not on attempts to make service "personal." Making an encounter look like a relationship can be alienating, building resentment and cynicism in both customers and providers and reducing potential profits. Acting like a friend to make a sale conjures up images of slick, manipulative used-car salespersons or lawyers chasing ambulances.

Pseudo-Relationships and Enhanced Encounters

We call service delivered in an encounter structure but made to feel like a relationship a pseudo-relationship. There are of two types of pseudo-relationships:

1. Familiar procedures and surroundings (same bank, different teller)
2. Knowledge about the customer (data kept in a database)

Pseudo-relationships have become far more sophisticated in recent years through use of database technology and the concept of "relationship marketing." Relationships are the model for all types of service, but encounter businesses should not claim they have a relationship with their customers. Instead, they should focus on the strengths of encounters—low cost, fast and reliable service, convenience, and professional management—to create what we call *enhanced encounters.*

Services don't have to be personal to be popular with customers and profitable for owners. Whole industries from eyewear to pharmacy have changed. Many of them did it by taking advantage of changes (in technology, government regulations, public taste, etc.) that opened an opportunity to bring a service to more people than could ever get that service through relationships.

Using these concepts, we offer a road map for service businesses so they can consider whether to offer service in encounters, relationships, or both. Some companies can gain a competitive advantage by offering service to some or all of their customers in relationships rather than in encounters. Customers are getting a shrinking percentage of their service transactions in relationships, which makes this simple format even more valuable. For many small entrepreneurs as well as larger professional firms, relationship businesses can give an edge, even over big chains. Relationship businesses can thrive with a much smaller clientele than encounter businesses, and they can market to those who can afford the cost of a relationship service.

In other cases, entrepreneurs can take a type of service traditionally offered in unsophisticated mom-and-pop shops and apply new technology and processes to deliver the service in a more convenient and lower-cost encounter structure. Just take a look at the many successful chain businesses that have made America incredibly prosperous in the 1990s.

The Plan of the Book

Services dominate the economy and many are financially successful, but customers still express dissatisfaction with the services they receive. Through ten chapters, this book explores the reasons for this and what we can do about it.

Chapter One looks at customer perception of some common business practices that result from mistaken ideas about what constitutes a relationship. At one time, all service transactions were in relationships, so this became the model. As the Industrial Revolution changed the way goods were produced, from hand-made to mass-produced, service followed a similar path. Chain businesses offer the same kind of efficient, standard operation as mass production manufacturing. Service at the chains is in encounters, not relationships.

Chapter Two explores in depth the differences between relationships and encounters. It explains that service involves an individual customer, an individual service provider, and an organization joined by tight or loose links. Organizations sometimes exert very little control, as is often the case when providers work with customers in relationships, or they can be strongly controlling, which is typical of encounters.

Chapter Three pulls together what was learned in Chapters One and Two and presents a model of every type of service business, using a triangle to show connections. In a relationship, the link between customer and provider is tight, but this link is always loose in an encounter. Encounters can be pseudo-relationships through a tight link between the customer and the organization.

In Chapter Four, we discuss encounter businesses, the most common strategy for delivering service and where we find the most dissatisfied customers. We look at what drives the design of service processes and what providers and customers want from an encounter business. What happens when the service process does not meet their needs? The chapter also explores specific business areas (eyewear, travel service, stock trading, and others) where delivery has been shifting from relationship to encounter, explaining how and why this happened. These examples suggest that opportunities exist in other areas to do the same.

In Chapter Five, "Machine Providers: Managing the Automated Service Process," we look at encounters, but examine one specific kind: when the individual service provider is replaced by a machine. This class of encounter, when used strategically, can be highly successful but also has its own set of problems. Encounters exist to make cheaper, more efficient service available to large numbers of customers, and using automated processes accomplishes that. We discuss the many ways businesses have implemented, or plan to implement, automatic service. We look at use of computers, particularly the Internet, as a means of providing service, along with the results for customers, providers, and organizations.

Chapter Six, "From Pseudo-Relationships to Enhanced Encounters: Forging the Customer-Organization Link," discusses how efforts by organizations to build "relationships" can end up being alienating. We explore the difference between being "pseudo" and using a business strategy that creates customer loyalty. You will learn how to make pseudo-relationships more satisfying for customers and more profitable for your business by creating enhanced encounters.

Relationship businesses are the oldest format and still work. Chapter Seven discusses how to have success in a service business built on real relationships between providers and customers.

Clearly technology is part of any service business and is becoming more important as we approach the new millennium. Chapter Eight discusses how use of technology is changing the way you should operate your service business. Technology has spawned new ways of providing service such as call centers and Web sites. The ways business owners choose to use technology affect both providers and customers.

Service is not always in the context of a customer and an organization, but it can be within an organization or between organizations. Chapter Nine looks at internal service and service between companies. It discusses outsourcing of service units and how relationships and encounters fit.

What does the future of service look like? Will customers

continue to feel dissatisfied? Chapter Ten brings us back to the central question and discusses the trends that will be important for success in the years beyond 2000.

Business Owners, Operations Managers, Consultants Need This Information

For anyone who is in a service business or who is thinking of starting a service business, making the right choice on how to structure the service is vitally important. Methods of dealing with customers that make business sense to the owner may look very different to the customer. Our aim is to give you a road map for the future and help you see your business through the eyes of your customers. What you discover in these pages may surprise you.

There are millions of entrepreneurs, business owners, executives, operations managers, and potential business owners who can put these concepts to work right away. Small and medium-sized businesses, which cannot afford expensive consulting services, may benefit the most. While having a relationship with a person and having a "relationship" with a firm may seem quite similar to a business owner, they provide very different experiences for customers. This vital—and misunderstood—distinction between the two fundamental ways to deliver service is the catalyst to structuring the business for maximum success. Only by understanding and building the correct framework can you be confident of attracting and keeping customers—and this book will help you do it.

Chapter One

Service Businesses: Successful but Still Merely Adequate?

Why So Much Dissatisfaction?

As a nation, we've moved into a service economy, and businesses everywhere want to be customer-focused and customer-driven. So why is it that so many people feel service is getting worse all the time? The American Customer Satisfaction Index, which annually tracks people's perception of service, shows a decline in satisfaction. Nor do companies think they are delivering quality service. Research by the American Management Association (AMA) found half of the companies surveyed about their customer service rated themselves as only "adequate." In another survey of 181 U.S. service firms, senior executives rated "being a leader in customer service" as the most important element in their business vision.[1] Both businesses and the customers they serve value good service, but the companies don't deliver it and the customers are not satisfied. What's going on here?

The problem with service is pervasive. It doesn't matter if we're talking about a trip to the doctor, a visit to the shopping mall, a phone call to the gas company, or a stop for fast food. We might be discussing ordering luggage or candy from a Web site or banking online. Wherever people are being served by a service worker or an automated process, there are complaints. Service, we are told, is impersonal. No one cares anymore. There is a persistent belief that it used to be different, that once upon a time, there was a golden age of service when waitresses always got the order right, doctors were all like the caring 1950s TV doctor, and butchers knew their customers by name.

This book is an answer to the questions of why people feel so negatively about service and explains what businesses can do about it. Customer dissatisfaction has its roots in a major change in America and the industrialized world, a change in the way people relate to one another in service transactions. Service involves two people, a provider and a customer. Unlike manufacturing, the "product" is consumed at the time it is delivered. The person who provides the service—the provider—is part of the product. That is apparent in service transactions between people who know one another. If you've had the same accountant for many years, that provider knows you and your habits and preferences. You know what papers to bring when you see your accountant and how the meeting will proceed. This is an example of one of the ways—the traditional way—that service can occur.

Compare that with what happens when you stop at McDonald's. You wait in line and talk briefly with a counter person, move aside to wait for your food, then carry it to a table. This process, well known by customers and duplicated in identical restaurants all over the world, is efficient. It gets the job done, but it is different in a fundamental way from seeing your accountant.

These examples illustrate the two ways service happens:

1. Relationships—the traditional kind of service: Customers see the same person each time and both parties expect to continue doing business together.
2. Encounters—the new form of service pioneered by corporations where providers and customers are interchangeable; the customer sees whichever provider is available.

Will reverting back to doing business in relationships solve our problems? No, but understanding this distinction is important in sorting out why service gets such poor marks. The widespread belief that better service existed in "the good old days" has some basis in fact but not because service was always good in the past. Almost all service was once based on relationships and the infrequent transactions between strangers were often less satisfactory than encounter service is today. Chain businesses like McDonald's, by establishing standards for a business, have actually resulted in better service than people ever got when their stagecoach stopped at the inn for the night.

Pretending It's a Relationship

Northwest Airlines is one of many companies that have tried to build good will by claiming they have a "relationship" with customers. But airlines, like fast food restaurants, are encounter businesses, with processes designed to move many people through the system as efficiently as possible. A 1998 strike by Northwest pilots left many customers angered by canceled flights and poor treatment. Northwest sent letters making special offers to many of its customers, including *Detroit News* columnist Laura Berman (Detroit is a major hub for Northwest). Berman's reply to Northwest's letter, in the form of a newspaper column, illustrates how some customers react to the idea that they have a "relationship" with an encounter business.

Mr. Rick Dow
Vice-President, Marketing and Advertising
Northwest Airlines

Dear Mr. Dow:

Boy, was I excited when I read your letter yesterday.

You wrote that because of my "special relationship" with Northwest and KLM Airlines, you were pleased to offer me a complimentary membership in WorldPerks Gold. Needless to say, I'm the person who's really pleased.

These perks are tantalizing: unlimited first-class upgrades, a 100-percent mileage bonus whenever I fly Northwest/KLM, first-class check-in when I'm flying coach, first-class companion upgrades, even gold luggage tags that get my bags special handling. Last week, I was squished in the back with the screaming babies, begging for the full can of Fresca. Today, I'm sitting pretty in Seat 1B with free Chardonnay and flight attendants greeting me by name.

But, uh, Mr. Dow, this offer smells funny.

Everybody knows you don't give a gold membership to every disgruntled flier who whines about Northwest's service. No, World-Perks Gold membership is a trophy, hard-won by serious road warriors who fly 100,000 miles a year to reach the WorldPerks summit.

These are travelers who suffer endless waits in airports, eat hot dogs standing up, sleep three or four nights in hotels every week, and spend premium dollars for their seats. You don't give them WorldPerks Gold: They earn it, one misery at a time.

Compare that with my "special relationship" with Northwest: In 1998, according to your automated WorldPerks line, I've flown 3,854 miles in coach, using discounted leisure fares. As customers go, I'm not worth two packs of honey-roasted peanuts.

So why are you being so nice?

Maybe because my Sept. 6 column described how Metro Detroiters, battered by Northwest's labor problems and a strike, were highly unsympathetic to your airline. To many of us accustomed to indifferent service, canceled flights, and America's worst airport, Northwest Airlines has become an object lesson in the evil of monopolies.

And Northwest does have a history of crude public relations efforts. Remember that ill-conceived attempt to give away 1,300 domestic tickets to civic and government leaders last May on Mackinac Island?

I asked author Elmore Leonard, who mocked Northwest breakfast sandwiches in one of his novels, whether he got World-Perks Gold club membership after being quoted in that Sept. 6 column. He said no. No gold card, no luggage tags, no free coupons or upgrades. "I didn't get any of that," he observed dryly, "because I don't write a newspaper column."

I know what he means. And although Seat 1B is enticing, I must decline your generous offer. It's too generous—and typifies what's wrong with your company's culture. Frankly, Mr. Dow, we don't have a "special relationship."

If you are serious about winning any kind of customer loyalty in Metro Detroit, you should provide consistent service. Take off on time. Stop canceling flights for "mechanical problems." Apologize for mistakes. Stop snarling at us.

We depend on you because we have no choice. If you want customer satisfaction, earn it fairly: one flight at a time.[2]

Management may have thought these offers build a "relationship" that would keep customers like Berman from defecting to other airlines, but airline customers are still dealing with strangers. Having strangers give your luggage special handling and hand you a glass of wine as you relax in the comfort of first class might be preferable to waiting in a long line of jostling, anxious people and squeezing into a too-small seat, but it does not turn an encounter into a relationship.

Nor does Berman or any other Northwest customer have a relationship with the vice-president of marketing who sent out the letters. Only the most naïve people would be flattered by the suggestion that they have a relationship with an organization's vice-president, whom they have never met, and some may be insulted by such an obviously ridiculous notion.

What the airline has done is confuse a connection between a customer and an organization with a relationship. People have relationships with people. An organization is not a person. Therefore, it follows that neither Laura Berman nor any other Northwest passenger has a relationship with Northwest Airlines.

What Northwest is doing with this letter is what many companies are doing to combat the "impersonal service" label. They keep data on customers, then make them an offer tailored to that customer in some way. To make it feel personal, the company claims to have a relationship with the customer. But that's not what it is. We call it a "pseudo-relationship," an encounter made to look or feel more like a relationship. Passengers do not personally know the ticket seller, the onboard steward, the pilot, the luggage handler, or anyone else they deal with in the course of taking a flight from one city to another.

Does that mean there is nothing an airline can do to make the encounter more pleasant for their customers? Of course it doesn't. Encounter customers are generally satisfied (if not actually happy) if they understand the process and if the process works as it should. Note that Berman thought the airline should clean up its act for *all* customers (i.e., provide consistent service, take off on time). In encounter businesses, service cannot be chaotic. While some customers can be given extras, there must be an underlying set of procedures that work for everyone.

Frequent customers can be rewarded. If the rewards have a standard set of requirements understood by all and the rewards are delivered as promised, this can be an effective way to keep customers. In its letter, Northwest offered extra frequent flyer miles, upgrades to first class, faster check-in, and gold luggage tags. In making this offer to Laura Berman, Northwest made two mistakes:

1. It offered the extras to someone who did not fit the set of standards for who should get them, leaving the airline open to charges of unequal and therefore unfair treatment.
2. It confused the issue by claiming it was giving these extras because of a "special relationship" between the airline and the customer.

Berman perceived the offer as a bribe, since she felt she did not qualify for the extras. She was not fooled into thinking she had a "relationship" (let alone a "special" relationship) with the airline.

While the offer she got was apparently not based on her past spending, but on her influence as a columnist, the idea of treating customers differently based on their value to the company is a popular marketing concept. Northwest Airlines stepped over the line by appearing to have no standards for who gets an offer. The incident Berman mentioned in her letter in which Northwest gave away tickets to attendees at a conference on Mackinac Island contributed to that perception. The tickets were given away at random as a supposed goodwill gesture, but ended up offending people who were not at the conference and did not get tickets and caused problems for those who took them. Many of these people's employers did not find accepting such a valuable gift ethical. Some attendees were offended by the "gift" (which they, like Berman, felt was a bribe) and refused the tickets.

It is important that encounter businesses have standards. Encounter businesses are egalitarian by design; they must treat everyone the same, or they risk the wrath of customers.

Relationship businesses operate differently. When customers have an actual relationship with a provider (because they see that same provider each time they receive the service), the provider can tailor the service for each customer. In other words, the service can be unequal. The stock broker who has a customer with a large and active portfolio will give that customer more time than he gives a customer with a modest and relatively inactive portfolio. But both customers are satisfied if each receives the exact service they need.

In the new service economy, people have fewer service relationships. Most of their service transactions are in the encounter format, but because relationships serve as the model for all kinds of service, both service businesses and their customers confuse patronizing a particular service organization—like Northwest Airlines or Hyatt Hotels—with having a relationship. In encounters where the customer has repeated transactions with one organization, the customer builds a tight link with that organization but not with any particular provider who works for the organization. A relationship business is one in which the customer sees the same *provider* (not just patronizes the same *organization*) each time.

Despite claims by companies that they are building what they like to call a "relationship" with customers, the truth is that most service is no longer personal and consists of stranger serving stranger. None of us like to admit this because we would rather cling to the notion that we have relationships, and companies exploit this desire in their marketing efforts. Some people might be drawn into this relationship rhetoric because they really want what relationships offer, but most people—like

Laura Berman—are not. Most people intuitively sense the difference between relationships and encounters even if they do not use these terms. And most people know they have fewer and fewer service relationships.

What is the cause of this decrease in service relationships? It is connected to the rise of the corporation as a business form and the proliferation of chain businesses. Chains offer customers something they want—low price and convenience. Their fresh approaches are part of the American success story. But they also represent a discontinuity in the way customers and providers interact. What forces were behind the rise of chain businesses? The roots lie deep in our past, when service went from being a relationship between providers who made items by hand and knew their customers personally, to a time when that no longer worked. The Industrial Revolution changed everything.

From Personal Service to Mass-Produced Services

The Industrial Revolution changed the way people worked and this, in turn, changed the way people received service. At one time, almost all service workers were independent business people: sewing clothes, making shoes, operating the general store, or hammering out tools in a blacksmith shop. These service providers did not work for a company; they worked for themselves and knew their customers personally. Because of this, these providers had good reasons to deliver what they promised. They depended on their good reputation to get and keep customers.

But along came new technologies that could mechanize some kinds of work, beginning with the textile industry. Cloth had been woven by hand by individual workers, but a number of inventions during the 1700s mechanized the process, resulting in the power loom. Machines were invented to replace other kinds of hand labor as well throughout the 1800s as the medieval guild system that had controlled who could enter common occupations gradually disappeared.

When mechanization first began to replace craftspersons, work habits had to change. This did not happen right way. It took some time before workers took seriously the idea of showing up every day at a specific time and working steadily for the benefit of an organization. In Great Britain, where the Industrial Revolution was born, workers in the mills in the 1840s were absent 20 percent of the year. Absenteeism averaged 33 percent in the week after workers received their monthly pay. In America, turnover rates in early factories were about the same as they are at fast food restaurants today. In the New York garment district in 1912, the turnover rate was 232 percent, and in Henry Ford's auto factory of 1913, it was 370 percent. (There was a very good reason Henry Ford offered to pay $5 a day wages—he was trying to reduce absenteeism.)[3] The shift from a nation of independent workers to a nation of wage earners did not come quickly or easily.

Here are some of the effects of this shift that created today's environment of encounter businesses:

1. Work moving to factories where goods were mass-produced, which meant work was separate from home
2. The need for capital to finance factory machinery, giving rise to the corporation as the dominant business form
3. The need for professional managers to plan and supervise the work done in factories, creating a new career field called management
4. Customers dealing with the goods-seller instead of the goods-maker
5. Women entering the workforce as mass-produced goods and new service businesses reduced the work that had to be done at home
6. An ever-increasing emphasis on efficiency of production to generate profits for the shareholders who financed corporations

In the industrial economy that replaced the agricultural way of life, families became units of consumption rather than production. As people moved from farm to city, they became customers for many kinds of goods and services.

The division of labor that characterized factories meant the workers did not need to understand the products they made.

Their part in making the product was just one step in the manufacturing process. The more that work could be broken down into small repetitive tasks, the more "efficient" it became. Henry Ford's assembly line exemplified efficiency and was hailed as the work of a genius. Each worker performed one task over and over. A worker's actual skills were unimportant, and he or she did not have a chance to learn new skills. Workers could spend forty years on the same job doing the same thing. But they were well paid and eventually the corporation provided them with useful benefits. For many workers, it was a good trade-off. American auto workers became the best paid unskilled workers in the world.

Changes for Customers

What exactly changed for customers? The artisans who made an item by hand knew their customers personally; whereas factory workers don't meet the people who buy the products they make. The products of artisans and craftspersons are customized; the products that are mass-produced are uniform and predictable. Uniformity became a goal to strive for: each light bulb made to the same specifications, each telephone receiver the same, each Oreo cookie exactly like every other, and later, each Big Mac made in the same way.

People stopped buying goods directly from the person who made them, but many services remained personal. People got to know the barber, the bakery owner, the butcher, the grocer and got advice from the guy at the hardware store. The Fuller Brush man, the milkman, and the vacuum cleaner salesman even came right to their door. Some people had bread delivered fresh from the bakery or groceries brought to their door. Many neighborhood businesses would extend credit to customers who couldn't pay right away. All of these services were available to ordinary working people.

Most of these businesses were small, family-owned operations, each with its own way of doing things and not requiring a lot of promotion or management. And they were not profitable for the owners in the way chain businesses are today. The owner of a neighborhood shoe store was not generally concerned with "growing the business." His goal was to make a living and service his customers.

Was Service Better in the "Good Old Days"?

If you had lived in the days of America's pioneers and had to travel, you would find leaving your circle of acquaintances a harrowing experience. The providers you encountered along the way would not know you. There would be no reliable Holiday Inn to provide a clean room and no cluster of fast food places to offer a quick and inexpensive meal. Instead, you would stop at a tavern or inn where, in contrast to your friendly hometown, you would be faced with strangers. You were at their mercy if the room was less than cozy and clean, the coffee was made from dish water, and bed bugs were crawling over the breakfast rolls. Those were exactly the conditions Carrie Stearns encountered in her 1853 journey by stagecoach from Ohio to the Kansas "frontier."[4]

The good service you got back home was because you had a relationship with the shoemaker, the blacksmith, and the storekeeper. The poor service on the road was because you did *not* have a relationship with the providers; they were strangers. Service in relationships worked, but service in encounters was not reliable. It was left to the corporation and its invention of chain businesses with standardized service processes to bring reliability to encounter service.

The Rise of Corporations

The high cost of mass production spawned the growth of a new institution, the modern corporation. Corporations are desirable when an enterprise requires more investment than one person can make. Their origin has been variously traced to the ecclesiastical universities of the Middle Ages that grew out of isolated monasteries and were chartered by kings, or to the building and supplying of ships for long voyages and the need to limit liability for the slow and risky business of sailing the seas and searching out new lands. Corporations, as they evolved in America, were different from neighborhood businesses in being owned by outsiders. Where stores and services had been grounded in a local community, shareholders in a corporation often had no interest in the community where the business was located.

The first corporations existed to do manufacturing, and this became a model for later corporations that provided a service. At the beginning of the twentieth century, men like Theodore N. Vail of AT&T, Walter Teagle of Standard Oil of New Jersey, Alfred P. Sloan of General Motors, and Andrew Carnegie, the steel baron, were establishing the corporate business form. General Motors' Sloan is credited with saying the "primary object" of the corporation was to make money. These business organizations were financed by shareholders who expected a return.

Jobs in twentieth century urban America were mainly a byproduct of the corporation. Daniel Bell, in his brilliant 1973 work, *The Coming of the Post Industrial Society*, writes: "In place of the farmer came the industrial worker, and for the last hundred years or so the vicissitudes of the industrial worker—his claims to dignity and status, his demand for a rising share of industrial returns, his desire for a voice in the conditions which affected his work and the conditions of employment—have marked the social struggles of the century."

Efficiency

Corporations, unlike neighborhood businesses, were concerned about worker efficiency since they had to make a profit for their shareholder investors. Many corporate managers listened to the ideas of Frederick W. Taylor in the 1890s. Taylor, a mechanical engineer for the Midvale Steel Company, developed his theories over many years but got his main insight while watching the movements of immigrants loading pig iron at a steel mill. Taylor used his system of "time study" to determine that a "first-class workman" ought to be able to handle 47 tons of steel a day. But the actual workers were handling only 12.5 tons per day. How to get them to do the work Taylor believed they were capable of doing? He began by selecting one worker he felt could handle 47 tons per day. He offered this workman, who had been getting $1.15 per day, a raise to $1.85 per day if he would follow all orders of a supervisor. The supervisor set the pace of work, and the workman did indeed load 47 tons per day. Other "first-class" workmen were trained to do the same, and production increased from 12 tons to 47 tons loaded per man per day.

Taylor had begun his career as a workman himself and worked his way up as foreman and then as engineer. He was thoroughly convinced that workers deliberately did less work than they were capable of doing (this was called "soldiering"). He felt by providing an economic incentive for them to work harder, they would produce more and the company would then make more money. This would end the antagonism between management and labor; they would not have to squabble over how to divide the surplus as there would be enough for everyone.

Taylor used a stop watch to calculate the best time for many kinds of work, eventually standardizing motions down to a hundredth of a minute, covering the time it took to climb a ladder, walk to a desk, or read a gauge. Such studies became known as "time studies" and were used by many industries to determine just how long a given task should take. Later, Frank and Lillian Gilbreth, influenced by Taylor, set up "micromotion studies," using a motion picture camera (new technology at the time) to record the motions of workers as they went about their tasks. The Gilbreths felt their work should be used alongside Taylor's to find the best way to do each job. Managers eventually combined these into what became known as "time and motion studies."

Taylor based his determinations of time on the basis of "a first-class man in favorable conditions." Determining the "favorable conditions" was the job of management, which had to decide the flow of work, the proper incentive for workers, and how to train workers. Giving testimony before the U.S. Congress in 1911, Taylor stated:

> Both sides must recognize as essential the substitution of exact scientific investigation and knowledge for the old individual judgment or opinion of either the workman or the boss, in all matters relating to the work done. . . .

Although Taylor thought it was all right to allocate more of the profits obtained from the new efficiency to management than to labor, his system always included more money for workers who performed at their best. He felt the reward should closely follow the actual work and favored paying piece rates beyond a certain standard level of output. He wanted to do away with any favoritism in pay and, in today's parlance, to "pay for performance." He called his system "scientific management."

"Efficiency" gained popularity precisely because it is an idea that can be applied to both human and machine labor. It fit the times. In 1912, *Harper's Magazine* wrote: "Big things are happening in this country. With the spreading of the movement toward greater efficiency, a new and highly improved era in national life has begun."[5]

Superhighways built in the 1950s joined cities together and gave Americans new mobility. The suburbs were built, beginning with the Levittowns in New York, Pennsylvania, and New Jersey. The Levittown houses, built by Levitt and Sons in the 1950s, used construction workers who each specialized in one task and made use of prefabricated sections. The Levitts built houses the way Henry Ford built cars, except the workers moved from house to house doing their part. The result was a "new town" of look-alike, but affordable, houses. Subdivisions sprouted along the big four-lane highways and expressways, as suburbs, were built across America. Main Street and neighborhood stores declined, and malls appeared. A new kind of business—look-alike chain businesses—began to blossom along the highways. Americans were on the move, and one of the places they liked to visit was McDonald's.

McDonald's did not invent franchising or the fast food idea. A&W root beer stands and Dairy Queen were there first. But Ray Kroc, who bought McDonald's from its original owners, perfected the idea of uniformity in food service. Every McDonald's had to operate in the same way. He spelled out exactly how franchisees were to grill the hamburgers, right down to putting down the hamburger patties in six rows of six patties on the grill and flipping the third row first because it is closest to the heating element. Each hamburger would have a quarter ounce of onions placed on top. The fries had to be made of the same kind of potato and be cut nine thirty-seconds of an inch thick. His operations manual had to be followed exactly, ensuring that McDonald's customers could count on getting the same burger and fries at each restaurant. Ray Kroc became very rich by making everything the same, and Americans loved the result. McDonald's used to post on its golden arches the number of hamburgers sold until the number got so big the signs just said "billions and billions served." Today, 50 percent of Americans live within five minutes of a McDonald's restaurant.

McDonald's helped bring about the idea that uniformity in a service, like uniformity of an industrial product, is good. Other service businesses tried the same tactic. American Airlines talked about a "reservation product." A spokesperson declared, "We at American aim at a certain level of standardization." Marriott Hotels decided to make "core services and perks consistent at 207 U.S. hotels."[6] This included such items as regular hours for room service and health clubs, free morning coffee, incoming faxes, and express checkout.

The year 1956 marks the first time white collar and service workers outnumbered blue collar workers. The rest of the century saw fewer and fewer 'help wanted' signs outside factories and more ads for work in sales, advertising, entertainment, restaurants, medical, computers, and all kinds of customer service.

America shifted from a manufacturing economy to a service economy. By 1998, more than 75 percent of all American workers were working in services. Many kinds of work once done in the home by family members have become businesses servicing the needs of two-income families. We now have professional child care workers in place of stay-at-home moms, security companies that protect our homes and property instead of neighbors keeping an eye on it, lawn and landscaping services to mow our lawns and tend our flowers instead of doing it ourselves, take-out food instead of home cooking (sixty-six take-out meals per person in 1997), and even learning centers to help our kids with their homework when mom and dad don't have time.

Mass Produced Service in the Information Age

Chain Businesses Take Over

Chain businesses have taken over the highways of America. To-day's consumers zip along the freeways built to move products from factories to warehouses, on their way to work, home, school, shopping malls, restaurants, sports arenas and places of entertainment, or to a vacation destination. Along the way, they can stop at McDonald's or eat in a place with waitresses like Denny's or Chili's. Each expressway stop has its cluster of fast-food chain restaurants, motels, and gas stations. At these establishments, Americans can get food, gas, and a room for the night quickly and predictably—where the coffee is not made from dishwater and there are no roaches lurking under the croissants. While the proliferation of chains has taken away the uniqueness of place that the old highways had, it has given ordinary Americans a chance to travel at reasonable prices and spend a smaller percentage of their income on food and clothing than ever before.

Today, the average American consumes twice as much as people consumed at the end of World War II, a tribute to the economy's ability to continue creating new products and jobs.[7] This process has been at work in the rest of the industrialized world as well.

"Knowledge Workers"

The term "service worker" covers a broad area. As work has changed from manual work associated with manufacturing to more "brain" work, a larger proportion of service work is done by people who are educated and well-paid. What workers produce becomes largely intangible as we climb ever higher levels of economic abstraction. Money is a representation of wealth. Credit and debit cards are representations of money. Now Internet transactions are another abstraction of money. In society as a whole, an explosion of multimedia technology reduces the distinction between reality and the digital world. Images of reality replace reality in politics, fashion, and recreation. Information is both the input and the output.

Corporate assets are increasingly viewed as intellectual property, not factories, buildings, or machinery. People who can create these assets are those whom corporations want to employ. Routine tasks, even highly skilled tasks like computer programming, can be left to contract workers or outsourced to the new service businesses that "partner" with today's corporations.

Peter Drucker popularized the term "knowledge workers" to describe workers with computer skills whose jobs involved manipulating information. The work involved in moving information products is mainly mental work. The modern office building is a hive of people sitting at computers, dealing with transactions with people in other physical locations and moving around bits of data, while factories are populated with robots and machines and only relatively few people.

Late twentieth century technology—computers, fax, cellular phones, the Internet—and new kinds of employment are bringing work back to the home. Many kinds of service work do not have to be done from an office building. Call centers, order tracking, or help desks, for instance, can be operated from anywhere—a small town in Idaho or in workers' homes scattered about the country. Some small towns, like Telluride, Colorado, have recruited and attracted well-heeled telecommuters. It seems we are coming full circle, with work and home life merging once again for many Information Age workers.

Most families now count on two incomes to help cushion the shock of frequent job changes and short-term contract jobs. The temporary help agency, Manpower, has been called the country's largest employer. With more than 3,000 offices in fifty countries, Manpower supplies workers of all kinds from food service to engineers. This is a trend that shows no signs of slowing down.

There is a new social mobility. People change careers, residences, families, and even identities with dizzying speed. Old support systems—community, family, church, and company—can no longer be relied on. No one really expects to stay at one company for an entire career. The downsizing craze has taught workers to look out for themselves. Loyalty—workers caring about their company and companies taking care of their workers—has eroded. "Service career" could be an oxymoron in the twenty-first century.

New Kinds of Service Delivery

How does a service business owner cope with these new realities? Managing with fewer workers is one answer. New technologies can replace human labor with machine labor. The ubiquitous ATM machine, available at every 7-Eleven and outside every bank, is replacing bank tellers. The phone tree ("press one to talk to a service representative, press two to place an order, press three to . . .") is replacing receptionists. Books, tools, plumbing supplies, gourmet coffee, and imported cigars are just some of the products being successfully sold from Web sites. Some high tech products have moved totally to the Web. Egghead Software, for example, has closed all its retail stores and operates only on the Internet.

Service transactions have become more impersonal. Instead of the neighborhood restaurant, people eat fast food. They make a stop at a no-appointment chain hair salon and get a haircut from the next available barber/beautician. They come home and use their computer to check how their stocks are doing through an online broker service. The customers' transactions are with an organization, not a specific person, and the organization must build some trust with these customers to keep them.

The shoemaker and blacksmith in George Washington's day also worked to build trust, but they did it by knowing their customers and supplying a custom product. In the world of colonial America, getting service was a different kind of experience for the customer than going to Wendy's or buying shoes at Payless is today. Today's counter clerks don't know their customers, and their customers don't know them.

Professional Services

What about professional services? Doctors, lawyers, architects, and psychologists offer service, too, and their work requires many years of education and necessarily involves a degree of customization for each customer. Customers often want to build a relationship with these kinds of providers, not just see whoever is available. But professional services, as well, under the direction of managers, respond to pressures to be more "efficient" and deliver the service for less cost. When these services are offered through an organization, managers can define a process for delivering the service, just as they do at McDonald's.

Consider the case of doctors, who are finding it harder to exist in small or solo practices. Medical care is dispensed mainly through managed care companies, large well-funded organizations that design and dictate every aspect of the service. While the doctors often dislike this kind of arrangement, there is little they can do to stop it when faced with consumers who cannot afford their prices. Medical care is a special case, since many consumers don't like managed care either. The third-party payers—insurance companies, corporations, and the government—are calling the shots. Their interest is in reducing costs and increasing efficiency, while delivering consistent, quality care.

When customers have to pay for services, many are interested in ways to lower the cost. No frills walk-in medical clinics appeal to people who have large deductibles, minimal insurance that doesn't cover office visits, or no insurance. The customer trades off the personal relationship with the doctor to get a lower price. At the other end of the scale, some doctors have started deluxe practices in which they take care of all the customers' medical needs and give each patient as much time as needed in return for a monthly fee that is totally outside the insurance system. These are small limited practices, but the doctors have the satisfaction of operating in their own way, providing good service without having to answer to an HMO financial manager or worry about efficiency. Raising the price and keeping it personal is one answer to the worker shortage, since this more independent way of operating will always attract providers. But it can attract only wealthy customers, leaving a vast number of consumers patronizing cheaper chain services.

What About the Customers?

Do customers benefit from service being delivered in a standardized way through large organizations? It is an important question because Americans spend a large part of their time and income being customers. The average household spends 45 percent of its income on services. We all play the role of customer over and over at work and in our personal life.[8]

Being a customer includes such tasks as getting your driver's license renewed, going to the dentist, making travel reservations, or standing in line to buy concert tickets. Students in college are customers of that college, just as we are all customers of the medical practitioners we see, even if they prefer to call us "patients."

There is no doubt that the existence of large organizations delivering service in an efficient manner has resulted in a plethora of low-cost services. Jiffy Lube pioneered the quick oil change business after its founder noticed how many service stations no longer provided mechanic services and that customers were dissatisfied with the slow and messy service of those that did. Taking a cue from Frederick Taylor, the Jiffy Lube workspace is designed for a three-person crew to handle eighty-five cars per day using a minimum of motions. Economizing on movements was also a goal of Xerox when the company benchmarked its warehouse operation against that of catalog clothier L.L. Bean. As a result, Xerox redesigned its warehouses to shorten the distance order fillers have to walk to get to materials and began arranging parts according to how often they were ordered. This has helped them deliver goods at a lower price.

Encounter businesses provide everyone with low cost service, whether it's fixing a car, cutting hair, serving dinner, or putting a cast on a broken leg. These are services many could not afford if they were available only through a one-to-one personal relationship.

No Longer Personal

Despite the fact that service is typically delivered through organizations, not by someone the customer knows, personal service—provider and customer having a "relationship"—is still held up as the ideal. Businesses talk about having a "relationship" with customers they don't know personally. Books and training materials on customer service often make comparisons with the "village shopkeeper" in discussing how to make customers feel like a business cares about them.

A book on online service, *Online Customer Care*, begins with such a comparison:

> Unlike the owner of the village store, the average call center agent is rarely knowledgeable about the particular needs of certain customers, their personal likes and dislikes, or trials and tribulations in their everyday lives. Impersonal, often sharing its secrets reluctantly, the agent's computer does not innately care whether Judy just lost her job, or Jack went to school with the store owner's father, or that Allison prefers the village store atmosphere to the cheaper and better-stocked supermarket. The call center computer system was not built to consider human circumstances.[9]

Real relationships have not disappeared, of course. You have real relationships with your family, friends, neighbors, and coworkers. And sometimes consumers have real relationships with service providers such as a family physician, an accountant who regularly provides tax advice, or a hairdresser who has been cutting and coloring their hair for years. People still do business with people they know, but they have fewer real relationships and more of what we call encounters.

Businesses like to claim their service is "personal" because they correctly assume that is what customers prefer. In research done at the University of Arizona, researchers questioned people about transactions they had with seven types of service providers—hairstylist, physician, mechanic, travel agent, bank employee, academic advisor, and insurance agent. Those who had a personal relationship with the provider had more interactions and were more satisfied than those who didn't. Not everyone has service relationships, but almost everyone in the study reported having at least one relationship in the services covered.

What characterizes a service relationship? It is the expectation of repeated interaction *with the same person.* This is not the same as repeated interaction *with the same organization.* In today's chain business, the organization substitutes for the person. Marketing builds an image for the company and its service to attract customers. *The Burgers are Better at Burger King, You're in Good Hands with Allstate, You'll Never Have a Better Neighbor Than Wal-Mart, Did Somebody Say McDonald's?* The organization must make the customers feel good about the organization. It does not want to call attention to the actual provider. The friendly Wal-Mart greeter in the commercial is not the same person the customer will see when he or she goes to Wal-Mart. The smiling kid behind the counter in the Burger King commercial is not the same kid the customer will see when he or she heads for lunch at Burger King.

Like the factory workers of yesterday, today's "fast food" service workers must be replaceable. Their work is one step of a process designed by a professional manager. Having enough workers is important, but an individual person in the provider role is not. It is the uniformity and predictability of the service that builds customer trust and makes the business profitable. Mass-produced products made huge profits in the Industrial Age, and mass-produced service is making huge profits today. But people still yearn for "personal" service, and companies still want customers to think they're getting it.

Conclusion

Customers are dissatisfied with service, but that dissatisfaction is rooted in societal changes in our industrial past. Trying to make service personal when it is structured to be fast and impersonal does not work. Service businesses must instead build on the strengths of their particular structure, whether they offer service in encounters or in relationships.

To summarize, the evolution of service has followed the major shifts in society:

1. Society went from agricultural to industrial, and service went from customers knowing the providers who made

goods by hand to knowing the persons selling the goods in neighborhood stores.

2. The next shift was from industrial to post-industrial and customers saw the rise of chain businesses; service began a changeover from customers knowing the service person to getting service from strangers.

3. Society is now moving from a post-industrial economy to the Information Age, and service is moving further away from face-to-face transactions to more *pseudo-relationships*, where companies use data about customers to tailor offers.

Society has moved from the infrequent and personal contacts of agricultural communities to the neighborly friendliness of the industrial period to the rise of encounter-style chain businesses of the latter half of the twentieth century and, finally, to the emerging new cyber businesses that transcend time and place.

How can your business benefit from an understanding of the evolution of service delivery? The rest of this book examines the basic ways you can service your customers—in relationships, in encounters, and in what may be the dominant format of the new millennium, the pseudo-relationship, and its more refined cousin, the "enhanced encounter."

Notes

1. "Service in the U.S." A study of service practice and performance in the United States by the London Business School at the University of Southern California and the University of North Carolina, May 1997.

2. Berman, Laura. "Dear Northwest Official: Free Perks Offer is Enticing, but It Won't Fly," *Detroit News*, October 4, 1998.

3. Zuboff, Shoshana. *In the Age of the Smart Machine: The Future of Work and Power* (New York: Basic Books, 1988).

4. Stratton, Joanna L. *Pioneer Women: Voices from the Kansas Frontier* (New York: Touchstone, 1981).

5. Rifkin, Jeremy. *The End of Work* (New York: Tarcher/Putnam, 1995).

6. Gutek, Barbara. *The Dynamics of Service* (San Francisco: Jossey-Bass, 1995).
7. Rifkin, Jeremy. op. cit.
8. Gutek, Barbara. op. cit.
9. Cusack, Michael. *Online Customer Care: Applying Today's Technology to Achieve World-Class Customer Interaction* (Milwaukee, Wisc.: American Society for Quality (ASQ), 1998).

Chapter Two

Encounters and Relationships: Understanding the Changing Structure of Service

The Structure of Service Organizations

The modern corporation is organized to provide service in encounters. It seeks efficient, cost-effective methods of serving customers in the same way that manufacturing sought efficiencies to turn out more goods at lower cost. But those who manage service companies often don't understand the difference between the way they operate their business and the way people used to get service. This chapter further clarifies the differences between relationships and encounters and the impact of each on a service business.

Selling Shoes: An Illustration of the Changing Structure of Service

Think about how your customers get service. If they need shoes, they probably don't have them custom made. That would be very expensive, and most people don't know where to go or who to contact to get custom-made shoes. Some wealthy people may still have a personal shoemaker (or bootmaker), but most of us don't.

That was once the way everyone got shoes. Each village would have a shoemaker (maybe several), and someone needing shoes would know the shoemaker and go see him. He'd have a nice visit with the shoemaker and discuss what he wanted and when the shoes would be ready. They'd also talk about events happening in the community and gossip about mutual friends. It would take up some time, but that would seem pretty normal in a world where there weren't that many goods to buy.

Fast forward to a large American city sixty to eighty years ago. Your customer might have had a neighborhood shoe store where he knew the owner. The owner might even know what kind of shoes the customer liked so he could go quickly to the back room and bring out a pair in the style and size the customer normally bought. While the owner was helping the customer try on shoes, he might ask about the customer's kids and remind him about an upcoming meeting at school. The customer would walk out of the store with a smile on his face, not only in possession of new shoes but also with some gossip and news. While anyone could walk into this store and buy shoes, the store owner depended on the repeat business of regular customers who lived nearby.

Neither of those scenes occur today. When your customers need shoes, they drive to a mall and visit a self-service shoe store or the shoe department of a large department store. The shoes are on display, and the customer takes the ones she wants to try on from the shelves or tables, seats herself and tries them on, often without benefit of help from anyone at the store. There are a lot of different shoe styles on display, but at self-service stores, customers have to dig through stacks of shoe boxes to find their size. There is usually no store employee around to look in the back room. When a customer decides on a pair to buy, she goes to a check-out station where she waits in line to pay.

This difference in the way customers buy shoes, from village to neighborhood to mall, illustrates the difference between relationships and encounters. In the case of village and neighborhood, the buyer and provider actually knew each other. Along with the transaction, they exchanged personal greetings and information. In the case of the shoemaker, the customer's relationship was with the person making the shoes. With the storekeeper, her relationship was with the person selling the shoes. The customer had been distanced from the manufacturing process, which had made the shift from hand-made to factory-made. The neighborhood store was a product of the industrial age, with shoes mass-produced and distributed mainly via the nation's railroads to neighborhood stores where they were sold one-to-one. The shoes were no longer custom made, but the store owner knew something about his goods, and his customers trusted his recommendations.

The customer buying from a neighborhood shoe store would generally feel confident about his purchase. If he got the shoes home and decided they didn't feel good or were the wrong color, he could take them back. The store owner, not wanting to lose a customer (and perhaps a friend as well), would exchange them or refund the money. These actions were part of what both provider and customer meant by the word "service."

The person who goes to the mall for shoes today does not know who will be working there or have any expectation of seeing that person again. She may deal only with the cashier during her visit to the store and may not even remember what that person looked like. If she needs to return the shoes, she will have to deal with the store's customer service department, not the cashier who took her money. The store's concept of "service" is a set of policies decided by managers who probably work in a different location and are carried out (or not carried out) by employees of the company.

The process of "service" has been rationalized and its very nature has changed. "Service" in a retail operation is having a big selection of reasonably-priced items at a store that is open enough hours to make shopping convenient for customers. There is very little traditional service component left in a mall store. The customer selects and pays for a product. He has little interaction with anyone who could tell him something about what he is buying. If a customer buying shoes were able to locate a store employee and ask if the shoes would wear well or if they were waterproof, he would probably be greeted with a dull stare from a worker who knew little or nothing about the many items in the store.

The neighborhood store probably had less merchandise than mall stores, but those who sold it were more knowledgeable. Going back further, to the cobbler who made shoes by hand, the customer dealt with someone who knew everything about the item he sold. But the cobbler had only one pair of shoes to sell that customer, the pair made just for him, which might have been that customer's only pair. The person who buys shoes at the mall today may grumble about poor service, but he can select from a large stock of merchandise. He probably owns numerous pairs of shoes and accepts the fact that some of his purchases don't work out. To this customer, "service" has a different meaning than it had to the customer buying his one and only pair of shoes from a craftsman.

Two Ways of Doing Business

When customers contact your business, they either deal with a provider they know and expect to see again or, more commonly, they deal with a stranger they do not expect to see again. These two ways of doing business represent a fundamental dichotomy. Dealing with a provider you know and expect to see again is to have a *relationship*. Dealing with a provider you do not know and do not expect to see again is to have an *encounter*. The one does not shade into the other. They are completely different experiences for both customer and provider. Because they are so different, the strategies, structures, marketing plans— every aspect of how you run a service business—are affected. Understanding how each functions will help you design a business that fits the kind of service you are offering.

In an *encounter*, the customer is dealing with an organization. The person who provides the service is a stranger, an employee of the organization. Since he knows nothing about the actual provider, the customer's expectations are shaped by what he knows of the organization. Customers, for example, know what to expect when they go to McDonald's because they know the McDonald's organization. They've been to many McDonald's restaurants over the years and most customers know the menu and the ordering process. From the viewpoint of the counter person (the provider), the work is the same for each customer. Customers are interchangeable. So are providers. The constant in these transactions is the organization. Organizations need a steady supply of providers and customers.

In a *relationship*, the individual provider and customer accumulate information about each other over time and draw on this information when they interact. Just as the shoe store owner knows that Joe Bonkowski likes to wear brown loafers and Mary Wang wears only Adidas, relationship providers use what they know about customers' tastes and habits to make the transaction successful. While customer and provider might become friends, what is necessary for a successful transaction is that the expectations of both be met. The provider hopes to make a sale of his product or service and the customer hopes to get the item or service she wanted in the time she wanted it. To the extent that these expectations are met, both provider and customer have an incentive to continue the relationship. Because of the repeated interactions, relationships become more efficient over time. If you've been going to the same barber for many years, you do not need to tell him how you want your hair cut; he knows.

While most service is delivered in encounters, many services are still provided through relationships. The family physician, personal barber, insurance agent, financial advisor, travel agent, or personal trainer are examples. These providers are often self-employed, but they can also work for an organization that has chosen to provide the service in a relationship. An insurance company may want its agents to service the same pool of customers and handle all the needs of those customers. The fact that the service is truly personal becomes a selling point. The company can then run a commercial asking, "When your house has been devastated by a tornado, do you want to have only a voice at the end of an 800 number? Or do you want to be able to call the agent you know and trust?"

Most people, not wanting to give their money to a stranger, would insist on having a relationship with a financial advisor.

Merrill Lynch created commercials featuring Tiger Woods's father in which he says of his financial adviser, "Dave is a personal friend of mine today." These commercials sell the fact that Merrill Lynch customers get a relationship; they deal with the same provider each time.

Many kinds of service can be structured to occur in either a relationship or an encounter. It can occur between the customer and an organization or it can be within an organization. Consider the following examples:

1. *Clerical workers.* When administrative assistants work for one boss, the working arrangement is a relationship. Both are employed by the same company, but one is a service provider to the other. On the other hand, the company could offer a pooled service in which customers for clerical services go to a central desk and use the services of whoever is available. This is structuring the service as an encounter within an organization.

2. *Computer support.* In companies in which each department has its own computer support person, the service is a relationship. When customers call a central support unit or go to a central desk and talk to whoever is available, the service is structured as an encounter. When the service involves a customer and an organization, it is usually structured to be an encounter. A PC user who has a problem at home with a software product calls a hotline for help. She is having an encounter, since she will talk to whoever takes her call. Each time she calls, she may get a different support person.

3. *Insurance.* Having agents sell insurance policies and then be available for the customer's continuing needs is a relationship. Selling policies online or through the mail, leaving customers to call a central office if they have questions or claims, is structuring the service as an encounter. In this case, the person who takes the order on the phone is neither a full service agent nor the same person who would service a claim. Typical of encounter service, the tasks of selling policies and servicing claims

have been separated, much like the tasks of making shoes and selling shoes were separated.

4. *Medical care.* A family doctor who takes care of a patient's total medical needs is working in a relationship. A walk-in clinic where the customer sees whichever health care professional is on duty is medical service structured as an encounter.

Tight Links, Loose Links

The encounter format always has a tight link between a customer and an organization, but not between a customer and a provider as with relationships.

In an encounter, the customer does not need to be concerned about the pay or working conditions of the provider. For example, if a person needs someone to clean his house, he can call a maid service. If he needs someone to take care of his yard, he can call a yard service. He and his wife send their children to a school rather than hire a private teacher. For all of these services, he deals with an organization. The organization takes care of the details of hiring, training, and paying the provider and the customer relies on the organization to provide value. If the yard service sends someone who trims the bushes too severely, the customer can call the yard service to complain. The organization can respond by sending someone else next time or retraining their employee. The customer does not have to deal directly with the provider when there are problems with the service. This can be a convenience for the customer, but it leads to a loose link between customer and provider and tends to tighten the link between the customer and the provider's organization.

If the customer were to deal directly with an individual gardener, she might have to negotiate the pay and hours. The customer might also have to pay taxes on the gardener's wages if she were unable to set up the arrangement as contract work. If the gardener did not do a good job, the customer would have to tell him and fire him, if necessary. On the other hand, if the customer found someone whose work she really liked, she could rely on having the same gardener each time. The fact that the customer would have to negotiate directly with the gardener and pay him directly would mean they would talk to each other and get to know one another. The gardener would learn exactly what the customer wanted for her yard. If the gardener was highly skilled and found many other people also wanted his services, he could charge more than the yard service. But the customer might happily pay it, knowing she had a great gardener, someone she knew and trusted. She wouldn't have to put up with the constant turnover of people employed by the yard service. She would have a relationship—a tight link—with her gardener.

Relationships are easy to understand as they have been around as long as there have been people on earth. One person interacts with another. They get to know each other and feel comfortable with each other. Encounters, as noted previously, are completely different and should not be thought of as mini-relationships. They are, in fact, nothing like relationships.

Sometimes customers try to make an encounter more like a relationship. If someone has breakfast at McDonald's every morning, she may get to where she exchanges personal greetings with the counter person (if the restaurant is not too busy). But since fast food restaurants average as much as a 300 percent staff turnover, the customer will probably outlast that provider. A customer at a no-appointment chain hair salon may try to get the same provider as last time, even though he is supposed to take whoever is available. Someone might do the same thing at a bank, waiting until "her" teller is free and undermining the "next teller" system most banks have. Some people who desire relationships will try to circumvent the encounter process. But from the point of view of the organization, these transactions are intended to be encounters, with any provider capable of performing the service.

Customers seem happier with the encounter form of service when there is little or no judgment needed on the part of the provider. Customers are not likely to insist on a certain counter person at McDonald's, but trying to get the same operator at the chain haircut place makes some sense. Cutting hair cannot be reduced to a few simple steps, so there is always going to be some variation in the technique of different hairstylists.

This is also why some people may resist taking whoever is available at the walk-in medical clinic. They want a certain doctor or nurse-practitioner with whom they felt comfortable on their last visit. Customers who resist the process managers have created are a problem for encounter businesses.

Conversely, some services are organized to be relationships but end up as encounters. For example, a professor with a large class may never get to know all her students. A medical specialist may see a patient only once or so infrequently he doesn't remember them when they come back. In this case, there is no chance for trust to develop, and the customer will feel she has had an encounter. But from the point of view of the organization, the transaction is a relationship. Students would be miffed if they came to class one day and found a different professor there; so would someone going to the eye doctor and finding a completely different doctor. These kinds of transactions are not very relationship-like, but they are still relationships.

Organizational Control

To ensure that carefully designed policies and procedures are followed, encounter businesses typically try to control the actions of service providers. In a relationship business, however, the organization may be just an association of providers with little or no management oversight. Service organizations can be created by a group of professionals, for instance, each of whom bills out his or her services to clients. An example is a law firm in which providers typically are partners. Each has his or her own clients, and each is responsible for recruiting more business for the firm. In this case, the practitioner will work to satisfy her clients because they provide her income. Losing a client would cost the practitioner income as well as prestige with her colleagues. These reasons for working hard substitute for organizational control.

Professionals often feel more loyalty to their profession than to their current employer. Professions that require many years of education, as for doctors, lawyers, or college professors, do not depend on a particular employer. You are a doctor or lawyer, for instance, whether you have a job or not. Well-educated workers can even exploit their employer to their own advantage. Stock brokers can research their own investments, professors can use university time to build a consulting practice, and accountants can recruit their employers' customers and start their own business. The loose organizational control over these kinds of professionals allows them to do this.

Where a professional works in a supporting role in an organization that exists for some purpose other than the type of work done by the professional, the organizational control is stronger. An example is an accountant who works in a manufacturing plant or a doctor who works for a drug company. The service provider works in a true relationship with his clients (who are other employees of the organization), but the provider's loyalty to the company that writes his pay check will be stronger than loyalty to the customers he services in the company. There may even be a conflict of interest as in the case of a company doctor who is asked to certify someone as able to work when the worker thinks she cannot do the task. The provider's link to his clients is looser because the organization he works for provides his pay, a potent form of control. This control may interfere with the trust that normally develops between customer and provider in a relationship.

In an encounter business, the organization, rather than the provider, determines how the work is done. Employees may be given some discretion in dealing with customers, or they may have none at all. Some kinds of work require the use of broad guidelines to service customers (like a computer support call center). In other cases, the organization may provide a "script" to cover all possible actions (like a hotel clerk who checks in guests using a company process). And in the ultimate situation, the organization has complete control. An example is when the provider is a machine such as a bank ATM.

When the organization has strong control over the service, the customer is more likely to attribute good or poor performance to the organization, not to the actual provider. If the fries are good at McDonald's, customers attribute this to the McDonald's organization, not to the kid who operates the fryer. If someone liked their last room at the Holiday Inn, she is likely to book at another Holiday Inn, expecting to receive the same kind of room and service received during the other stay. She would generally not attribute the cleanliness of the room to the maid who cleaned it but to the organization that hired and trained the maid. She trusts the organization and expects it to perform the same way again.

The degrees of organizational control are pictured in Table 2-1.

Table 2-1   Organizational Control

Organizational Control	Service Format	Link Between Customer & Provider
None ↓	Independent practitioner	Tightest ↑
Some control ↓	Relationship provider in group practice organization	Tight ↑
More control ↓	Relationship provider who is an employee of an organization	Medium ↑
Strong control ↓	Encounter provider who is an employee of an organization	Loose ↑
Total control ↓	Machine provider	Not applicable ↑

Strong organizational control is Frederick Taylor's idea transferred to the service sector. Automobile assembly plants, as established by Henry Ford, followed Taylor's model of placing all production and scheduling decisions in the hands of management. The workforce assembling the cars didn't need any kind of engineering knowledge or control over the pace of production. Taylor's ideas about finding the most efficient movements for completing tasks found a home in the fast food business, and then in many other kinds of service work.

Some organizational experts, including Peter Drucker, have pointed out that this need not be so. Back in 1954, Drucker questioned this division of function:

> It does not follow from the separation of planning and doing in the analysis of work that the planner and doer should be two different people. It does not follow that the industrial world should be divided into two classes of people; a few

who decide what is to be done, design the job, set the pace, rhythm and motions, and order others about; and the many who do what and as they are told.[1]

But that is the way manufacturing, and later service, went. As the planner and the doer become separate people, the planner gains useful experience and the doer does not. This creates a boundary between managers and providers. As Shoshana Zuboff wrote in her study of factory automation, "As production jobs offered less opportunity for skill development, they came to have little relevance for the kinds of expertise needed at supervisory levels, and the boundaries between these classes of organization members became more rigid."[2] Encounter businesses are characterized by the separation of managers who design the service process from the providers who do what the managers tell them.

The growth of encounter businesses may account for why the United States has a higher percentage of managers than any other country—about 12 percent of the labor force.

The Differences

Table 2-2 summarizes the important differences between relationships and encounters that usually (but not always) apply.

The following sections will look at some of the ways relationships and encounters differ for providers and for customers. It is important for business owners to understand and consider all of these differences and their implications.

Role of Managers

In encounter businesses, managers are responsible for the success or failure of the business. They play four roles in the delivery of service in encounter formats:

1. Design the service delivery system.
2. Implement the delivery system.
3. Enforce the delivery system.
4. Alter the delivery system.

Table 2-2 Encounter vs. Relationship

	Encounter	Relationship
Role of manager	Design jobs and maintain compliance to standards	Facilitate, coordinate, determine profitability
Customer's access to service	Walk-in, phone call, or unattended	Appointment or prior arrangement
Speed of service	Designed to be fast, but depends on the number of customers at any one time and a complete transaction may involve more than one encounter	Slower in the beginning; gets more efficient over time
Cost	Lower per transaction	Higher per transaction
Feedback	Indirect—the customer generally has to give feedback through the organization via a Customer Service department, a form to be sent in, or an 800 phone number	Direct and informal—the customer and provider discuss the service
Provider incentive	Provider gets the same pay regardless of the number of customers	Provider makes more money when the business has more customers
"Emotional labor"— display of appropriate emotions	Provider may be told how to behave with customers, such as having to smile, call the customer by his name, or say "Have a Nice day"	Customer and provider build a personal relationship, so the provider is usually not coached on how to act
Planning for peaks and valleys	The organization can hire more workers for peak periods	Difficult—the provider must deal with all his/her customers personally and work harder during busy times
Worker satisfaction	Often very low—most aspects of the work are controlled by the organization and the pay may be poor as well	Providers generally like the autonomy of this format which lets them learn new skills and increase their earnings
Whose convenience?	Organized for efficiency, often having the customer do some of the work, and may provide such conveniences as being open 24 hours or having a drive-through	Appointment times must meet the needs of both customer and provider; customer must find an alternate if provider is sick or on vacation
Measuring efficiency	Organizations put in place many ways to measure the efficiency of their service such as counting the number of calls a worker took or having an auditor pose as a customer	Measurement not emphasized—business strives for customer satisfaction more than efficiency; some may have no way to measure efficiency
Customer loyalty	Little loyalty on either part	High for both customer and provider
Profits	Unlimited	Good, but limited

Most of a manager's day-to-day time is spent on the last two activities. Managers make sure that the service is being delivered according to the company design and constantly seek ways to improve the process for greater efficiency and profit. Encounter businesses are profitable precisely because they are managed. The work is structured by the organization so the customer can depend on the service or the experience being uniform. Each time the customer uses the service, she knows what to expect. The consumer experience at a McDonald's, a Day's Inn, or Jiffy Lube should be about the same in Chicago, St. Louis, or Atlanta. This familiarity brings with it a comfort level that appeals to many customers, so maintaining and enforcing it is very important.

Ray Kroc, who built McDonald's into the worldwide chain it is today, always felt the worst thing a McDonald's franchisee could do was to deviate in any way from Kroc's formula for success. Each restaurant had to follow the operations manual completely. He was so convinced the business he'd bought from the McDonald brothers could be successfully duplicated that he copied their building exactly when he built his first restaurant in Chicago. Uniformity is serious stuff at McDonald's. Maintaining uniformity, a source of customer loyalty, is an important part of managing an encounter business.

Managers must also select people to do the all-important customer contact work. They can try to hire "service-oriented" people and encourage employees to "go the extra mile," but in many businesses this doesn't result in much, if any, reward for that employee. Many books on customer service are full of anecdotes about incidents in which an employee went beyond the normal effort to please a customer. But encounter businesses are structured so there is little to motivate workers to deliver outstanding service. Efforts to get providers to please customers often come down to pep rallies that simply urge providers to work harder. Managers must find ways to reward good providers.

In relationship businesses, a lot less money is spent on management. Relationship providers are generally not very concerned with efficiency and may not even have a way to measure it. Managers in a relationship business are more concerned with developing profit and loss statements for client engagements than with telling providers how to do their work. The work is usually of a highly customized nature; the principles that apply in encounter businesses don't apply in service firms that sometimes literally sell the services of a specific person. The practitioners may have a common method of approaching their work or common practices during an initial client meeting, but beyond that, the service may be individually tailored to the client's needs and preferences. Price is not as much of an issue for customers of this kind of service.

Independent practitioners manage to operate without an organization or professional managers. These practitioners, of course, must learn to manage such tasks as computing and paying their taxes, buying insurance, and figuring out if their service is profitable. Some businesses of this type are operated by people with great talent at what they do but whose limited management skills make them targets for better-financed, larger-scale organizations. Their customers may get frustrated with their slipshod way of operating, which may include not returning phone calls promptly, running over budget, failing to make and keep a schedule, failing to provide an itemized bill, being late for meetings, and many other behavioral deficiencies not as likely to be found in a professionally managed firm. These behaviors can drive away customers who may prefer the more organized workers at the encounter business.

Customer's Access to Service

Relationship providers usually make their own arrangements, generally by appointment, to see customers. There may be a receptionist or assistant who sets up the provider's schedule, but the provider is in control. He or she can choose to work more hours or set up a meeting at a restaurant or an early morning hour if that is what suits the customer. Because relationship providers want business, they usually make it easy for customers to get to them. They may give their best customers their cell phone number, their home phone number, and their e-mail address. Providers who work out of their home only need to check their answering machine, fax machine, and e-mail to keep in touch with customers. In a relationship business, the provider may call the customer from time to time to see if the customer needs anything. The customer may give the provider ways to contact her, including a home phone number. There is a joint desire to keep in touch and trust enough to share personal information.

Encounter businesses, on the other hand, develop a standard procedure for dispensing service that applies to all customers. Most chain businesses operate on a walk-in basis. The customer may walk up to a counter and sign in and wait to be called. Or the customer may stand in a line and wait for his or her turn. Since the customer is interacting with an organization and does not know the provider, there is no routine exchange of personal information. The provider may obtain information about the customer (either by asking the customer to complete a survey or by collecting it in the course of doing business) and may have someone call the customer later to ask about the service or to offer more services. But the person who follows up will generally be a different person than the one who provided the service.

Speed of Service

One of the reasons chain businesses exist is to provide fast service. When the business doesn't rely on a specific person to provide a service to a specific customer, it can have a procedure for serving a lot of customers quickly. Sometimes this involves making the customer a coproducer. For example, airlines can have customers "write their own ticket" by having them use a Web site to order tickets and faxing back a confirmation. They can have customers line up in reverse order of their seat assignments so they can be seated onboard more quickly or employ a "zone boarding" system, as United Airlines has done with their shuttle service, in which people assigned window seats board first.

Fast food restaurants expect customers to clean their tables. Some economy grocery stores have customers bag their own groceries. These measures are a help to the customer who wants fast and inexpensive service, but they would not appeal to the customer who wants to be pampered and doesn't mind paying for it.

Sometimes speed is actually equated with service. Commercials for Marathon gas stations, for example, say adding "pay-at-the-pump technology" makes their stations more "user-friendly." They make an assumption that customers would actually rather pump the gas themselves and put a credit card through a machine than have a person wait on them. For many customers, that is undoubtedly true, but perhaps not for all. When Xerox set up its copier repair service, it decided to dispatch whichever repair person was available for emergency repairs rather than assign a specific repair person to service the same customer. Xerox had determined that customers are more interested in having their copiers fixed fast than in having a relationship with the repair person. However, Xerox did assign a lead repair person to each account.[3]

But "fast" service is not always fast. Bill Wilson, an economist with a banking company, Comerica Inc., asks audiences when he gives speeches to raise their hands if they think service has declined. He says when he first started asking this question a few years earlier, he might see a quarter of the people raising their hands. More recently, everyone is raising their hand. Wilson says longer lines and poorer service are a form of inflation. He gives the example of going to a fast food place like McDonald's or Carl's Junior. Two years ago, he says, it would have cost $1 and a three-minute wait. "Today," he notes, "you still pay $1 but you wait twice as long in line and the guy serving you would be rude. That's a form of inflation, because time is money."[4]

Frequent flyers have a similar complaint. It takes more time than it once did to complete a flight from one city to another because there are fewer non-stop flights and each dash through an airport to get a connecting flight is time-consuming. In addition, the flights take longer because the listed times include built-in buffer time to keep the flights from being considered late and to provide adequate time for people making connections. And the time spent on the plane is less pleasant than it once was because of fewer attendants; often there is no food except for the ubiquitous peanuts.

Relationship services usually take longer, especially in the beginning as the parties get to know each other. As the provider learns more about what the customer wants, she can sometimes deliver the service faster. A masseuse with regular customers will learn how each customer likes his or her massage, can be in and out of a client's home or place of business quickly, and go on to the next appointment. Consultants learn how their customers think and sometimes can quickly lay out a solution to a business problem. A graphic artist who does regular work for a manager can put together a presentation for that manager from hand-written notes because he knows what that manager likes and how he thinks.

The down side is that the provider cannot be split in two when two customers want his services at the same time. He will have to reschedule one of them and maybe work extra hours to keep both happy. Customers who want the personal touch of a relationship must be willing to accept the fact that their provider has other customers; there may be times when they simply cannot get the service they want. The professional service firm must sell the skills of its practitioners so the customer will be willing to make compromises to retain that person's services.

Cost to Customer

Getting service in a relationship usually costs more than getting service in an encounter. Encounters are set up to service more people for less money, and relationships are not. The additional costs of a relationship are not just financial. The customer must take time to make an appointment, perhaps adjusting her own schedule to fit with the provider's. She must accept having limited access to the provider, finding a substitute for the provider when the provider is sick or on vacation and accommodating the provider's idiosyncrasies. These are some of the other "costs." Like relationships with family or friends, business relationships carry with them a certain amount of emotional "baggage."

A prescription may cost less at a chain drug store, which competes heavily on price. On the other hand, many people would rather make time to visit an independent pharmacy when their favorite pharmacist is on duty and pay a bit more to get their prescription from someone they know.

Medical care is an obvious example of a service traditionally delivered in a relationship that is increasingly being delivered as an encounter to save money. Insurance companies and managed care organizations, which pay most of the bills, are not the recipients of the service and have every motivation to cut costs by providing service more efficiently in encounters. Machines and technology are increasingly used to diagnose illnesses. These machines are generally more reliable than human judgment, and they can help reduce costs. But customers don't like impersonal medical care and are not ready to accept the judgment of a machine. Combining technology with a relationship service staffed with nurse-practitioners would lower costs, but the obstacles would be the probable opposition of the American Medical Association (AMA) and convincing customers they were getting first-class care.

Some people prefer a relationship but settle for an encounter because of cost. They might wish they had their own accountant, but go to H&R Block because it is cheaper. They might like to go to the expensive hair salon, but they go to BoRics or Supercuts to save money and time.

The Feedback Loop

Managers in encounter businesses need to include in their process design a way for customers to provide feedback. The person buying shoes and then coming back to report a problem needs to be able to find the person who handles complaints. Studies show that most customers who are dissatisfied with a service never bother to complain, thinking it would do no good. However, in some cases the customer may take out his wrath on the unfortunate provider on the spot. The provider will feel she's been abused, especially if she is not empowered to do much about customer complaints.

Here are some comments left at a Web site for McDonald's and other fast food workers (www.mcspotlight.org):

> My daughter, a manager, has been sworn at, had food thrown at her, and even has had death threats made against her because the french fries weren't hot enough.

Is it right for someone to ask us to wait while they sit at the menu board on drive-through for five minutes to see what they want, holding up the cars behind them? No. Is it right to completely change your order at the drive-through window, holding up the others behind you? No. What about the customer who comes inside screaming and yelling (bothering our other customers) about how he wanted extra pickles but we didn't put enough on? How about the customer who walks through the door cursing at us that his wife was just here and after she got home, the food was messed up, only to find out that the food he is holding wasn't purchased at our restaurant, but at Wendy's or another BK or something. Are they right? What about all the people who curse at us because they want a breakfast sandwich at 12 in the afternoon and we won't do it.

(What about) the women who yell because the toy their kids got yesterday is the same one they got today? The people who eat 75 percent of their fries before they take them back because they are cold and want new ones? They get mad when we refuse to give them new fries. How about the people who live fifteen minutes away and complain that their food was cold when they got home; well duh!! These are all things that happen all the time where I work.[5]

These minimum wage workers are left to deal with all kinds of customer complaints and may have to decide whether to replace the fries the customer claims are cold or look for a different toy for a crying kid. If there is a manager in the restaurant, he or she could be called to deal with the problem, but some restaurants operate without full-time managers. Even when a manager is on duty, she may have little skill in dealing with these problems.

Although the above quotes involve provider perception of unreasonable customers, complaints are not always unreasonable. If the customer really got cold fries, he might not bother to complain but he might not come back again either. Organizations try to keep complaints down by closely supervising and controlling providers, by supplying them with scripts for every possible occasion. But even the best manager cannot foresee everything or actually control the behavior of low-paid people who don't care very much whether they hang onto their job or not.

Chain drug stores may have clerks give customers their prescription drugs instead of the pharmacists, who are busy filling the prescriptions. *Detroit Free Press* columnist Bob Talbert wrote about his experience with a chain drug store and got plenty of reaction from his readers.

As Talbert related it, he called in a new prescription and expected it to be ready in a few hours. When he came to get it, he found himself in a long line. An old man ahead of him was slowing things down because he didn't understand why he was getting a different drug than his usual one. The store had substituted a generic version, but the clerk's mumbled explanation left the man confused, and he wandered out of the line saying he would call his doctor. Finally, it was Talbert's turn. Already upset about the wait, he was even less happy when the clerk told him his prescription was not ready and to come back in two more hours. Two hours later, Talbert was back, waiting in another line. When he finally got to the counter, he was told they had no record of a prescription for him. Barely controlling his rising anger, he told the clerk he had called it in earlier in the day. The clerk looked around and found it had been shoved aside. Now he was told they'd have it ready in twenty minutes.

Talbert said that when he tells this "prescription-from-hell" experience, he hears even worse stories from other people. A father had to wait four hours for pain relief for his daughter who was in agony after dental surgery; a disabled man paid for a cab to take him to the drug store to get a prescription called in the day before, but it was not ready. When he checked on it the next day, it still was not ready.

Talbert attributes the poor service to the dominance of drug store chains.[6]

After running the column on drug stores, Talbert was deluged with about 250 letters and calls from readers who had had bad experiences with chain drug stores. It was one of the biggest responses he'd ever received from a column. He wrote: "Your comments and complaints about chain drugstores confirmed my premise that the chaining of American businesses is helping eliminate personal service in everyday commerce."

Many also wrote Talbert about their good experiences with neighborhood, non-chain stores. Only one reader wrote and suggested people complain, but she said to write to the chain management with all the details, adding "Phone calls are a waste of time. You'll just get a clerk who has no interest and no authority."

A Detroit-area drug store cooperative called Sav-Mor began running radio ads using the line "Does your pharmacist know you?" Its ads explain that Sav-Mor stores are independently owned and offer personal service "because the owner is in the store." This is a direct counter to the chain stores where the owner is a big corporation. The chain stores are going to have more difficulty getting customer feedback than the owner who is in the store and can talk to his or her customers directly.

Some organizations provide feedback cards for customers, but these usually go to the headquarters of the company, not to the store or the employee the customer dealt with. This would seem like a pretty remote way of complaining about cold fries or a prescription not being ready on time.

In a relationship, feedback is easily handled by the customer telling the provider what she thought of the service. The customer deals directly with the provider and they can work out problems between themselves. Relationship providers always understand their customers can go elsewhere so they are motivated to work out any problems. People do leave relationship providers, of course. They may no longer need or want the service, or maybe their circumstances change and they can't afford it any more. They might move away, or they might hear about a different provider they'd like to try, but the provider is likely to know the reason the customer left. On the other hand, in an encounter, an organization is likely to never know the reason why it loses a particular customer.

Desire for Customers

For encounter providers, customers are not always a blessing. Seeing the line snake out the door at Wendy's cannot be fun for the person behind the counter. He gets paid no more for serving all those customers than if the place was empty. The airline ticket clerk is not overjoyed at seeing a bunch of nervous, tired people lugging suitcases and clamoring for her attention. The hairdresser who is directly paid by her clients, however, is quite happy to see a full appointment book. The medical specialist with big overhead on his office and staff is glad to see a waiting room full of people. The insurance agent who works on commission eagerly checks her voice mail and calls right back when someone wants to buy more insurance.

In some situations, there may be no competition for customers because of a monopoly (as in government services) or more demand for the service than existing vendors can satisfy. In this case, the service can be structured to be efficient with less concern for the customer's convenience since the customer has no choice. There is only one place drivers can go to get a vehicle license plate, so they must put up with the process the state has set up. Customers who are locked into an HMO because it is all that's available to them will have to accept the level of personal care HMOs offer. If there's only one drug store in your town, people who need a prescription filled will have to get it filled there whether the drug store offers personal service or not. When the customers have no choice, the service is almost always offered in an encounter if this is the most efficient (and profitable) way to provide the service.

Emotional Labor ("Have a Nice Day")

Managers designing encounter jobs train their providers to do their work in a certain way. This may include the way employees are supposed to behave toward customers. Wanting customers to feel welcome, managers may require employees to smile, wear name tags, address customers by name, or say "Have a nice day."

In his insightful book, *The McDonaldization of Society*, George Ritzer relates his feelings about the scripted performance of the counter clerks at Roy Rogers roast beef fast food restaurant:

> An example of scripted interaction, the Roy Rogers chain used to have its employees, dressed in cowboy and cowgirl

uniforms, say "Howdy, pardner" to every customer about to order food. After paying for the food, people were sent on their way with "Happy Trails." The repetition of these familiar salutations visit after visit was a source of great satisfaction to regulars at Roy Rogers. Many people (including me) felt a deep personal loss when Roy Rogers ceased this practice.[7]

The scripted words of the Roy Rogers counter workers were part of their job, and clearly some customers enjoyed hearing them. But the words repeated over and over throughout a worker's shift would have little meaning to the person saying them. Ritzer adds, "The Roy Rogers employees who used to say 'Happy Trails' really had no interest in what happened 'on the trail.'"

The policies at the Safeway grocery chain are an example of an organization managing the way its workers must act toward customers. Safeway employees received a memo in 1998 that exhorted them to:

Greet with a smile. Make eye contact.
Don't be mechanical.
Don't be overzealous.
Role play with checks before beginning shift.
Thank customer by last name. Don't thank randomly.
Develop a battery of appropriate [parting] comments.
Don't be repetitious!

A Safeway spokesman defended the policy, saying, "It's a personalization of service. Service is a very important key to our company, and we have been for quite some time fine-tuning [it]."

Not all Safeway employees saw it that way. Some female employees complained that male customers misunderstood the smiles as come-ons. The United Food and Commercial Workers union filed a complaint in May 1998 with the National Labor Relations Board, alleging that Safeway's customer service policy was illegally imposed. "They've got battalions of MBAs who are coming up with these policies at the corporate fort in Pleas-anton who don't take into account the real life implications," said union lawyer Matthew Ross.[8]

The union wants workers, especially women, to have more freedom to choose not to make eye contact with a potentially threatening customer or to refuse to carry groceries out to a man's car at night.

Not all customers like scripted pleasantries. A column by Traci Hukill that appeared in *The Sonoma County Independent* had this to say about a visit to Safeway:

> But customer service is nothing new, and Safeway isn't alone in the conspiracy to befriend the existentially isolated consumer. Wal-Mart checkers have been stumbling over my surname for a good five years, and I hear tales of similar "personalized" friendliness at Nordstrom and other department stores. That the practice is becoming more common makes it no less gratingly superficial, only easier to overlook.
>
> In truth—and this is spleen talking—the economic motive for implementing institutionalized chumminess is so vile that it all but eradicates the sweetness of a smile from a stranger. From the corporate standpoint it's business as usual: Work that bottom line, and tap every resource if you must in order to do it.

She went on to call forced friendliness "the ultimate manipulating tool." Then she adds:

> The era of the friendly corner market is a distant memory for most communities, especially in the suburbs. And yes, many of us are nostalgic for the "good old days" we never actually experienced, days when Bruno the Butcher and Maggie the Vegetable Lady knew our kids' names and what kind of steaks and tomatoes we liked.
>
> But Bruno the Butcher would never mispronounce my name. It's fine to hear a clerk rattle off your name if you're a Smith or a Williams, but what if your last name is Wierzchowicz or Gzsanka? Of course, if your Safeway checker has followed the rules and engaged in a little light role-playing with checks before his shift, he may not stumble at all. Don't count on it, though.[9]

In encounters, both customer and provider follow a routine that each learns. It can be reassuring or irritating to the customer.

Planning for Peaks and Valleys

Encounter businesses can plan for peaks and valleys in the business better than relationship providers can. H&R Block can employ tax preparers only during the tax season, adding more people as April 15 approaches. Fast food places can have more workers during the lunch rush, and grocery stores can add more checkout clerks during rush times. No individual worker has to take on an unfair work load since more workers can always be hired.

A relationship business, on the other hand, usually can't add people. Tax accountants plan for April 15 by clearing away other activities and expecting to spend more hours working that month. Professors plan to be busier at exam time. The relationship provider must put up with a schedule that can be unforgiving and relentless. She cannot just hire someone else to replace herself. Her clients expect to get her, and she must not disappoint them if she wants to stay in business. A professional might hire an assistant to help with some of the work, but she cannot clone herself.

Worker Satisfaction

Encounter business managers typically break the work down into individual tasks. The insurance company that sells policies through an 800 number, for example, hires different employees as policy providers and as claim providers. This enables them to train people more quickly for each job. By limiting the content of the job, they can employ people who earn less money than full-service agents, who handle all the services needed by their clients. This results in savings for the customer, but the customer must accept service that is less personal and the pro-vider must accept a job with less content.

For the provider, encounter jobs offer little opportunity to develop any new skills. Doing the same task over and over doesn't teach anything new. The repetitious nature of the work actually erodes skills the worker may have but is unable to use. Most encounter jobs do not prepare workers to be managers or give them skills they can use to get better jobs. This leads to dissatisfaction for workers, who may quit out of boredom or frustration.

If an encounter worker has any ideas about how to add to or improve the service, management probably doesn't want to hear about it. Encounter firms operate on the idea that it's not the worker's job to improve the service. And service workers are usually paid low wages. An article, part of a series in the *Arizona Daily Star* on Tucson's call centers, reported:

> Today, most Tucson call centers are non-technical. They offer customer service for companies such as United Parcel Service, AT&T, and Sears. A few provide service in the form of directory assistance, including Lucent and InfoNXX. Others collect data, such as Opinion Research, set up appointments with insurance agents through Anderson Financial Network Inc., or take reservations for American Airlines or Greyhound Lines.
>
> Jobs at this level don't require much training. Many of the call centers offer near-poverty-level wages although agents at American Airlines start at $7 an hour and, over time, can earn up to $19.66 an hour.[10]

The *Daily Star* series included an editorial entitled "Tucson's Sweat Shops" that expressed the wish that the city had never gone after call-center companies because the quality of the jobs provided was so poor. Workers are not likely to feel good about working under the conditions described in these articles. The same could be said for many service businesses.

As noted before, when the customer perceives an encounter service as good, he or she usually attributes it to the organization. When the service is perceived as poor, the customer is likely to attribute it to the provider. This leaves the provider in a lose-lose situation. If he is pleasant, the customer thinks it's because the organization has trained him to be that way, and if he is rude, it is because he is a rude person. This is in line with research on bureaucratic encounters that shows people tend to think of encounter providers as cold, impersonal, uncaring, and unwilling to go beyond the narrow requirements of the job.[11]

Relationship businesses, on the other hand, usually involve a variety of tasks that can be highly satisfying. Workers are hired for their skills, and this fact alone makes them feel valuable. If they are self-employed, they have the satisfaction of working for themselves. The rewards of the business are all theirs.

Whose Convenience?

Encounter businesses compete on certain kinds of convenience. No-appointment, walk-in services are always available as contrasted with relationship services that require an appointment. Chain drug stores may have twenty-four-hour service, whereas the friendly pharmacist in an independent drug store cannot work all day and all night. Catalog sales with a twenty-four-hour toll-free number serve the customer's interest by being available at any hour. Web sites, too, allow ordering at any time of day or night.

The customer of a walk-in service does not know how long he or she will have to wait, so the service is not always quick. There is little he or she can do about it when confronted with a long line. Chain businesses operating on a walk-in basis need to determine their busy times and try to add more help or find a way to shift some of the business to another time, possibly through incentives (senior discounts on Monday from 9 a.m. to 4 p.m., for example). Customers like the convenience of first-come first-serve when there is no wait, but they like it a lot less when there are many other customers.

Some encounter businesses are structured for the convenience of the organization, which has designed the process for efficiency without thinking how it affects the customer. For example, the customer may have to engage in more than one encounter to complete a transaction. Consider the process of renewing vehicle license plates. In many states, customers must first put their car through an emissions or smog test and present a certificate showing the car passed the test. The customer goes to an inspector for the test. If the car fails, she must go to a mechanic who works on the car, then back to the inspector. She then can go to another person to get the license plate. This process serves the need for the provider to have specialists perform different tasks, but it is hardly convenient for the customer.

A Michigan Blue Cross customer who wrote a letter about a claim called the office when he had received no response. He discovered he could not talk to the person to whom he'd written. Instead, he had to talk to the "phone representative." Blue Cross apparently found separating these functions served efficiency, but for the customer, it meant explaining the problem all over again to a new person.

Phone encounters where customers are passed from one person to another and end up describing their problem over and over to each successive person are among the most annoying for customers.

Look at this example of a hypothetical interaction between a woman calling a road service and the people working for the road service. It's 1:00 in the afternoon, and the customer calls her road service and says, "My 1992 Ford Taurus won't start. The battery is dead."

The clerk asks standard questions and concludes with "What kind of vehicle do you have?" The woman again states that it is a 1992 Taurus, to which the clerk asks, "What year?" Time passes, it's now 1:45 p.m., and no help has arrived. The customer calls back. She gets a different clerk and describes the problem all over again, giving the same information.

The clerk is unable to find the woman's records in the computer and asks, "Did you use the same member number when you called before?" The customer is now really exasperated and demands that the truck be sent soon. The clerk is annoyed at being yelled at and again asks what kind of car the woman has, concluding, "You need towing, right?"

The customer tries to control her anger as she says in slow, deliberate words, "Wrong! All I need is the battery charged."

The clerk again asks, "What year is your car?" Before hanging up, the customer is assured someone will be there soon. Fifty minutes later a tow truck shows up.

The driver gets out and says to the eager customer, "Lady, where do you want the car towed?" Incredulous, the customer explains she only needs the battery jumped. The driver reluctantly jump starts the car; the woman drives to a service station and buys a battery, has it installed, and returns home to find her phone ringing. "Hello," says a voice. "This is Janet with the emergency service. I understand you need a tow truck."

This customer did not get good service. No one was actually responsible for helping her. The tasks at this emergency service had been broken down into answering the phone, entering the call into a computer, and dispatching the service. These functions did not work smoothly together. Each person working for the service would have thought they had done their job, and none of them could have seen or understood the frustration of the customer.

Would the manager of this service have a way of knowing the customer had been treated badly? Encounter services, as stated before, often lack any kind of a feedback mechanism. Would this woman bother calling back and asking for a manager to whom she could relate her unhappy experience? Probably not. Studies show very few dissatisfied customers actually complain; they just don't come back.

Making the customer a "coproducer" is a common characteristic of encounter businesses. When the customer gets something in return for doing some of the work, this can be mutually beneficial.

Fast food places put the customer to work doing some of what servers would do in a full-serve restaurant, such as carrying their food to a table and cleaning their table when they are finished. Salad bars and smorgasbords are a way of getting customers to wait on themselves, but the payoff for the customer is getting exactly the foods he wanted in the quantities he wanted (more tomatoes and less lettuce, for example). Some furniture stores offer lower prices if the customer will take the furniture home in the crate, possibly having to assemble it when they get home. Not as convenient as the expensive store where the salesperson spends time with each customer and arranges delivery and setup, but it is a good tradeoff for many customers. Self-serve shoe stores keep costs down by having customers find their own shoes and try them on by themselves.

Measuring Efficiency

Managers often devise "metrics" to determine if the service met the organization's criteria for success, but sometimes their measurement does not take into account the way the customer experiences the service. If the manager used time on the phone to determine how well his people were doing, he might find each conversation with the woman calling the road service was suitably short and that the clerk asked the right questions. But that would not take into account the fact that the woman had to call back and supply the same information numerous times. It would also not measure the fact that when the truck finally arrived, it was there to deliver the wrong service, and the customer had to intervene to get the service she had requested.

Use of metrics encourages providers to work toward making the numbers look good. Call center support people might close a service request before the problem is really fixed or turn one request into several to make it look as if they did more work (actual occurrences reported by one call center manager).

Encounter businesses rely on a number of methods of finding out if the customer was pleased or not. They often use short surveys for customers to complete, or they may employ a "mystery shopper" to pretend to be a customer, then evaluate the service. Chain businesses send out "auditors" to check on the way service is being dispensed.

Dots, a low-cost women's clothing chain, keeps a stack of customer surveys on the counter near the cash register. The survey card says in big letters, "Did We Deliver?" It goes on to say, "Thanks for shopping at Dots. Our customers are extremely important to us. We are committed to not merely meeting your expectations, but to exceeding them. Only you can tell us how we are doing." The card goes back to company headquarters, not to the store where the customer got the card.

Some businesses, like the Days Inn chain, have company

auditors come and rate the service, awarding zero to five "sunbursts" (the company logo is a black and yellow sunburst). Its guide to motels and online reservation service lists the number of sunbursts next to each motel name. The customer can feel good about booking a five-sunburst motel, assured of a standard level of quality.

McDonald's uses surprise inspectors who show up at random times and places to inspect each restaurant for compliance with the McDonald's way of doing things.

Metrics typically aren't used in relationship businesses since customers can tell the provider what he or she wants and whether the service was satisfactory. The provider can use this direct feedback to alter the service to suit the customer.

Customer Loyalty

Everyone wants loyal customers, but what does that really mean? Basically, you want your customers to come back. In relationship businesses, as long as the customer continues to need the service and is satisfied, she will continue to come back. It's generally in her interest to keep using a provider who knows her and her preferences. Whether it's medical care, investment advice, insurance, legal help, or hair coloring, a customer will stay with a provider she knows and trusts.

In an encounter business, the customer knows only the organization. If he is displeased with the service, he will probably go somewhere else next time. If he is merely satisfied that the organization providing the service is about the same as other providers, he may go somewhere else.

A chain business builds customer loyalty by minimizing the role of the provider in the mind of the customer. The organization must reinforce the idea that the organization, not the provider, creates the quality experience. This will build an incentive for the customer to return to this business.

Since an encounter is between a customer and an organization, the customer knows he has banked at Gigantic National Bank for ten years, but the person behind the teller's window may not know that and may treat him the same as a new customer. A teller could refuse to validate a long-time customer's parking ticket, for instance, and lose that person's business. Or a woman whose check to Visa got lost in the mail receives a threatening letter from the card issuer despite the fact that she'd had the card for twelve years and never missed a payment. To the woman, it is an outrage that she could be treated so shabbily by a service she'd retained for so many years. These cases illustrate the fact that a person cannot truly have a "relationship" with an organization. The customers know how long they've been dealing with that organization, but the person they deal with doesn't. Employees at the provider organization come and go, and unless the organization has a process for identifying long-time or special customers to their employees, they risk losing those customers.

Organizations do not have to treat all customers the same. Organizations can use technology to identify repeat customers and have a process for making this known to their employees. Keeping current customers is cheaper than getting new ones and providing some kind of special treatment is a recognition of that customer's value over his or her lifetime. In his book *Customers for Life*, Carl Sewell estimates his customers spend an average of $332,000 on vehicles in their lifetime. When he goes out of his way for a customer, he is not doing it just for that customer's business today, but for his business forever.

Profits

Both relationship businesses and encounter businesses can be very profitable, but there is no doubt that encounter businesses have more potential for profit. When the business can be duplicated, the profits can be duplicated. Online encounter businesses can also be very profitable, since they can have an almost unlimited number of customers at their online store without the expense of operating a real store.

Relationship businesses can be either small mom-and-pop kinds of services or professional service firms that typically charge a lot of money. A law firm may not be huge, but if each lawyer bills his time at $300 to $500 per hour, the profits can be considerable. Relationship businesses usually exist because the people working in them want to earn a living, but the really big money is in encounter businesses.

Conclusion

It is important to understand that relationships and encounters are totally different ways of providing service. Although the word "relationship" is heavily used by marketers, real relationships are between people, not between a person and an organization. The many organizations seeking a "relationship" with their customers are really providing encounters but are trying to make them feel like relationships.

Encounters always involve a customer and an organization where the customer does not know the provider. Relationships are simpler. The customer always sees the same provider.

Here is a summary of some of the considerations that flow from the differences:

- Relationship businesses can be started with less money and need to attract fewer customers than encounter businesses.
- Relationship businesses need providers with excellent skills and the business acumen needed to manage accounts.
- Relationship providers can only have as many customers as they can service, and in busy times, they must work harder. As a result, sometimes their customers have to wait, do without the service, or go elsewhere.
- Relationship providers are generally more satisfied with their work and earn more money than encounter providers.
- Relationship services usually are more expensive for the customer; they appeal to customers who are more interested in getting exactly the service they want than those who are looking for the best price.
- Encounter businesses require a lot of money to get started and must have good management to succeed.

- Encounter businesses must have well-designed processes for providing the service and for customer feedback.
- Encounter businesses can continue expanding as long as the managers can find and hire providers and can attract enough customers. This means profits can keep growing, too.
- Encounter businesses service customers efficiently, but customer loyalty is usually weak, whereas relationship providers are not as concerned with efficiency and usually have very loyal customers.

Encounters and relationships are different, but perhaps because encounter businesses are still an evolving form, there can be many customer problems. The next chapter deals with service models, and the following three chapters look at ways service encounters can be improved for greater customer satisfaction.

Notes

1. Braverman, Harry. *Labor and Monopoly Capital: The Degradation of Work in the Twentieth Century* (Monthly Review Press, originally published 1974).
2. Zuboff, Shoshana. *In the Age of the Smart Machine: The Future of Work and Power* (New York: Basic Books, 1988).
3. Heskett, James L. *Managing in the Service Economy* (Boston: Harvard Business School Press, 1986).
4. Gallagher, John. "Can't Get No Satisfaction," *Detroit Free Press,* June 3, 1998.
5. McSpotlight Web site (www.mcspotlight.org).
6. Personal communication with Bob Talbert, February 12, 1999.
7. Ritzer, George. *McDonaldization of Society* (Thousand Oaks, Ca.: Pine Forge Press, 1996).
8. From ABCnews.com, "Fighting the 'Corporate Fort,' " October 22, 1998.
9. Hukill, Tracy. "You've Got a Friend at Safeway, Inc.," *Sonoma County Independent*, June 26–July 2, 1997.
10. Hogue, Ruthann. *Arizona Daily Star* series on call centers, November 18, 1998.
11. Gutek, Barbara. *Dynamics of Service* (San Francisco: Jossey-Bass, 1995).

Chapter Three

Customers, Organizations, and Providers: Managing the Links of the Brave New Service

What Is the Best Way to Structure a Service Business?

Is there a best way to structure a service business? Does the nature of the business drive its structure? Let's look at the three basic elements of a service business and see how having either tight or loose links between these elements affects the business.

The COP Model of Encounters and Relationships

Our service model includes three elements: the *Customer* [C], the *Organization* [O], and the *Provider* [P]. By placing these elements into the points of a triangle and visualizing the connections as loose or tight links, you can apply the concepts explained in the last two chapters to any service business.

This model excludes only the individual practitioner or

Figure 3-1   The C-O-P Model

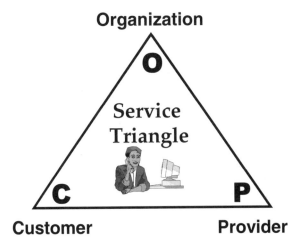

Organization

Service
Triangle

Customer   Provider

one-person business (where there is no organization). Any other service business fits into one of the models shown in Figures 3-2 and 3-3 on page 62. In our models, the *organization* is represented by the owners and managers who run the business and encompasses the brand image of the service products. The *providers* are the customer contact workers who deal with customers and actually provide the service. The provider could also be a machine or automated process. The *customers* are everyone who purchases the service offered by the organization and dispensed by the providers. These models, each the same except for the type of links connecting C-O-P, will be used throughout the remaining chapters as a conceptual framework.

Figure 3-2 shows the four ways an organization, individual service provider, and customer can be linked in a service relationship. What is common to these relationships is a tight C-P link.

The first relationship model involves tight links between all three components. An example is a business in which providers work for a high-prestige consulting company or a high-priced law firm where providers are well-paid and gain prestige from their position with the firm. Customers also value their ties to the firm and develop a close working relationship with a specific service provider.

Figure 3-2   Relationship Models

  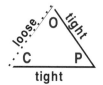

tight	tight	tight	tight
A good model, but describes a very small number of businesses.	Here, the customer has a tradition with the company and deals with the same provider each time, such as an assigned phone representative.	In this model, the provider may be the founder and "star" whose clients value him highly and whose firm is well-known.	This is a business in which the organization serves only as a means to bring together customers and providers.

Figure 3-3   Encounter Models

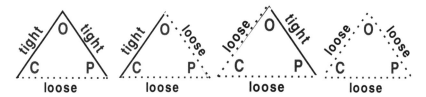

loose	loose	loose	loose

**Pseudo-Relationship or
Enhanced Encounter**
characterized by a tight C-O link

The customer knows and trusts the organization which also keeps the loyalty of its employees.	The organization offers good value to the customer and enjoys repeat business, but has a high turnover of employees.	Here, the company has done a good job of hiring and training employees, but has not built a strong image with customers.	This is an encounter business which does little to gain repeat customers and has high employee turnover—not useful for most business.

The second type of relationship has tight links between the customer and provider and between the customer and organization. Providers may have developed their skills on the job, such as phone representatives for a mail order/Web business, or they may work in a partnership where they are not partners. In this model, the provider may quit the organization to go to a better opportunity, leaving the customer to decide whether to follow her or stay with the company.

The third type of relationship has strong C-P and O-P links. The organization may be identified with a "star" provider, the person who built an advertising agency, consulting firm, or polling service, for example. Customers are linked to the organization through their tight ties with an individual provider whose services are highly valued. This could describe any well-known academic who has set up a partnership firm in which he has part ownership in order to do consulting or the top partner in a professional firm where the provider is strongly identified with the organization.

The final type of relationship has a tight link between the customer and provider, but both have loose ties to the organization. This is good for providers, but not for the organization which risks losing both its providers and its customers. Beauty salons where providers rent space, doctors or therapists sharing a practice, and attorneys sharing an office fit this model. Here there is a steady turnover of both providers and customers, with customers following service providers when they leave to go to a new office or firm.

Figure 3-3 shows the four ways an organization, individual service provider, and customer can be linked in a service encounter. The common feature of encounters is a loose C-P link. The first two of these models are characterized by a tight C-O link; the customer is loyal to the organization. These types of encounters we call pseudo-relationships or enhanced encounters. (The difference between them will be described in detail in Chapter Six.)

The first model describes any encounter firm where the organization has loyal employees as well as loyal customers. The organization provides well-designed processes for the provider to interact with the customer. This might describe a high-priced hotel chain where both the desk clerk and the customer checking in feel the process works well.

The second model describes businesses where employee turnover is high, a common type of encounter business. Fast food restaurants and most retail sales fit this model. The organization keeps customer loyalty through competitive pricing and procedures that can be quickly taught to new employees.

The other types of encounters have loose C-O ties. The third model might describe a start-up company or a company selling something like long-distance phone services, where customers are confused about many similar offers, but the providers tend to stay with the firm.

The final model, characterized by loose links on all three sides of the triangle, is an encounter business which does little to gain repeat customers and has high turnover. This model fits services that are quick and low-cost where customers are transient, like a newsstand at an airport.

As Figures 3-2 and 3-3 show, most service businesses have at least one loose link. In the case of encounters, there will always be a loose C-P link. Organizations compensate for this by providing the customer with convenience, reliability, and low cost. A tight C-O link means the organization has built customer loyalty.

Relationships and What They Mean

Much of this book deals with the misuse of the term "relationship." But some companies really do establish relationships between their providers and customers. There is a risk involved in this strategy because it loosens links between customers and the organization and possibly between providers and the organization. When a company is based on the skills of the providers rather than an encounter process, that company and the service it provides cannot be duplicated. You can duplicate a process, but not a person.

Providers who work in relationship businesses bring special skills to their work that they use on the customer's behalf. The customer values this skill, and his appreciation brings satisfaction to the provider. This creates meaning in a way that encounters do not. David Maister talks about the importance of meaning in the work of professionals. He says it is the job of those supervising young professionals to help them see the meaning in their work:

> Rarely have I heard of young professionals becoming demotivated because of too much work; most often (all too often) demotivation results from too much *meaningless* work. And since almost no work done by a professional firm is in fact meaningless (it is all or should be valuable to clients), this syndrome represents a failure of management.[1]

This quote shows the difference in the way workers in relationship jobs and encounter jobs are treated. Firms of consultants, lawyers, and accountants try to develop the skills of their providers through individually tailored work assignments and mentoring. No such consideration is given to the average encounter worker who may be put through a canned training program in which each provider is treated the same. Because encounter work doesn't allow for individual differences, neither does the preparation for the work.

Making Relationships From an Encounter Business

Some service organizations that would normally operate as encounter businesses have tried assigning a specific representative to each customer so customers can actually build a relationship with their provider. This will usually please both customer and provider. Research shows customers like relationships, and providers benefit because working in relationships means more variety and greater autonomy in their work.

But there are some drawbacks:

- The customer may be upset if her provider leaves the company.
- The customer may not always be able to reach his provider.

A company that has built up goodwill with the customer (a tight C-O link) will probably be able to keep the customer if the provider leaves, but the customer may be unhappy about having to work with a new provider. The organization may allow the customer to choose a new provider, or one may be assigned. The new provider will need time to understand the customer's needs. Relationships are based on repeated interactions, so someone new is at a disadvantage and may not be able to service the customer effectively in the beginning. The organization may offer incentives for customers to stay, then bring the new provider up to speed as quickly as possible. If the customer has a contract with the organization, such as an insurance policy, a health club membership, or a computer support agreement, it may be difficult for her to switch to another company right away, even if she is unhappy about the loss of her personal provider. She may still leave when the contract expires.

Customers who call and find their provider is on vacation will have to leave a message or talk to someone else. This may be only a small inconvenience if the customer really likes the personal service or values the privacy (would you talk to anyone but your financial adviser about your investments or anyone but your lawyer about your divorce settlement?). Where the service does not require privacy, it may be perceived as a drawback. If no one else can locate the information on that customer, it may drive the customer to another company in which the service is in encounters and any provider can access information on any customer. It depends on which the customer values more—privacy or convenience.

In a relationship business, the most important segment of the service triangle is the link between customer and provider. An organization of relationship providers must strengthen this bond, which is the basis for the business. But it also presents a dilemma. The tighter the C-P bond, the looser the C-O and O-P bonds are likely to be. Organizations risk losing their customers and their providers if they don't have another tight link. They can try to bind their customers to the organization by building up the image and reputation of the company and by supplying the methodology and technology used by providers (making it difficult for the providers to offer the service without the organization). Or they can try to bind the providers to the organization by making their pay and working conditions highly desirable. This will keep providers from leaving and taking customers with them, but it may loosen the link between the provider and the customer since the provider forms his primary loyalty to the company and not to the customer.

CDW—Building Tight Links

One direct sales company that offers "personalized expertise—your own highly trained account manager for every order, every call, every time" is CDW, a $1.4 billion Fortune 1000 computer products company founded by Michael P. Krasny. CDW calls itself the country's leading "direct solutions provider." Founded in 1984, CDW had a customer base split 70 percent business/30 percent consumer in 1994 that had shifted to 90 percent business/10 percent consumer by 1998. They market to the small to medium-sized business and provide each customer with a personal "Direct Solutions Provider." CDW offers competitive prices on a comprehensive selection of more than 80,000 brand name computer products, including hardware, software, networking, peripherals, and accessories. While it doesn't manufacture any product or write custom software, CDW has grown at a fast rate (according to *Fortune* magazine, "one of America's 100 fastest-growing companies"), based on its high-quality service. Because their account managers work directly with the customer, they can do custom configurations or install a customer-specified software load.

CDW has taken catalog and Web-based sales beyond "mail-order" by having highly skilled people work directly with customers. In an industry noted for tales of over-controlled, low-paid workers toiling away in sweat-shop phone rooms, CDW stands out. It ranks on *Fortune* magazine's list as "one of the 100 best places to work." It also received an award from its local Better Business Bureau for demonstrating ethical practices toward customers, suppliers, coworkers, and the community. CDW is reversing an incredible number of practices found in other companies that sell to the public by phone:

1. Instead of outsourcing phone rooms, CDW's workers are all under a single 218,000 square-foot roof in Vernon Hills, Illinois, outside Chicago.
2. CDW uses technology as a tool for its account representatives. Its annual report says, "Our enabling technology approach does not replace people interactions, rather, it frees up account managers, targets their efforts away from paperwork to direct customer contact, speeds their response time and improves their effectiveness."
3. Instead of paying minimum wages and providing few benefits, CDW pays salary, commission, and has such extras as free meals for late night workers and on-site child care; all workers are called "coworkers."
4. Instead of hiring people with few skills and giving them a script to follow, CDW trains their workers through CDW University and promotes from within.

CDW founder Michael P. Krasny says, "It's really very simple—service the customer. Success is not complicated. It's actually very simple. People try to overcomplicate it." He added, "If servicing the customer ever becomes a deterrent to growing your business . . . I think I'd like to retire."[2]

The headline on the first page of CDW's catalog proclaims: "Introducing That Special Someone You've Been Waiting For." It goes on to promise:

> [The direct solutions provider] assigned to you personally . . . will use his expertise to help you select the right top-name brands . . . and build a custom-configured solution that's right for your business. Finally, a one-stop resource for everything you need, including great savings in time and money. It's exactly what you should expect from a billion-dollar Fortune 1000 company. So call CDW or visit www.cdw.com to meet your personal account manager. And begin a rewarding new relationship.

Krasny explains that the account representatives are grouped into "streets." If a customer's representative is not available, another person on the same street will take care of the call. This is a response to one of the weaknesses of relationships: the provider is not always available.

CDW does not sell customer information to other companies. This is important in building trust with customers. The customer can establish a real relationship with her service representative, but this is necessarily a distance relationship that requires extra indications of good intentions, such as the company's pledge to keep information confidential. Since the customer does not determine the provider's pay or working conditions, the relationship is not as tight as that created with professional service firms. The organization is a strong player in this triad and must prove its trustworthiness as well.

Krasny's methods do not arise from anything learned in business school; they come from his own experience and feelings about how to service customers. He began the business from his home, selling computers through newspaper ads. Asked how he came up with the idea of providing personal account representatives for each client, he answered "When there was just me selling, people would call and ask for 'Michael.' When I added other people, they got their own customers who asked for them." His purely intuitive business model has built strong customer loyalty and sales positioned to go over $2 billion.

The following list illustrates some of CDW's "Philosophy of Success . . . based on our company's foundation—the Circle of Service—where everything we do revolves around the customer":

1. What's right yesterday may not be right today. What's right today may not be right tomorrow. And what's right tomorrow may not be right today. Conclusion: Don't be afraid of change.
2. It's only good if it's Win-Win.
3. Pay attention to your weaknesses. If you dwell on your successes, you will suffocate on your weaknesses.
4. Smile. People can hear you smile through the phone.
5. Good luck many times comes disguised as hard work.

6. Treat every customer as if they were your *only* customer. If you don't, they may be your *last* customer.
7. Pigs get fat; hogs get slaughtered.
8. Perfection is unattainable. If you strive for perfection, you will achieve excellence.
9. The higher in an organization you get, the more that is expected of you, the less you are told.
10. People do business with people they like.
11. Success means never being satisfied.

CDW's triangle would probably have tight O-P and C-P links. Its loosest link may be C-O, but that matters little since the provider works for CDW and cannot easily take his customers if he leaves: CDW's partnership with vendors and processes for filling orders are part of the reason customers buy from them. The provider, if he worked for a different company, might not be able to duplicate them. In addition, CDW has launched a branding campaign to build awareness of the organization. They come very close to tight links all the way around the triangle . . . a unique situation for a company that essentially sells the same products as many other companies. Research shows that customers are more satisfied and have more interactions when they do business in relationships. Could that explain the success of CDW?

Relationships in Which the Provider Works in a Strong Organization

There are benefits to customer and provider working in a relationship, but a strong intrusion by the organization tends to loosen the link. The customer may trust the provider a bit less, knowing the provider's major commitment is to the organization. The provider may value the customer a bit less, knowing she gets paid whether the customer likes her or not.

Social service agencies are examples of organizations that have a tight link to employees, but a loose link to customers. Clients deal with one social worker, but do not pay this provider directly and the social worker is bound to the priorities of the organization. Service is based on the policies of the organization, which do not necessarily match clients' individual needs. Schools are another example. In K-12 or vocational education, schools employ teachers who follow a set curriculum or course outline. The course of study is not customized for any student and students do not directly pay their teachers. This tends to tighten the bond between the student and the school rather than the student and the teacher. Students, like other kinds of customers, have gained a little more influence in recent years. Most institutions of higher learning have a system that lets undergraduate students rate faculty, with these ratings counting toward raises, endowed chairs, or promotions.

The duration of the service in these settings is mainly determined by the organization rather than the customer. The social service agency can decide to terminate a client. A student's graduation is based on his or her meeting the requirements of the school, not on ties to any individual teacher. The school expels or graduates the student. All of these factors tend to weaken a customer-provider relationship.

When we're talking about graduate school, the links between customer (student) and provider (professor) get much tighter, especially in doctoral work. Studying under a prominent professor can mean a lot to the student, and the student may continue to work with the professor on research after completing her degree. They generally maintain their relationship through professional conferences.

Despite limiting factors, tight relationships may develop between social worker and client or teacher and student. A provider brings to his work a degree of skill at what he does and many bring an ability to relate well to other people. The personal charm of the provider can be an important factor in getting and keeping customers. People are so used to encounter service where their interaction with the provider is fleeting that many have become used to judging providers on superficial qualities. Some of this spills over into relationships in which the person who is attractive or good at conversation may attract more clients than someone less charming. It is difficult for clients to actually judge the competence of professionals, so they may fall back on other, easier methods of evaluation. Despite this, relationship providers often bring a genuine concern for their customers to their work.

When the provider has a heavy financial stake in the company, the result is a tight O-P link. If the provider has devoted many years to developing the client base and skills needed to qualify for partnership in a professional firm, for example, she is not likely to leave. However, her customers will have their main allegiance to her, and it may be difficult to shift any of her work to junior staffers. Prestige and name recognition may accrue to the partners rather than to the firm. Individuals at the firm may become well known and simply operate on their own, without regard to the growth and best interests of the firm. There can also be rivalries and jealousies among partners who vie for the title of "best producer" for the firm.

Carried to extremes, some members of professional firms become "stars" who are sought after for their fame and who command very high fees. Lawyers who handle famous cases, architects who design extraordinary public buildings, and consultants with best-selling books are examples. These people do not really need the firm; they could go it alone and make big money. Dealing with "star performers" can be a challenge. Their star quality can disrupt the operation of a professional firm, but if they leave, it could be devastating for the firm as well.

Relationship With Two Loose Links

Where only the customer-provider bond is tight, you essentially have an association of professionals who neither have built a reputation for their firm nor have a big stake in it. They may simply share offices and bill out their services independently. The organization plays a weak, almost incidental, role. It may exist just for shared facilities: three lawyers who share an office and a secretary, two medical specialists who share an office and cover each other for vacation time, or four beauticians who rent space together. In this case, each practitioner develops his or her own client load, and none has a big incentive to promote the company or work together effectively. A strong organization can provide a vision that comes from a leader. In a loose association, each person has to find his or her own motivation.

Many relationship companies are not corporations but are organized as partnerships. While corporations exist "forever" under their charter, partnerships depend on the continued participation of the partners. Partners are direct owners of the business in a way corporate managers are not. They are directly responsible for the success or failure of the business. They have strong incentives to build good customer relationships because they depend on the repeat business of those customers to make their living. The organization, if there is one, is not a major player and often does not need to be.

Relationships are about filling a need, not about perpetuating an organization. Some professionals are happy to simply close their business when they retire and do not see a need to perpetuate it beyond that. So the role of the organization in a relationship partnership is not as important as in an encounter business in which a corporation has been established with the awareness that it will outlast its founders.

The Pseudo-Relationship

Two types of encounter formats, as shown in Figure 3-4 on page 74, superficially resemble relationships—what some other commentators refer to as "relationship marketing." These formats have a tight C-O link, a weak C-P link, and may have a tight or a loose O-P link. Pseudo-relationships have one or both of these elements:

1. The customer knows the organization.
2. The organization has information about the customer.

These models can apply to either pseudo-relationships or enhanced encounters, depending on how the business pursues its strategy of building a tight link with customers. We'll discuss creating enhanced encounters in depth in Chapter Six.

Customer Knows the Organization

Customers may choose a store, hotel, airline, or fast food restaurant because they know the organization. This may be from

Figure 3-4   Pseudo-Relationship Model

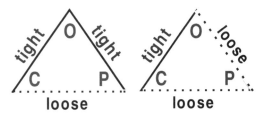

personal experience with shopping at Sears, staying at Hyatt Hotels, flying on Delta Airlines, or eating at Wendy's; it may also be from seeing ads or commercials that seem to give the service a legitimacy. Chain businesses build customer goodwill through the uniformity of their service, providing a familiarity and dependability that has nothing to do with the actual person who will deliver the service. The C-P link is always loose, but the customer gets a sense of comfort from knowing the organization.

Even if the customer is not always pleased, brand loyalty may keep him coming back for a while. Sears, Roebuck is one company that was able to turn itself around from a near-fatal plunge in sales partly because of its favorable image with the public. Despite poor customer ratings at its low point in sales in 1992, the company's research showed that through the years, American families had maintained a positive, trusting image of Sears as a good, honest place to shop. This helped the company work its way back from near disaster.

McDonald's is another example of a strong brand image. It is the favorite restaurant of so many children that it becomes a place for families to accumulate happy memories. Watching your kids play in the ball crawl and enjoy their Happy Meal toy creates an aura of good feeling around the golden arches. The fact that McDonald's also delivers the same food at each restaurant in a perfectly dependable way explains its success despite an employee turnover rate as high as 300 percent. The link between McDonald's and its customers is tight enough to overcome the sometimes lackluster service at the counter and the lack of much choice on the menu. Besides, so many people have either worked at McDonald's or know someone who has that customers forgive occasional slow service or long lines at the drive-through. Familiarity becomes a powerful driver of customer loyalty.

On a more high tech note, the "Intel inside" logo and the short musical jingle that goes with it have become very familiar. Although the processor in a personal computer is invisible to the average user who wouldn't know a processor chip from a potato chip, many customers will still make sure they buy a computer with "Intel inside." It is all too easy for computer makers to substitute a different manufacturer's chip, so Intel is creating a strong brand image for itself so customers will ask for it.

For the customer to feel this sense of familiarity, the business must have been around long enough to have a public image and for customers to have some experience with the company. The bond is tightest when the customer has had repeated contact with the organization and has been pleased with the result. Businesses with big advertising budgets have the advantage in creating a brand image. Branding is really a substitute for the old pre-industrial model of customer knowing the provider, but it substitutes an organization and uniform experience for an actual relationship.

Organization Knows the Customer

As businesses compete for customers, many of them compile data about their customers in an attempt to build "relationships." But data and information are not the same thing. And having data about someone does not make a relationship. The data a company has about a customer may not have been given willingly or even knowingly. Information about a customer can be obtained in a variety of ways: freely given upon request, captured during a transaction, or extracted from a purchased data base. It can be used in many different ways, some of which can be offensive to the customer. Here's one example from an article on relationship marketing in the *Harvard Business Review* by Susan Fournier, Susan Dobscha, and David Glen Mick, in which a customer relates his story:

The company has what seems to be a good idea . . . Each year around the holidays, it sends out a reminder to its customers, telling them what they ordered the year before and for whom. The problem is, several years ago I ordered presents for the physicians who took care of my mother when she was hospitalized for an emergency medical condition. And each year now, the company reminds me of that awful time. I even called the company and explained that I don't generally buy presents for the people on that list. I told them why, and I asked for those names to be deleted.[3]

Someone who had a real relationship with the person quoted above would know that he did not want to be reminded of a difficult time in his life.

Of course, every contact with a customer can be an opportunity to sell her something, and using data you have on file about that customer can facilitate a sale. Companies that retain information from each contact can build a picture of the customer's buying preferences so that any provider can deal more intelligently with that customer. Relationships get more efficient over time because of what the customer and provider know about each other. While this is always true of a relationship, the customer's encounters with an organization can also build efficiency into the sales process.

Don Peppers and Martha Rogers, authors of the 1993 book *The One-to-One Future*, advocate keeping track of *all* transactions. Their idea, a breakthrough insight that has influenced marketers ever since, was that companies could use this information to send customers only the sales pitches they want and provide them with attractive offers tailored to their individual needs. They urged marketers to look at the long-term possibilities in dealing with customers, trying for "share of customer," not "share of market." The customer was no longer to be regarded as part of a "segment" but to be looked upon as a unique individual. Peppers and Rogers say:

Over a longer period of interaction, the customer and marketer, not unlike long-time friends, or business partners, or spouses, develop their own "context" of understanding that provides a more and more familiar background for every new conversation.[4]

But this ignores the fact that the customer is dealing with different people for each transaction. It is only through the organization that the provider knows anything about the customer. The data on the customer can be helpful in making the transaction quick and efficient so the customer need not supply her address and credit card number again. The provider should be able to call up that customer's buying history on a computer screen very quickly, thereby having fast access to the customer's previous orders. Customers must believe that this kind of personal data is only used to provide more convenient service.

If customers find their names have been sold to other companies that bombard them with unwanted messages, they will lose trust in the organization that gave away their names. Many Web-based businesses are new companies without a long history with the customer or an image of being dependable and honest, like Sears, for example. And yet they ask their customers to trust them with all kinds of personal information.

The 1998 (ninth) survey by the Graphics, Visualization and Usability Center (GVU)[5] showed that 51 percent of people say they have deliberately entered false information at Web sites that requested personal information. Customers are so distrustful of how organizations will use personal information that many prefer to simply make something up rather than give truthful answers. This is another indication that even repeated transactions with a company do not constitute a "relationship." The person on the other end of the phone or Web site is still a stranger to the customer.

What can companies do to make customers feel more trusting about data-gathering? Companies should make sure their employees use data in a sensitive manner. Customers may be uneasy when they realize the information they gave to one employee is now known to all employees. This may prompt some customers to lie or conceal information they would provide if they could deal with only one provider in a real relationship.

Customers intuitively know they cannot have a relationship with a company. Again, quoting the *Harvard Business Review* on relationship marketing:

Ironically, the very things that marketers are doing to build relationships with customers are often the things that are destroying those relationships. Why? Perhaps we are skimming over the fundamentals of relationship building in our rush to cash in on the potential rewards of creating close connections with our customers. Perhaps we do not understand what creating a relationship really means; that is, how customers' trust and intimacy factor into the connections we are trying to forge. Relationship marketing is powerful in theory but troubled in practice.

This article goes on to explain that customers have too many offers coming from too many companies. They are confused and overwhelmed and have no sense of "relationship" to the companies pursuing them. They may not even have positive feelings for the companies vying for their business. What happens when someone who doesn't smoke gets a free pack of cigarettes in the mail with a coupon for more? Or someone whose baby has died gets free diapers? Or a deaf person gets a catalog of music CDs? Would someone who had a "relationship" with these people make this kind of mistake? Of course not!

Companies are using data to make a lot of assumptions about individual customers. For example, Web sites that require registration provide clues to customers' interests and buying habits that are then used to send offers via e-mail. Tower Records' direct-to-consumer division uses a "collaborative filtering system" to pull out addresses of those customers who might consider buying a category of music such as jazz. Then, the company sends e-mail to these customers promoting Web sites where they can buy jazz CDs.[6] These methods do reach customers, some of whom are interested in the product being pitched, but they are no more personal than a stranger's smile. All such pitches are based on assumptions. Some of those people who bought jazz CDs, for instance, may have purchased them as gifts for someone else and may never buy another jazz CD. A relationship provider would know that, but a database "knows" nothing. What the database doesn't know can hurt the organization making the pitch. A travel service might assume a woman who took a trip to Japan was on vacation while a man going to Japan was on a business trip. That can be insulting to the businesswoman who sees her retired husband getting mailings about business trips while she gets mailings about vacations. In a relationship, a provider would learn something about the customer's habits, likes, and dislikes—the kinds of things you know about someone you see regularly—like the fact that the well-dressed couple with the suitcases is on *her* business trip, not his.

Knowing someone's address and shirt size does not tell you anything meaningful about that person. Like the superficial judgments service providers make of their customers based on a two-minute transaction, organizations also make superficial judgments. Mary bought a Hanson CD, so she might buy a Backstreet Boys CD. David ate at McDonald's today, so he might come back tomorrow if we give him a coupon. Keisha bought an expensive sweater last month, so she might buy other items from our premium catalog. Andy visited three Sci Fi Web sites, so he might like to get an e-mail about a special offer on a Sci Fi magazine. These are all big leaps based on very little. New kinds of software can search databases for patterns—related buying habits revealed in large masses of data—that can make these kind of pitches more accurate. But they are still just based on averages, not on knowledge of any one customer. Using aggregated data to look for trends is different from thinking that you can get at an individual customer's future purchases. Statistical probabilities are not relationships.

Eventually, all of these methods will suffer from the same overuse as the gimmicks of traditional direct mail marketing such as using the customer's name in big letters in the mailing, providing a phony check, or making the mailing look official (as if it came from the government). The only enduring form of one-to-one contact is a true relationship in which a customer and a provider actually know one another and have repeated interaction over time.

What gives data gathering a bad name is all the companies that purchase huge data bases of names based on common attributes—all homeowners, for instance—and target them by telemarketing or mailing. Instead of cultivating long-term customers, these tactics use a shot-gun approach to attract new customers. According to Peppers and Rogers, "You won't generate trust and promote a long-term relationship with a customer or prospective customer when you use detailed, personal information to make a one-time sale to a stranger." They cite cases of what they regard as insensitive use of information, such as getting addresses of people convicted of drunk driving and sending them a solicitation to buy a breath analyzer or using driver's license height and weight data to target overweight ladies for large-size clothing. They also state that in 1991, Lotus Development Company was going to release a set of disks containing names, addresses, likely income levels, and shopping habits of 80 million U.S. households—almost every household in the United States. When Lotus got 30,000 protests, they withdrew the product. This shows an overwhelming fear on the part of the public about too many companies having too much information about them. In a real relationship, information each party has about the other is acquired naturally over the time and experiences shared between the parties. The "data" does not exist in a computer database but in the minds of the people who have the relationship.

Peppers and Rogers clearly thought data create a relationship when they wrote *The One to One Future*. In a discussion of the "economies of scope, not of scale," they say, "The deeper a relationship you have—the more information about the customer in your possession—the less likely it is that your competitor will be able to wrestle that particular customer away from you."[7]

We must respectfully disagree with Peppers and Rogers. What such companies have is a pseudo-relationship. They have data, and data and information are not the same thing. Compiling data on customers may or may not pay off, depending on the quality of experience the customer has with the organization.

Customers do not share marketers' enthusiasm for one-to-one marketing. Fournier, Dobscha, and Mick wrote in the *Harvard Business Review*:

> The number of one-on-one relationships that companies ask consumers to maintain is untenable. As a result, many mar-

keting initiatives seem trivial and useless instead of unique and valuable. Every company wants the rewards of long-term, committed partnerships. But people maintain literally hundreds of one-on-one relationships in their personal lives with spouses, coworkers, casual acquaintances. And clearly, only a handful of them are of a close and committed nature. How can we expect people to do any more in their lives as consumers?

The May 1998 *Wired* magazine contained a long article by Chip Bayers that took a look at whether Peppers and Rogers' "one-to-one future" was coming to pass. He concluded that most marketers are gathering far more data than they have any idea how to use and that many successful Web marketers are not anywhere near "one-to-one" in their methods. For example, the Excite search service was collecting forty gigabytes of data every day. It was impossible to deal with such massive amounts of data in any meaningful way. The article quoted Donna Hoffman of Vanderbilt University, who said, "In theory, any site can know a great deal about what its users are doing. But in practice very few sites have the technical expertise or the marketing expertise to know what to do with the data." Bayers pointed out that the bookseller Amazon.com has been very successful by simply showing visitors other books similar to the ones they select. Amazon.com asks nothing of visitors and very little of buyers. They do assign buyers a unique ID that identifies them so they don't have to enter personal information the next time, but they give up the chance to collect a lot more data. Could that actually be a source of their customers' loyalty? In early 1998, Amazon.com reported that 58 percent of its customers were repeat buyers.

Bayers concluded that Internet marketing is "all about using the trick of technology to deliver a personalized message that isn't really personal at all . . . the consumer, it is hoped, will perceive a one-to-one relationship; the truth will be somewhat different."[8]

How Organizations Build Tight Links to Customers

Peer-to-peer help can be useful in some kinds of service businesses to substitute for the customer having a relationship with a provider. Overworked computer support operations could start a user group where computer users share tips and ideas. While some tech support managers might feel threatened by the idea of computer users helping each other, it would reduce the frustration level of customers who can't get the help they need right away. Customers can "let off steam" in these user meetings and often will find they are all having similar problems, making them feel less ignorant. Often, someone in the group knows the solution to a common problem. This reduces the load on the help desk.

Another solution is one used by Home Depot that offers onsite classes to educate customers. Home Depot personnel hold demonstration classes showing how to lay floor tiles, hang drywall, put in plumbing, or whatever their customers need help with, and they tell customers to call at any time when they need help with their project. Customers can also chat with each other about their home improvement projects during these demonstrations. Obviously, the customers of these classes will buy their supplies at Home Depot. It also serves to grow the base of customers willing to try "do it yourself" projects as they perceive that help is as near as their Home Depot store. Home Depot can offer this service because its workforce includes many full-time skilled employees who earn above-average salaries. An article in *Fortune* on Home Depot notes:

> Home Depot succeeded where others faltered by being the first on the block (now almost every block) to recognize just what the core customer wanted: everything. They built radical "big box" stores (the typical new store is 108,000 square feet) and loaded them with every imaginable home product, under one humongous roof. Nothing fancy, just rows and rows of building materials and good old-fashioned toolbox stuff. Then they hired carpenters, plumbers, contractors, and other industry professionals to stroll the aisles in bright-orange aprons with their names handwritten on the front, and drilled them in the founders' mantra: This is a service business, not a discount hardware store. Help customers solve their problems, don't just sell them a wrench.[9]

Home Depot has tight C-O and O-P links. Home Depot is building an image for itself of being a dependable place to buy home improvement products and get the help needed to use those products. Such a scenario necessarily includes a tight O-P link as its employees must buy into the corporate culture of helping customers. If customers went to Home Depot and found employees standing around talking to each other instead of offering to help, or received only blank stares when they asked what kind of glue to use to install bathroom tiles, they would soon lose faith in this picture of Home Depot as a helpful place to shop.

Following this model, lawyers could hold legal clinics in how to write a will or how to get a divorce. Many law firms do provide specialty clinics for their corporate customers. This lets those attending learn together, benefiting from the experiences and questions of everyone attending. These kinds of clinics, if advertised to the public, would help establish a friendly image for the firm and enable them to offer help at a low cost.

In a real relationship, the customer comes to trust the provider. This is especially important in professional services (doctor, accountant, consultant, etc.) where the customer may not be able to judge the actual competence of the provider. The feeling of trust is an important element in the customer continuing to return to the same provider. David Maister notes in his book *Managing the Professional Service Firm*:

> Just as with my garage mechanic, when I find a professional service provider whom I trust, in whom I can have confidence, and who provides me with peace of mind and reassurance, I will tend to remain with that provider. Indeed, on most technical or professional matters outside my own area of expertise, I am as much shopping for trust, confidence, peace of mind, and reassurance as I am for "cold" technical expertise.[10]

Organizations can try to build this kind of trust with their customer, too. Building a strong brand image through use of logos and celebrity spokespersons helps accomplish this. For instance, it is easier to feel you have a relationship with Mickey Mouse than with the Disney organization, with Ronald McDonald than with McDonald's Inc., with Snoopy rather than with Met Life, with Joe Camel rather than a big conglomerate.

Ronald McDonald is such a well-known character he was reported to be familiar to more people than Santa Claus. There is a story making the e-mail rounds on the Internet told by a man who played Ronald McDonald in southern California. The man was visiting a hospital one day and at the end of his round, he heard a small voice call "Ronald, Ronald" as he passed through a corridor. Stepping inside, he saw a boy "about five years old, lying in his dad's arms, hooked up to more medical equipment than I had ever seen. Mom was on the other side, along with Grandma, Grandpa and a nurse tending to the equipment." The boy was obviously in very serious condition. He made one request of Ronald: "Will you hold me?" But Ronald, who was with two "handlers" from the McDonald's Corporation, was supposed to observe a rule not to touch any patient—this could pass germs. Ronald played and talked with the boy, but soon the request was repeated. The man decided to risk losing his job and grant this dying boy's wish. He sent the "handlers" out to the car and asked the parents to leave, too. Then he held the boy, who told him of his fears his brother would get lost on the way to school when he had to go alone, and that his dog would not know where to look for bones the boy had buried for him. It was clear the boy knew he would never be going home. Ronald gave the parents his phone number—another McDonald's no-no—and told them to call if he could do anything. A few days later, the boy's mother called to let him know the boy had died. The mother reported that before he died, her son said "Momma, I don't care anymore if I see Santa this year because I was held by Ronald McDonald." The McDonald's corporation discovered what he did but did not fire this kindly Ronald.

We're not sure if this Ronald story is true or not, but it illustrates the mythic power of a character like Ronald McDonald, a spokesperson created entirely by the corporation but capable of building an incredibly tight link between McDonald's and its customers.

Other companies create a composite character to represent their workers like "Mr. Goodwrench," who will fix your car using "Genuine GM Parts." Mr. Goodwrench would probably be the loser in a contest between a trusted neighborhood mechanic and the unknown technician represented by Goodwrench at the big dealership. But most people no longer have a trusted personal mechanic, so they look elsewhere for someone to fix their car. Organizations can jump into that void, building an image of trustworthiness through friendly characters who stand for the service of the organization.

How Organizations Build Tight Links to Providers

A tight O-P link often results in good service to the customer because the customer deals with a person who is satisfied with his or her job. While some businesses must pay minimum wage and operate with high turnover, companies that can build a culture of customer service and train and empower their employees can have an advantage. Companies like Marriott and Men's Warehouse have built reputations both for being a good place to work and for good customer service.

Sears, in its turnaround effort, recognized that its employees were a key element. When a top-level Sears executive toured stores across the country and asked hundreds of employees, "What do you think is the primary thing you get paid to do here every day?" the answer he got in more than half the cases was, "I get paid to protect the assets of the company." He felt this was the wrong answer. It was clearly an answer they had been given, and it said nothing about the customer. The answer he wanted to hear was "I get paid to satisfy the customer." He also found employees did not always trust the company, partly because they had misinformation. Employees thought the company made an average of forty-five cents for each dollar sold, but the actual figure was two cents.

Sears initiated a program to reorient its corporate culture toward customer service, giving employees authority to issue refunds or adjustments up to twenty-five dollars without supervisory approval. Sears offers extensive orientation for all employees to teach them the facts of the business. An article in *Harvard Business Review* written by Sears executives states: "It is an issue of trust and of business and economic literacy. Unless employees grasp the purpose of the system, understand the economics of their company and industry, and have a clear picture of how their own work fits into the employee-customer-profit model, they will never succeed in making the whole thing work."[11]

Because not all customer problems can be anticipated, companies should consider giving employees some leeway in dealing with customers (as Sears has done), especially customers who are very unhappy. The Northwest Airlines strike and the flying public's reaction to it illustrate this. *Detroit Free Press* columnist Doron Levin received many e-mails from Northwest customers complaining about shabby treatment from agents on the phone following the settlement between Northwest and its pilots. Despite having balloons and candy at their check-in counter at Metro Airport, Northwest got poor marks from those who contacted Levin. One e-mailer told of an agent insisting on adding a thirty-five-dollar fee for returning World Perks miles that were not used because the customers booked on another airline when the strike came. Levin wrote in his column that Northwest got little sympathy from a public whose loyalty it did not know how to win. He called it "incomprehensible" that Northwest did not acknowledge, let alone rectify, customer complaints. He suggested that Northwest "authorize and train every employee to do whatever it takes—within reason—to make a customer happy. Give free drinks. Distribute more $50 discounts for future tickets. If this step hurts earnings for a few quarters, so be it."[12]

Giving employees some authority to fix problems by waiving a fee or giving a gift certificate not only makes the customer feel better but also empowers the provider in a way that might make him or her feel better as well.

Businesses That Are Just Encounters, Nothing More

There are still two models left, shown in Figure 3-5, that describe encounter businesses that do not have a tight C-O link. Not every service business is trying to build "relationships." Some have recognized that no such thing is possible. A gas station at an expressway exit that serves mostly transient customers or a food stand at an airport may not see a need or opportunity to build any tight ties with customers. Many kinds of routine government services (people who issue business licenses or work permits, for example) may see different custom-

Figure 3-5 Encounter Models

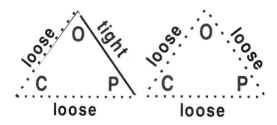

ers every day, besides having captive customers, and never think they should have a "relationship" with the people they service.

In some of these cases, there may be a tight O-P link. Government workers, for example, usually have good pay and benefits and a low turnover rate. In other cases, employees may have little attachment to either the organization [O] or the customer [C]. Regardless of the customer's experience, the business may still make money. A hot dog stand at an outdoor concert full of hungry people may take in a lot of money even if customers have to line up, the hot dog is not great, and the guy serving it is taking his time. Someone who arrives at a small airport and needs a ride and finds the only taxi in town charges an outrageous amount of money will still pay for it if he has no choice.

Many customer call centers would fit into the "all loose links" model. Their employees don't have much loyalty to the organization and neither do their customers. If customers must call an 800 number to order a concert ticket or a software upgrade, they have to endure waiting on the line for a person and can do nothing about it if the person is not helpful. The worker they talk to may be a minimum-wage person who is only at this job until a better job offer comes along.

Conclusion

There is no one answer to the question of which way to go in providing service, in relationships or in encounters. The answer can only come by understanding the differences.

Do you have a relationship business, or can you operate in relationships? If not, then you should probably try to establish a tight link between your organization and its customers. Use the service models introduced in this chapter to help model your own business and consider where you have tight links and where you have loose links.

When you use strategies that build a tight C-O link, you:

1. Take an encounter and make it more effective by giving the customer a set of expectations that are reliably fulfilled.
2. Gather and use information about the customer to deliver the products and services she seeks in a faster and more convenient way.
3. Don't promise what you cannot deliver—you are *not* building a "relationship" with customers.

Notes

1. Maister, David. *Managing the Professional Service Firm* (New York: The Free Press, 1993).
2. Personal communication.
3. Fournier, Susan, Susan Dobschas, and David Glen Mick. "Preventing the Premature Death of Relationship Marketing," *Harvard Business Review*, January/February 1998.
4. Peppers, Don and Martha Rogers. *The One-to-One Future* (New York: Doubleday, 1969).
5. "The 9th GVU WWW User Survey," (http://www.gvu.gatech.edu/user_surveys/survey-1998-04/).
6. "Marketing by E-mail: Sales Tools or Spam?" *New York Times*, December 8, 1998.
7. Peppers, Don and Martha Rogers. op. cit.
8. Bayers, Chip. "The Promise of One-to-One: A Love Story," *Wired*, May 1998.
9. Johnson, Roy S. "Home Depot Renovates," *Fortune*, November 23, 1998.
10. Maister, David. op. cit.
11. Rucci, Anthony J., Steven P. Kirn, and Richard T. Quinn, "The Employee-Customer Profit Chain at Sears," *Harvard Business Review*, January/February 1998.
12. Levin, Doron. "Northwest's Return Relies on Service," *Detroit Free Press*, September 18, 1998.

Chapter Four

Encounter Businesses: Devising Processes, Designing Jobs, and Creating Encounters

Why Encounters?

The smokestack industries brought lots of uniform consumer goods to the masses and a comfortable middle-class way of life to workers. The continuous creation of new manufacturing jobs and constant improvements in manufacturing techniques meant ever-climbing productivity and profits. But there was a down side to it, especially for workers. Most of the manufacturing jobs were boring, some were dangerous, and most did not lead to promotions to better jobs. Workers felt they did not get their fair share of the profits and, in some industries, they formed unions to try to get more. Sometimes management and workers battled it out. In 1937, Henry Ford became so incensed at his workers for wanting a union that he ordered his security people to attack organizers in the "Battle of the Overpass" outside the mammoth Rouge plant in Dearborn, Michigan. United Auto Workers (UAW) president Walter Reuther and others who were with him suffered severe injuries. Henry Ford won that battle, but he and his fellow tycoons lost the war. The auto industry eventually learned to live with the UAW, and the union movement took hold in other burgeoning industries like mining, steel, and trucking.

Encounter businesses offer exactly the same kind of situation that led to the unionization of manufacturing industries, only most of the jobs don't pay as well as those in manufacturing and the jobs are scattered. The reasons for offering service in encounters are the same as the reasons for mass production of goods—greater efficiency and lower price. The captains of industry like Henry Ford and Andrew Carnegie built factories that turned out complex products. They were not in the business of providing services, which were thought to involve simpler tasks that could be delivered one to one.

The success of McDonald's, which delivered hamburgers and french fries, rather than cars or bales of steel, served as an example of service provided through a corporation. It began to occur to entrepreneurs that they could make big profits in establishing a national chain of businesses that delivered a service. And as the new millennium begins, manufacturing will actually imitate services as manufacturers see customer service as the means to differentiate themselves from their competitors and earn more profits.

Corporations establishing chain service businesses may not have considered what the change could mean for the provider-customer transaction. Most have continued the analogy of friendly personal service within the encounter framework. It has taken the form of requiring providers to wear name tags, smile, and "be friendly." But the providers are now employees of big companies, and their pay and promotions come, not from customers, but from an organization. The intervention of organizations in the customer-provider interaction has produced a fundamental change in the way service happens.

Encounter service is characterized by:

1. High volume of customers served
2. Standardization of procedures and services to customers, devised by managers

3. Efficiency of delivery
4. Limited, defined set of tasks performed by the provider, usually for low pay (or less pay than if he or she worked in a relationship)
5. Potentially high profits for owners

These characteristics closely parallel those of manufacturing. Delivering service in high volume can lead to high profits. To deliver in high volume, procedures usually need to be standardized. Standardization should result in greater efficiency. With an efficient process in place, low-skill providers can be used while employing higher skill managers and people who support the technology that enables the business. That is the basic formula for operating an encounter business.

Do Customers Benefit From "Fast Food" Service?

While the "chaining of America" with look-alike encounter businesses reflects the organization side, what about the customer side? Don't customers benefit from an abundance of goods and services? Don't customers love to spend a day at the mall where anything they could want is on the shelves? Don't they appreciate cheap fast food? Does anyone want to go back to the days of overpriced and understocked neighborhood stores? It would seem not.

We also have a new group of consumers: children. Parents of small children can hardly resist their pleas for the latest TV-advertised toy; parents of teenagers are aware of all the must-have cool clothes and beauty products sold from the pages of *Seventeen* and other teen magazines, as well as items hawked by fabulous-looking young people on MTV. These media teach young people to be consumers even before they have jobs, building their desire to join the world of work and get their share of the abundance it produces. In former times, couples wanted children partly because they were necessary farmhands and partly to care for them in their old age. Homes were units of production, but in the post-industrial age, children have become consumers by the time they are out of diapers. They are a new market for new goods and services.

Looking around at the chain businesses that fill every strip mall and shopping center, you can easily arrive at the conclusion that consumers have pretty much abandoned their side of relationships in search of bargains and variety. They have accepted service from strangers in return for having many more places to spend money and more products to spend it on. But, like a ghost from the past, the vision of the village shopkeeper greeting customers who were his neighbors and friends continues to haunt consumers. Americans freely choose to patronize chains, enjoying the large stock, convenient hours, and low prices, but the complaints about poor service indicate many feel something is missing. The problem is, they really can't have it both ways.

Devising Processes

Whatever criteria a business uses to measure efficiency generally drive the design of an encounter service. For example, the process will look different if the designer wants to keep all providers busy all the time than if the designer wants to minimize customer waiting time. If the measure of efficiency is how little time a provider spends on the phone with a customer, the process will look different than if the measure is the amount of information the provider gets about a customer or is based on customer satisfaction surveys.

Sometimes businesses facing competition decide they've been measuring the wrong thing. One business that has decided to rethink its process is New Century Energies in Denver, Colorado. Suzette Tucker-Welch, director of market research and evaluation, reports that monitoring workers at their call center for length of time on the phone and number of calls handled, is not a good measure of serving the customer. Workers feel pressured to finish calls quickly so their numbers will look good. With competition coming to the markets served by New Century, the company wants to emphasize satisfying customers rather than getting rid of them as fast as possible. New Century is bringing in a consultant to help redesign their processes.

Customers who are told their order "isn't in the system" or "it's not in the computer" feel frustrated. Realizing the problem is not the fault of the clerk only increases their frustration. However, in these phone support situations, the clerk on the phone is the only outlet for resolving the problem. Some customers will resort to screaming and cursing at the clerk, even when they know it does no good. Venting their anger provides some immediate relief but does not solve the problem.

A first-person article in the *Los Angeles Times* by a man whose new baby stroller was broken by an airline highlights the explosive anger engendered by a system that provides no way to deal with customer complaints. As he describes it, "I had just spent six hours on a crowded flight from Florida where I'd gone with my wife and two children to visit my mother-in-law. From the beginning, it had been one of those awful holiday travel experiences, complete with cranky kids, disgruntled flight attendants, and a plane that, like the Grinch's heart, was at least three sizes too small." When he retrieved his baggage and found a large crack in the stroller, a fellow passenger said he'd seen the baggage handler throw it. The handler as well as an onsite customer service representative said the airline was not responsible.

He goes on to describe what happened next:

> Finally, a supervisor informed me that the airline was not liable for the damage. Never mind that the stroller had been broken while in the airline's custody on one of its planes.
>
> I looked at him for a moment, waiting for an explanation. Not only did he fail to offer one, he refused to meet my eyes. All I could think about was how much it would cost to replace the stroller and that it had been brand new.
>
> "What?" I yelled. "You've got to be kidding!" Then I slammed my fist down on the counter, and security was called. I wish I could say I feel bad about how I acted, that it was an unfortunate overreaction, borne of frustration and the stress of a holiday trip. [1]

The airport personnel were the only people available for him to talk to and their handling of the matter left him feeling "somehow less than human . . . as if I do not count" (as he says later in the article). He was too angry to let the matter drop and describes his efforts to reach someone over the phone:

> The morning after we returned from Florida, I spent nearly three hours on the phone to various departments getting absolutely nowhere. First, I called a general information number, only to learn that there was no line for customer service, that if I wanted to complain, I would have to do so by mail. Then, I requested a supervisor and discovered that there was a customer service number, but no one except a supervisor could give it out.
>
> There's a nice bit of obfuscation, I thought as I punched in the extension, where I spent twenty minutes on hold before being told that the person I needed was unavailable for the week.
>
> Feeling optimistic, I asked whether there was anyone else I might talk to, a query that got me put back on hold, before I found myself disconnected altogether.
>
> I called back. The number was busy. So much for Round 1.

Not to be deterred by these roadblocks, he next went back to the airport and attempted to find someone. He writes, "I started with the baggage service office before moving to the claims department and finally passenger services, where the manager's secretary said her boss was out for the day but promised he would call me back." He never got the call back, but finally the airline gave him a twenty-five dollar credit for his trouble—only after he learned about a document called "Conditions of Carriage," which states that the airline is not responsible for strollers. This document governs the airlines' responsibilities toward passengers, but the airlines' customers generally don't know it exists and are not given a copy unless they request one.

The workers at this airline could have explained the policy at the time the man discovered his broken stroller and could have offered the twenty-five dollars then—if they had known the policy and were empowered to assist customers who suffer a loss like this. A little sympathy here might have gone a long way, too. Instead, they caused a customer to feel that the airline had "raised customer avoidance to an art form, relying on a mix of miscommunication and indirection to keep disgruntled passengers at bay."

When workers have to repeatedly tell customers they can't help, it just breeds indifference on their part. Not caring becomes the armor they wear to keep from taking on the pain and anger of their customers. They can comfort themselves by thinking what martyrs they are for taking abuse from customers. This reinforces their lack of interest in helping customers, who in their minds become "the bad guys."

Service workers always remember the stories about abusive or stupid customers. These stories, like urban legends, get told and retold, reinforcing the idea that the customer is a jerk or an idiot. Among computer support people there is a story that has been retold for many years about a customer talking to a support person on the phone about a software problem. The support person told the customer to "make a copy of the disk and send it to me." Later, an envelope arrived from the customer. Inside was a paper copy of a floppy disk. The customer had placed the floppy disk containing the software on a copy machine and "made a copy." This story may or may not be true, but the fact that support people love to tell it over and over illustrates their primary feelings about customers.

Managers can react to customer complaints by blaming their workers or bringing in motivational speakers to tell them "the customer is always right," but what they should be doing is looking at their processes to see what is causing the problems that customers complain about. Chart out the service and look for a feedback loop from customer back to the organization. There should be a short loop for revision of an order and a longer loop for comments on the service once it is completed.

This can be applied to a simple service, such as eating at a fast food restaurant. The customer comes into Wendy's and orders a spicy chicken sandwich and coffee. Machines are whirring in the background, music is playing through a sound system, and the clerk doesn't hear the order correctly. The customer moves to the "pick-up" area after ordering and paying for the food. The customer sees a "frosty" placed on her tray with the sandwich. She protests to the person who puts it there:

"I ordered coffee, not a frosty." Now the whole system is upset. The person who placed the frosty did not take the order and is not working the cash register. She removes the frosty, tells the clerk at the cash register, who must now stop listening to the customer in front of her and deal with the fact that she over-charged the previous customer, since the frosty costs more than the coffee.

Managers devising encounter processes must accept and factor in that mistakes will happen. Clerks will misunderstand food orders. People will click the wrong button on a Web site. People will type the wrong zip code, or leave off their office number, or be victims of a baggage handler who carelessly throws their new stroller. The easy thing to do is blame "stupid" customers or providers. The right thing to do is to design proc-esses that have a way of dealing with these mistakes. If custom-ers can get a problem fixed quickly, they are less likely to abuse providers, and providers are less likely to feel powerless and un-happy about their work.

Designing Jobs

An encounter business begins with a concept. Service work has its legendary figures who came up with new ideas that took off and made them rich. Like Fred Smith who wrote his college term paper on a new idea for a company that moves packages overnight using its own fleet of planes and trucks. It was an idea his professor felt wouldn't work, but Fred went on to found Federal Express. Or like Wayne Huizenga's whose idea for a company called AutoNation put the powerful auto industry on notice that it's time for change. He built gigantic used car lots where sales representatives worked on salaries, and customers could peruse a computer listing of all the vehicles or walk the immense area of the lot with more than 1,000 vehicles, know-ing they would pay exactly the price shown on the sticker. Then there's Ross Perot, who chafed under the restrictions at IBM where he toiled as a salesman and dreamed of starting a more nimble company, one that would take over other companies' systems work for a fee. He founded EDS (Electronic Data Systems) and his concept of "facilities management" propelled him into fame and fortune.

These are stories about someone seeing an unmet need and devising a way to fill it. The concept can begin with diagrams on a piece of paper showing all the elements of the business and how they connect. It works its way into a detailed plan; implicit in the idea is the need for people.

Only the deviser has the excitement of taking a risk, of rolling the dice, of beginning something new. He or she must communicate that to others who come into the fold, such as managers and workers hired by the managers, although they will never experience it in quite the same way. Every circle, line, and notation that appeared on the original diagram gradually becomes a person doing a job, working to fulfill the concept. The idea becomes a business. As it moves into daily operation, the excitement of the original concept can fade with time. That excitement may never filter down to the bottom rung, which in any encounter service business, is the people who actually see or talk to the customer. These people are working in jobs designed by someone else. They are the clip-art people at the bottom of the diagram, the place where organization and customer meet.

Managers must decide what the jobs in their organization will look like, what kind of people are needed, how much to pay them, and what training to provide before turning them loose on the customer. The organization can plan for a tight link between organization and its workers or accept a loose O-P link and try to build a tight O-C link.

Is Good Customer Service Always Important?

It is important to consider whether the employees you hire can kill your business if they fail to perform. Is what you provide so attractive to customers that they will put up with poor service? In some businesses, it is clear that service is traded off for a lower price. Customers do not expect personal service at warehouse discount stores or discount grocery stores where customers bag their own groceries. The business saves money by having less staff. Such a business may be better off hiring minimum-wage workers and living with high turnover than trying to attract a more permanent and committed staff. They still need to keep shelves stocked, the store clean, and prices clearly marked, or customers may not feel it is worth the other drawbacks of shopping there.

Reader's Digest looked into the state of customer service for a December 1998 article titled "What Ever Happened to Customer Service?" It concluded that many businesses can operate without employees doing much to please customers:

> The sad fact is, stores can get away with poor customer service because customers let them. Customer-service expert John Goodman estimates that about half of customers continue to do business with firms they feel have mistreated them. This is "behavioral loyalty," explains Jeff Ellis of Maritz Marketing Research Inc. "We may bad-mouth a store after a bad experience, but we go back because it's close to our house or carries items we like." Many shoppers we interviewed admitted they returned to stores where service was poor.[2]

On its Web site, *Reader's Digest* opened a forum on the issue where anyone could leave a comment on the subject of customer service. In just a few weeks, it had accumulated more than 500 comments, many from retail workers. A small sampling:

> . . . with this in mind, next time you go to the "Mega-Mart" environment and complain about service, remember the old adage, "Pay peanuts and only monkeys show up" and then maybe you can understand why that guy or gal getting paid minimum wage is so disinterested in helping you.

> I politely asked, "Could you please call me back when the computers are up?" She said indignantly, "We don't call people back!"

> I have worked in discount retailing for the last twenty years. I have been physically shoved, sworn at, and spit on. I have been told that all clerks get minimum wage for a minimum brain.

I was a manager at Taco Bell, the worst job in the world, and we had the place running nicely until they replaced my boss with someone who keeps the place a mess and ignores customers but puts out orders faster. Tell me, which is more important, a clean, polite store or a fast one?

We all must understand what discount/wholesale pricing chains do to other quality stores with great service and higher prices. It shuts them down because they are willing to sacrifice good old traditional customer service to grab market share and volume.

These comments reflect the idea that many businesses operate without personal service and survive because customers are more interested in price. The business owner must understand this tradeoff. Companies operating with low-wage workers who receive little training should not try to claim they offer great service. If they offer anything, it should be great prices. As one of the more insightful writers commented at the *Reader's Digest* Web site:

It is unreasonable for us to expect the same attentive expertise in a Wal-Mart with thousands of product offerings that we enjoyed in our corner store with limited variety. Progress forces us to adopt new paradigms. We welcome the age of abundance, enjoying the variety, selection, competition, and convenience super-commerce offers in our lives. But we regret loss of personal intimacy and comfort we cherished in the past. Is it unreasonable to expect to have it both ways?

The desire of customers to "have it both ways" explains a lot of their dissatisfaction.

When Customer Service Matters

Some customers look only at price, but others want high quality service. Poorly trained employees who have no reason to care about customers or the company's bottom line can do a lot of damage in businesses where service counts. Banks, insurance companies, retail businesses selling high-priced items can lose a lot of money when customers go elsewhere. They need employees who can provide good service, but their hiring practices may not bring them the kind of people they need. Some current trends in employment that do not encourage providers to care about customers:

1. Short-term employment
2. Part-time employment with no benefits
3. Contract work
4. Work performed in a different location from other company employees (usually the case with call center workers)

Training alone cannot change the resentment workers may feel about their situation, which can be expressed toward customers in slow or indifferent service. Service businesses must accept the fact that encounter employees do not have relationships with customers, and this is not a weakness of their employees. It is systemic, arising from the nature of stranger interacting with stranger.

Despite the lack of built-in incentives, encounter workers do sometimes go the extra mile. The extra mile is efforts beyond the mere acceptable—employees doing things customers really appreciate and remember.

James H. Donnelly, Jr., author of *Close to the Customer,* relates an incident that happened to him on a flight from Salt Lake City to Lexington, Ky., with stops in Dallas and Atlanta. He'd had nothing to eat and was disappointed when only peanuts were served on the first leg. Then there wasn't time to get any food in Dallas, as he had to run to get the flight to Atlanta. Again, no food, but he decided he could stop at the popcorn stand in Atlanta and get a big bag of hot buttered popcorn to eat on the last leg. However, the plane arrived late, and the popcorn stand was empty. Before boarding, he complained loudly to the ramp agent about the lack of food and his thwarted desire for a bag of popcorn. As he tells it. "Just as the door [to the plane] was about to be closed, the ramp agent came on board carrying a freshly popped piping hot bag of microwave popcorn. I'm sure the other passengers wondered 'who is this guy?' when he brought it to my seat. He had rushed to the flight crew lounge, which was equipped with a microwave oven and popcorn for use by flight crews between flights, and prepared the snack just for me." [3]

This service worker went beyond the acceptable, making a lasting impression on the customer. But what made him do it? His boss might appreciate his extra efforts, but they probably brought him no extra reward. The truth is, he probably felt sorry for the hungry passenger. He was the kind of person who could put himself in the passenger's place and wanted to help.

Another good story was on the *Reader's Digest* Web site (which was mostly full of complaints, but not entirely, as this tale attests):

> At the Scotty's on Big Pine Key, Florida, customer service is alive, at least from Kelli and Tom (a manager on duty). During our preparations for Hurricane George, we were short of wood to cover the windows and went to Scotty's. The truck was due at 4:30 p.m., it was 3:30, and people were already lining up. Kelli, the cashier, had been on duty since 6 that morning. She was still friendly and helpful, even with the stress of the impending storm. We waited and waited, along with many others who eventually left. At 6:00 p.m., we decided to go and put up what wood we had in hopes of getting the remainder of the wood the next morning. Both Tom and Kelli said that they would call us when the truck got there so we could get what we needed. We left our number, but really had no hope that they would call, considering the madhouse that would occur when the truck got there. At 7:15 p.m., the phone rang. It was Tom asking how much we needed so he could set it aside for us. I left for the store which was 7 minutes away. I was #20 in line when I got there, but there was our wood. I can't begin to express how much this meant. They were VERY busy and yet still called. There were plenty of customers to buy their wood, but they REMEMBERED!!! Thank you Kelli & Tom. I know you closed at 7:00, but for ALL of us in line, we really appreciated you keeping the store open for us . . . also, thanks to the guys loading the vehicles . . . it was a long day for all of us. THANK YOU!!

The customers who got this kind of service from Scotty's will be customers forever. But it may not be anything the owner did that produced this kind of service. It may be that Kelli and Tom are people who empathize with others, who could easily see themselves as the ones needing the lumber, and that provided their motivation. Business owners could solve their worker problems if they hired only people like Kelli and Tom, but that is also totally unrealistic. There will never be enough people like Kelli and Tom for businesses to hire.

Stories of legendary customer service are often offered by consultants in seminars on how to give good customer service in hopes of motivating more providers to be like Kelli and Tom. But pep talks rarely make a difference in the long run on how people behave.

What Skills?

As the skills needed to perform a service job decline, there is more emphasis on personal characteristics of the provider. Studies show that customers prefer dealing with someone attractive and articulate, so some organizations look for these qualities in the people they hire. Being attractive as a condition of work is usually not a stated job requirement, nor is having an omnipresent smile, but employers are looking for those qualities in their public contact workers. For telephone work, having a pleasant voice with no accent is highly desired. The customer at an encounter business knows nothing about the provider, so she tends to gravitate toward someone attractive. But while these people meet one unstated requirement—because they conform to the customer's stereotype—they may not be the same people who will go the extra mile as Kelli and Tom did at Scotty's.

Organizations also turn to training firms that offer seminars in customer service. This kind of training concentrates on how to interact with customers rather than on the skills (if any) of doing the job. Where the work requires a set of skills that takes years to develop, it is less feasible to expect job candidates to have all the desired personal qualities. At the other end of the scale, jobs people normally keep for only a short time, such as working in a fast food restaurant, are usually filled with whoever applies, attractive or not. And it is less cost-effective to pay for training when the employee may be gone in a few months.

Some organizations infuse their employees with a philosophy or method unique to the company. Disney tries to do this at its giant Disney World complex and has the lowest employee turnover rate in the amusement park business. All employees spend a day and a half in a course called "Disney Traditions." They then get specific training for their job. The kids who sweep the park clean get four days of training. Their job is not just to sweep up but to answer any questions from the "guests" who visit the park. To the extent that the employees buy into the Disney philosophy, they will be happier on the job. Disney tries to make sure it gets people who like its way of doing things by always having more than one person interview applicants, even kids applying to sweep the streets. For Disney customers, the quality of the experience is crucially important. Disney cannot risk having rude or ill-informed "cast members" (as all employees are called). So the training is much more about the Disney way of treating customers than it is about the actual job the person does.

Following Disney's lead, calling all employees by a common name like "associates" has become more popular in business. Other service companies have also adopted the term "guests" for their customers.

Turning Relationships Into Encounters

Some kinds of businesses have remained primarily relationship businesses, and only rarely or recently have encounter versions turned up. These include:

1. Optometrists ("Eyewear")
2. Massage therapists
3. Stock brokers
4. Travel agents
5. Dry cleaners
6. Florists

Optometrists ("Eyewear")

At one time, most Americans got an eye exam from an independent optometrist who also sold them a pair of glasses. Glasses were "dispensed" by an optician who fitted them to the wearer. Contact lenses, which cost more than glasses, also required professional services for proper fitting and to make sure the wearer knew how to insert and remove them and care for them.

All that has changed as both glasses and contact lenses have become commodities to be purchased without as much need for professional services. Optometrists were able to keep the eyewear business to themselves at one time by refusing to give their customers a copy of their prescription. But the Federal Trade Commission has required eye doctors to release prescriptions for glasses; it did not require the release of prescriptions for contact lenses. However, twenty-four states have passed laws requiring optometrists to release contact lens prescriptions to their clients. These changes created a market for chain businesses like LensCrafters and PearleVision to offer the public a large selection of designer frames. It also paved the way for mail order contact lens businesses like 1–800-CONTACTS.

Are eyeglasses and contact lenses medical devices as optometrists claim, or are they a commodity, which anyone should be able to sell? Some state regulators agree with optometrists that contact lenses are a medical device and should be used only under the care of an eye doctor. But others disagree. Consumer's Union, publisher of *Consumer Reports* magazine, has studied the issue and thinks people should have a right to their prescription. Consumer's Union says it is just like any other prescription, and customers should be able to get their lenses wherever they want. In 1997, they surveyed optometrists in Texas and found 65 percent of them would not release copies of prescriptions.[4] Texas has since passed a prescription release law.

This may be a case in which people continue to engage in relationships because there is no alternative, but many consumers would just as soon not have the service if they could get a lower price by obtaining their lenses through mail order. Others who are less price conscious may feel the personal service of an optometrist is worth paying for. Obviously, chain eyewear businesses benefit from selling glasses and contact lenses as commodities, going for volume business by offering walk-in service and a huge selection, encouraging customers to buy two pairs or to buy fashion sunglasses along with their regular glasses. The existence of chain eyewear businesses has created a market for eyeglass manufacturers, who produce many fashion lines endorsed by celebrities. With only optometrists selling eyeglasses, this business would never have grown the way it has. It takes the kind of business acumen possessed by successful entrepreneurs to create a market for a product like fashion eyewear.

Along with fashion eyeglasses, the chains have created a new product: fashion contact lenses. These are purchased without a prescription because buyers have perfect eye sight—they don't need them for vision but merely want to change their eye color. Contact lenses worn only for color furthers the idea that eyewear is not a medical product but a fashion accessory.

Chain eyewear stores tend to be in malls, next to stores selling the latest clothing and electronic gadgets. Customers are free to browse through the selection of frames, view samples of colored and coated lenses, and look through pamphlets about the many kinds of tints and coatings available. The chains offer more convenience as well. LensCrafters initiated one-hour service so customers can do some shopping and come back in an hour to pick up their glasses. The lenses are made on the premises, and the frames are in stock. Other eyewear chains have started offering the same one-hour service.

This is a radical change from the medical clinic atmosphere of the neighborhood optometrist who typically offered a limited selection of frames and slow service. Without the income from selling glasses, it's more difficult for an independent optometrist to make a living.

Governmental actions hurt the financial interests of independent optometrists, who once had the eyewear business all to themselves. They do not have as powerful a lobby organization as medical doctors have in the AMA or they might have been able to keep control of eyewear sales. Harvey P. Hanlen, OD, president of the American Optometric Association, wrote in a letter to the *Detroit Free Press*: "The key point to remember is that good eye health and clear vision are more important in the long run than saving a few dollars on contact lenses."[5] Apparently, optometrists have not convinced the public that this is so.

Stockbrokers

The rise of discount stockbrokerage firms has given more people a chance to invest in the stock market. Unlike full-service brokers, the discount houses will deal with customers who have only small sums to invest. But they do not try to be financial advisers to their customers; the people they service must do their own homework on what to buy and when to sell. Full-service brokers work in relationships, getting to know their customers and their financial status. At one time, this was a very close relationship, and customers would generally follow their broker if that broker went to another firm. The big brokerage firms have an interest in keeping this from happening, however, and have tried to build a stronger link between the organization and customers. Operating a discount brokerage business is one way to do that, servicing a new kind of customer concerned with fees and/or wanting to use the many available resources to manage their own investment portfolio. Traditional stockbrokers would not be interested in many of these customers because the time and effort of establishing a relationship with them would not pay off. Discount brokerages like Charles Schwab, Quick & Reilly, and Kennedy Cabot grew rapidly in the 1980s and 1990s, providing brokerage service in encounters to a new kind of customer. For $20 or $30 per trade, these discount brokerages compete on price, not on financial advice. Customers call an 800-number and put in their request to buy or sell; their phone conversation with the "next available" financial services consultant is tape recorded so that orders can be verified. The customer saves money, but the trust that underlies service relationships is missing.

Mergers have created giant companies that are offering encounter-style broker services. For example, Kennedy Cabot merged with Price Waterhouse to form Waterhouse Securities where buying and selling stocks is even less expensive. The Waterhouse Securities web page offers $12 flat fee trading. Customers can buy and sell via the Web, through punching codes into a touch-tone phone, or by speaking with an Account Officer. Its Web site states:

> At Waterhouse Securities, you always have the choice of speaking with an Account Officer. And it's not just a person at an order desk—when you open an account you have your own Account Officer, who is registered with the New York Stock Exchange. Your Account Officer is there to give you personal attention when you need it and is backed up by a team of brokers, so there's someone you can speak with 24 hours-a-day, 7 days-a-week. You have Technical Support available 24 hours-a-day as well.

The "Account Officer" is not the same as the experienced stockbroker of the full-service firm, who will not just be "someone you can speak with" but will understand the customer's needs and contact customers when appropriate opportunities arise.

New technology makes it easy to buy and sell without talking to a broker. Many big investment firms are offering low-cost Internet trading through subsidiaries. For example, Morgan Stanley Dean Witter operates Discovery Brokerage Direct at www.discoverbrokerage.com.

Travel Agents

Travel agents are finding much of what they do can be easily replaced by technology. Many people find it faster and easier to book their own airline tickets and hotel rooms at Web sites than to work with a travel agent. Web sites offer lots of information about the destination, and services like TravelWeb, Travelocity, and Expedia offer quick and easy online booking. Airlines, seeing the possibilities of customers doing their own booking, have been reducing the amount they'll pay to agents for booking flights. In response to shrinking commissions, many travel agents have had to start charging fees for their services. For anyone not overly concerned about price, using a travel agent may still be the most convenient way to arrange their travel.

Southwest Airlines is an example of a newer business that caters to people who like a bargain. Its Web site lets customers choose both points of their trip, then see the scheduled flights between those points. The customer selects the flight he wants, prints a copy of his schedule, and within an hour or so, gets a faxed confirmation from Southwest, which becomes his ticket. He goes to the airport, shows some identification and the fax, and boards the plane, taking whatever seat he chooses.

For both stockbrokers and travel agencies, providers who want to work in relationships have to offer value-added services. Those who merely sell tickets and reservations will not survive the competition with the discounters and the Internet.

Massage Therapists

Entrepreneurs have been creative in finding other kinds of relationship businesses that can be turned into encounters. One such business is massage, a service that has never had a large clientele. Between having a bad name from the many "massage parlors" that double as houses of prostitution and the expense of real massage therapy, most people have never thought about having a massage. But with a new encounter format that standardizes a back rub in a public setting like an airport, massage therapy could find a lot of new customers. Amid the noise and hustle of the airport, getting a massage may seem odd, but it's located where there's plenty of stressed-out people who can benefit from this quick and inexpensive service.

The Massage Bar, headquartered in Seattle, has four locations (two at Seattle-Tacoma Airport, the Washington State Convention Center in Seattle, and the Nashville airport). It uses a unique custom-built hexagonal table equipped with headrests, where the customer, fully clothed, sits on an ergonomically designed chair and leans forward into the padded cradle of the headrest while the practitioner works on her back and shoulders. The location is in the open, where anyone passing by can watch.

"People are stressed, they're in a hurry," says Massage Bar owner Cary Cruea, who opened the first of two bars at the Seattle airport in 1994. "They sit in cramped seats on airplanes, carry heavy luggage, and they're anxious about flying." She is scouting other sites for her $1 million business.[6] Cruea is a professional massage therapist who wanted to bring the benefits of massage to as many people as possible. It took her six months of negotiations to get an agreement with the Seattle airport officials, who had turned down other massage businesses.

The Massage Bar's own description of the service:

As you approach the Massage Bar®, a Licensed Massage Practitioner (LMP) will greet you and explain our services and answer any questions you may have. Should you choose to have a massage, the LMP will ask you to read and sign a medical waiver, and assist you in sitting in the ergonomic massage chair. The LMP will ask you if there are any areas that may need special attention. After you are comfortable, the massage will begin.

Your upper and lower back, neck, shoulders, arms and hands are the focus of this massage. We can provide you with a Single Shot®—15-minute massage or a Double Shot®—30 minute massage. The LMP will communicate with you throughout your massage ensuring your comfort level.

The massage is intended to provide a relaxing and stress reducing 15 or 30 minutes during your travel time. We do not do injury treatment or diagnose illnesses. You will leave the Massage Bar® in a relaxed state of alertness, a state you will want to visit again and again. Quite a change from how most of us deal with air travel.

The Massage Bar has taken what has always been a custom service and created two standard service products. This is simple for the customer and very nonthreatening to those who know little or nothing about getting a massage. But the business probably benefits from the fact that most potential customers—air travelers—tend to be upper-income people who do understand massage. Massage Bar's customer survey shows over 90 percent of their customers have had a massage before.

Practitioners wear green Massage Bar shirts and talk to their customers to customize the service as much as possible while giving the massage. This service would appeal to people who have a regular masseuse and already know the benefits of massage as well as newcomers who are intrigued and don't mind spending fifteen dollars. A study already cited shows that people who get service in relationships tend to get the same type of service from other providers as well, indicating encounter-style massage will have wide appeal.

Other airports having massage businesses are Chicago O'Hare (Spa Nation), Denver International (A Massage, Inc.), Orlando International (Profiles Express), and Pittsburgh International (Touch 'N Go). Some of these offer a longer, more custom massage, along with a quick low-priced massage.

Another massage business started in New York is called The Great American BackRub Store. Unlike the Massage Bar, Bill Zanker, founder of Great American Back Rub, hired someone with a track record at the Supercuts haircut chain and raised 6.5 million dollars with his 1995 IPO. This has enabled him to open more stores and franchise his concept. The company's stock is traded on the NASDAQ as RUBB. Zanker had previous experience in an encounter business as chairman of the Learning Annex, Inc., a national chain offering inexpensive educational programs.

The process for getting a massage at Great American is similar to the Massage Bar, but its locations are stores that also sell massage and stress reduction products, including oils, bath salts, back supports, and electronic and mechanical stress reduction devices. Approximately 20 percent of revenues are generated from the sale of such products.

Dry Cleaners

Dry cleaners have typically been small neighborhood operations with the dry cleaning machinery visible behind the counter where the owners hustle to wait on customers. Most use a smelly, possibly carcinogenic chemical called perchloroethylene ("perc") to clean clothes. The only inroads by chains in this business have been One Hour Martinizing, the most successful with about 700 stores, and Dryclean Depot, a discounter with eighty stores.

But there's something totally new on the horizon that

could mark a real changeover to encounter-style dry cleaning. Two men with degrees from the Harvard Business School who started the Staples office supply business have sunk their money into a concept one of them developed because he missed the excitement of a start-up. Thomas Stemberg says he got the idea for a chain of dry cleaning stores from his own experience. He was quoted in the *Wall Street Journal* saying dry cleaning "is a market that needs to be served with lower prices and far greater convenience."[7]

He and associate Todd Krasnow have started Zoots, a dry cleaning chain, in their home state of Massachusetts; they plan to expand the concept to other states. Their concept is small stores with the actual cleaning done offsite. Customers can apply for express service, where they leave a credit card number on file, drop off clothes to be cleaned inside a Zoots bar-coded garment bag at a drive-through, and later check a Web page to see if their cleaning is done. The Web site can also give them a locker number where they can pick up their clothes anytime. Every step of the service can be done by the customer without having to talk to a provider. To attract environmentally sensitive customers, Zoots uses a hydrocarbon process they say is safer for the environment. Prices are unisex and reasonable.

But will customers go for convenience and price over the more personal service they get at the independent places? The *Boston Globe* ran an article about Zoots that included an interview with a local dry cleaner, Anton of Anton's Dry Cleaners, who owns forty stores in the Boston area. He says his experience tells him dry cleaning is "one business you can't McDonaldize." He flatly stated, "This is a business about personal relationships."[8] It's also been a tough business in recent years, as the trend has been toward casual clothes.

Unlike Zoots, which will do light clothing repair like sewing on buttons, Dryclean Depot will only clean the clothes. Their stores are big. Customers often have to stand in line and wait their turn at the counter, then must pay in advance. Dryclean Depot takes in about ten times as much clothing as the average neighborhood dry cleaner. What they offer is a lower price, charging a flat $1.75 for each garment and 99 cents for laundering a shirt.[9]

Another start-up called Hangers is planning to clean clothes with a new process that doesn't use any harsh chemicals, but the equipment needed for this process is twice as expensive as the machinery for the old process. This might answer one of the reasons chains have not taken over the dry cleaning market: liability. The perc chemical can cause serious health problems at high-exposure levels. Spills can contaminate groundwater if not cleaned up quickly. This has made banks reluctant to loan money for dry cleaning businesses, plus the Environmental Protection Agency has threatened to put additional restrictions on cleaners that use perc.[10] Customers of the chain dry cleaners are dealing with employees, not mom and pop. Zoots customers will have to depend on the process put in place by the professional managers who started the business. They certainly have a good track record, as evidenced by their success with Staples. But as Anton, the Boston dry cleaner, says in the Globe: "You have all these guys in the ivory tower making assumptions, but most of them have never pressed a pair of pants."

Florists

Flowers are an unusual product in that they are most often ordered as gifts, and the recipient is often in another location. Small flower shops have worked out arrangements via association with FTD or Teleflora for sharing orders. Flower shops have traditionally been local independent businesses, but inroads have been made by two national businesses.

The closest thing to a national chain of floral shops is 1–800-FLOWERS, which bills itself as the world's largest florist with $300 million in sales and more than 2,000 employees. They operate retail stores in New York, Los Angeles, Chicago, Dallas, Atlanta, San Francisco, San Diego, Orlando, San Antonio, St. Louis, and Phoenix, and have seven service centers. There are approximately 1,800 independently owned partner florists (including about 120 company-owned or franchised stores), who are chosen, according to company information, for their high quality standards, superior customer service and delivery, and ability to meet 1–800-FLOWERS' volume requirements. 1–800-FLOWERS, which began because f-l-o-w-e-r-s has the same number of digits as a phone number, is accessible through its stores, via the Internet, as well as by calling 1–800-FLOWERS. Unlike the mom-and-pop floral shops it hopes to displace, 1–800-FLOWERS operates twenty-four hours a day, seven days a week.

There is one very successful floral mail order company founded by a woman who saw a better way to service customers who order flowers. Ruth Owades started Calyx & Corolla in 1989 with $2 million. She observed that most flowers were cut, transported to a wholesaler, transported to a distributor, transported to a retailer, and then finally transported to a customer. This whole process took six to ten days from the time a flower was cut to when it reached the customer, and the customer was getting flowers that were far from fresh.

Owades thought this process could be improved so customers could order more conveniently, and the flowers could be sent anywhere and arrive fresh, only one day old. Her plan involved working closely with the growers, who would package and send the flowers directly to customers. Flower growers, she found, were mostly small family operations. She put a lot of work into finding growers and training them in her methods, but it has paid off with a successful business that competes with the mom-and-pop flower shops on convenience and having a better product. Calyx & Corolla established a strong upscale image for itself right from day one. It prints a glossy catalog and also has a Web site (calyxandcorolla.com).[11]

Because its products are most often ordered as gifts, flower sales do not need stores. This is a natural area for mail order, phone order, and Web-based sales. A business that makes it easy to order flowers to be delivered anywhere, with no confusing delivery charges, should have an edge. The 1–800-FLOWERS Web site had some customer testimonials. Here's one that every business would like to receive:

> This was my first time sending flowers this way. It was PERFECT!!! Excellent service, delivered as promised. Very impressive. You and your network keep up the good work. Service is everything.

Other Businesses

Services usually delivered in relationships provide opportunities for entrepreneurs to find a process for delivering the service in encounters. The opportunities are best where the service could be provided at a much lower cost than current providers charge so a service could appeal to a wider base. The Massage Bar is a great illustration of this. A personal massage in your home would be more expensive than most people could afford. But at the Seattle airport, thanks to entrepreneur Cary Cruea, anyone can afford a fifteen-minute massage.

The rising popularity of coffee houses illustrates that you don't always have to charge less. Starbucks sells an expensive cup of coffee, but it built its business on the idea of a better cup of coffee in an attractive setting. Having coffee becomes an experience. Brilliant marketing teamed with consistently good coffee pushed Starbucks from a local Seattle success story to a national corporate sensation in the early 1990s. Starbucks serves more than 4 million customers a week and has more than 20,000 employees in the United States, Canada, and Asia. But like many big chain businesses, Starbucks has had some labor problems. Wanting more pay, some of its Canadian workers have joined the Canadian Auto Workers union. Starbucks typically pays about $7.50 an hour to start and provides benefits.

Some types of businesses have resisted becoming chains. Here's a short list:

- Jewelry stores
- Furriers
- Plumbing and heating companies that serve residences
- Bars

Jewelry stores like to promote their unique jewelry designs, and customers usually don't buy in a hurry, so there may be little to gain in operating a chain of jewelry stores. At the high end, wealthy customers want personal attention and one-of-a-kind jewelry. The same could be said of luxury fur sales, where the coats and wraps sold are custom tailored for the buyer.

Although jewelry store chains have made inroads, independent jewelers still control 80 percent of the market, according to the *Wall Street Journal.* Jeweler Jules R. Schubot, whose business is in suburban Detroit, says he's not worried. His customers know him and his wife, who will often call a customer about jewelry she thinks that customer would like. The article says independents like Schubot have a good chance to keep their customers, despite competition from expanding national companies like Tiffany and Cartier which have moved into the area. It states:

> Usually economies of scale allow chains to sell for less, and that is how they steal market share. But price shopping isn't a big factor in high-end jewelry because the product is supposed to be unique; Tiffany, for instance, designs most of its own jewelry.[12]

Something else explains the existence of so many independent plumbing and heating businesses. The providers work in an industry heavily unionized and regulated by the government. Plus, they depend on charging for time; there would not be much efficiency gained by turning their work into a chain business. Fixing a backed-up sewer or a non-functional furnace cannot really be standardized; it depends largely on the knowledge and skill of the provider. Some kinds of specialized plumbing services that can be standardized are offered by chains. Roto-Rooter, which cleans sewers using a special patented machine, is a national company with franchised locations.

Bars are often independently owned, too, although there are some exceptions. Chain businesses that serve liquor are usually primarily restaurants. The neighborhood bar still exists in large numbers. Perhaps this is a business where speed and efficiency are not what people are looking for.

Medical Care: No Longer a Relationship Business

Everyone agrees that the delivery of medical care is undergoing massive changes. What many don't see is that it's reversed the service triangle, turning what had always been a relationship into an encounter, as shown in Figure 4-1. Medical care used to be given by doctors in private practice. Insurance companies, which would be the organization in the triangle, paid bills for individual customers. One doctor might deal with a number of different insurance companies, plus some customers would pay cash, so there was a very weak link between the doctor and any organization. Insurance companies did not limit members' choices as much as they do now, so the link between customer and insurance might have been weak too. What was strong was the doctor-patient relationship.

Figure 4-1   Medical Models

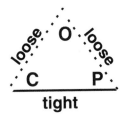

Former Medical Model

Customer (patient) and provider (doctor) have a tight link. The doctor works independently, with a loose link to the insurance companies that pay part of the bills. The customers feel more loyalty to their doctor than to their insurance company; some customers pay cash.

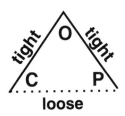

New Medical Model

The customer (patient) is bound to the organization (managed care company) by contract. The provider (doctor) is also bound to the organization by contract. The customer-provider link is loose, since the organization ultimately determines the behavior of both.

Doctors increasingly have little access to customers except through organizations. If most people are in managed care, then they must get their doctor through the organization. Half of all doctors in practice now work on salary. Those who don't often have contractual arrangements with HMOs.

Many managed care organizations tell members that they can choose their own doctor, but let's look at the reasons the link is still loose, even if members do choose from among the HMO doctors.

1. Customers might change jobs and have to change health plans, which means getting a new doctor.
2. The doctor they selected might leave the HMO, and she

can't take customers with her since they are bound to the HMO.

3. The customer's employer can switch health plans, which probably means getting a different doctor.
4. People are aware that the doctor they see is limited by the HMO in what treatments he can provide and in using his judgment about referrals for specialty services—these are controlled by the HMO.

Even though there is a promise of choice, the tight link that binds the doctor and the patient to the organization means people can't really count on a long-term relationship with a doctor in the same way they once did. In fact, a 1998 survey by VHA, a nonprofit healthcare membership organization, and Deloitte & Touche, indicates that 25 percent of consumers changed physicians within the last two years.[13]

Doctors have lost the autonomy they once had in the practice of their profession. By tradition, professionals define and control their work which once brought a great deal of satisfaction. Doctors are in revolt against managed care and not just because it reduces their income. The *Los Angeles Times* ran an article on doctor disaffection in California, where 85 percent of insured adults are in managed care plans. One doctor decided to quit his HMO, where he was expected to see a new patient every twelve minutes. He opened an office and just said no to HMO contracts. His income dropped by a third, but he feels much happier in his work. They quoted him as saying "I'd rather make less money and keep my reputation."[14]

A study of young California doctors found that one third of them wouldn't go into medicine again if they could do it over.[15] The satisfaction they expected to get out of their medical career is not there. These doctors, who expected to be able to serve their customers in relationships, have been forced to work in encounters. The HMO method of working fits most of the characteristics of an encounter:

- Providers are considered functionally equivalent.
- Service is standardized based on the rules of an organization.

- Service is egalitarian; all customers get the same amount of the provider's time.
- The feedback loop is between the customer and the organization, not the customer and the provider.
- The provider is paid by the organization and gets the same pay no matter how many customers he or she sees.
- The organization has a way to measure efficiency (counting the number of patients seen and tracking referrals for tests, etc.).

Once doctors had no organization at all to deal with. They were independent practitioners who dealt directly with their customers. When customers started using insurance to pay for care, doctors had to deal with the requirements of these companies, and the link with their customers became a bit looser. With doctors working directly for HMOs, their main bond is with the organization, not with their customers. This puts doctors in the same situation as the car mechanic who works for a dealership or the chain drugstore pharmacist.

Mature Professions Create Opportunities for Encounter Businesses

One of the effects of widespread encounter systems is the tendency in mature professions for the most-educated professionals to withdraw from the clients they originally served. This is a process Andrew Abbott called "professional regression."[16] Abbott said that because professionals withdraw from the public (by doing research, being a specialist, or doing consulting), clients lose confidence in them. High status and highly paid professionals in these fields are not seen by the general public, which does not value their work and their roles are not understood. Some examples of invisible high-status professionals are physicians who work on such specialized areas that they mainly do research and consult with other physicians, and college faculty who focus exclusively on research rather than teaching. Managers, too, can become gurus who don't actually manage but tell others how to do it.

As some members of a profession move into work the public does not see, the work of dealing with customers becomes the province of providers with less education. Eventually, it becomes an opportunity for an encounter approach.

Libraries are one venue where a profession is changing. Libraries used to have more people educated in Library Science staffing the desks. Now the staff members who are educated as librarians work mainly behind the scenes, designing library systems and doing administrative work. Librarians, in fact, have been reinventing themselves as Information Technology workers, as the very definition of a "library" is changing from rooms full of books to electronic compilations of content. Information has become a commodity to be bought and sold rather than a public service. As a profession mutates into a higher tech format, the work tends to pay better and become more male-dominated. Where once information experts were women helping library patrons find the right book, they now are just as likely to be computer-savvy, and male.

In some cases, the professionals themselves initiate this kind of regression, as a response to the observation that providers who work with customers generally have less prestige and pay. By moving their work away from customers, they upgrade themselves to a higher level. Sometimes a paraprofessional job will be invented to do the work of dealing with the public. Paralegals, physician's assistants, and college graduate assistants are examples. Management looks at the tasks of the professional and determines that some of the work is so standard that it could be done by a person without a professional education who is trained in the work. This process can end by undermining the profession, especially where there is no strong professional organization, as the public does not see the difference between the highly educated practitioner and the paraprofessional.

Optometrists and pharmacists are in danger of losing their work. Neither group has a strong professional representation. Some of the tasks done by both can be taught to persons without a professional education. Both kinds of businesses have been vulnerable to chains. The process may end with most optometrists and pharmacists working on salaries for large national chains. This process does not generally bode well for their personal incomes. When a profession undergoes this kind of retrograde process, it usually means less pay and the profession becomes more female-dominated, as is happening with pharmacists. Many pharmacy jobs are part-time, with fewer opportunities for the pharmacist to excel or build a reputation.

The practice of law also has moved into encounters. Some companies have started offering prepaid legal services that mainly involve free phone calls to a lawyer or paralegal and simple services like writing a will or selling a home. A string of legal clinics can offer only very limited legal services, and attorneys taking jobs in this setting will not get experience at more complex legal work. It is likely paralegals will do the actual customer contact work in these businesses.

Opportunities for entrepreneurs exist in areas where a service is very expensive for customers and an encounter-style business could staff it with cheaper providers. The massage businesses cited earlier are an illustration of this. In many more common kinds of health services, this is happening in a way that affects everyone. Medical clinics use physician's assistants (PAs) and nurse practitioners (NPs) instead of doctors to see their customers. The doctors on staff may spend most of their time consulting with the PAs and NPs, who are paid less than a medical doctor. This holds down the costs at walk-in clinics but removes the traditional caregiver—the doctor—from the customer. However, the PA or NP could build relationships with customers, and this might enable more people to have a relationship with a health care provider. The research that shows people are more satisfied with relationship providers would indicate this is a good choice for more health care organizations.

Customers who no longer have access to a neighborhood pharmacist and cannot afford expensive drugs may choose alternative therapies or visit the health food store where someone will actually talk to them about their health problem. They may leave with bottles of vitamins and natural substances sold in these stores that may or may not be effective. They trade using the services of highly educated providers working in a highly regulated environment for the services of less educated people in a largely unregulated environment.

Some medical specialty services hire people with no training at all. The weight loss field is an example. Weight loss clinics employ nurses and dietitians who do not normally see customers. The people employed to see customers are called "weight management consultants," and they are paid about $8 an hour plus a commission.

Sometimes customers who must give up an expensive relationship provider find they can enhance an encounter service by doing some of the work themselves. Drug companies have taken advantage of this by appealing directly to their ultimate customers rather than to doctors by running ads on TV for various prescription medications. Since so many people no longer have the luxury of a long-term relationship with a primary-care physician, drug companies are talking directly to the customer, devising mini-health plans that cater to individuals. There is a lot of money at stake because 80 percent of all medications sold are for long-term conditions, according to *Prevention* magazine. *Prevention*'s Survey of Consumer Reactions to Direct-to-Consumer (DTC). Advertising shows fully one-third of the 163 million adult Americans who have seen or heard a DTC drug ad have spoken to a doctor about the medication. Of those, 15 million asked a doctor for the drug, and 80 percent actually left the doctor's office with a prescription order.[17]

This reflects the growing trend toward everyone taking more responsibility for their own health care and doctors taking less responsibility and operating more as walk-in encounter services, dispensing prescriptions their customers request. Medical care in general has moved from delivery in a relationship between doctor and patient to a service provided by corporations with an interest in making a profit, some say by providing less care. Arnold S. Relman, professor emeritus of medicine and of social medicine at Harvard Medical School and editor-in-chief emeritus of the *New England Journal of Medicine,* has written:

> We have been witnessing a massive shift in the control and ownership of medical care to private, for-profit businesses. Most of the control is indirectly exercised through investor-owned, managed care insurance plans, but an increasing number of inpatient and outpatient medical facilities are also being acquired and managed by investor-owned corpo-

rations. These medical care businesses have become one of the largest sectors of the U.S. economy.[18]

The winners in this new system, says Relman, are the employers and the HMOs. The losers are the providers and the customers. This is the ultimate "tight organization" scenario. Those working for the organization give up their autonomy and control and also get less income. Those receiving the service deal with providers who must provide less costly service in order to personally prosper.

Licensing and Government Regulation

Some professions have tried to set standards for entry into their field with licensing, testing, or registration, or there may be a requirement for long years of expensive education. The result of these restrictions is that service may be very expensive, and there may be a shortage of providers. This can lead to more people seeking alternative methods and do-it-yourself activities. There have been a number of studies on the relationship between quality service and restrictions on who can provide the service, but none has shown that restricting entry into an occupation results in better service.

Restrictions on who can do certain kinds of work often means lower-paid providers work under the direction of someone with the right credentials. So the legal hotline is staffed with a paralegal, the lady giving a kitten its shots is a veterinary assistant, and the drugstore clerk fills a prescription that involves getting the right bottle from a shelf in the back room.

Professionals who see this happening may try to protest (as the optometrists protested having to give customers their contact lens prescriptions) or they may invoke the regulations governing their occupation or use their professional association to try to restrict who can do work in their field—but in the end, if the service is expensive and unavailable to a large part of the population, it becomes an attractive target for reworking into an encounter business.

The same principles can apply to skilled trade work where unions have limited who can do certain kinds of work. Everyone has heard jokes about the high cost of calling a plumber, yet what they do is not overly difficult to learn. Plumbing, like some other trades such as carpentry and electrical work, is controlled by unions and government licensing regulations. Legally, someone can only call themselves a plumber if they have been through an apprenticeship that leads to "journeyman" status. They may go on to become a "master plumber." The Department of Labor regulates these trades and controls licensing exams. This is contrary to current trends in work life that emphasize constant learning and frequent job change, even changing fields, as technology plays havoc with skills learned during youthful years. But not so in plumbing. Apprenticeships are given out (with much favoritism, many say) in youth and, theoretically, if you don't start then, you can never be a plumber.

Union plumbers belong to the United Association, which spends over $100 million annually on training programs involving approximately 100,000 journeymen and apprentices in more than 400 local training facilities.

New plumbers must go through a five-year apprenticeship program, and the United Association offers training toward certifications in valve repair, welding, backflow prevention, medical gas installation, safe removal of refrigerants, and other areas of specialization. There have been few changes in the way plumbing is done in the last fifty years. This could be a result of tight restrictions on who can do plumbing, which leads to a dearth of national plumbing companies that might invest in new methods.

In practice, union requirements have substantially broken down as people who didn't go through apprenticeships learn the work and are employed doing plumbing (even if they can't actually call themselves a "plumber"). Many community colleges offer programs in plumbing and other skilled trades such as lineman, sheet metal worker, carpenter, and electrician that culminate in a licensing exam.

But restrictions on who can do some kinds of work are an obstacle to starting an encounter service, as business owners can run afoul of union rules and government regulations. When licensing for a profession is local, or licenses are issued by state government, the added red tape and lack of mobility of providers are additional barriers to operating a chain business.

What Are the Drawbacks of an Encounter Business?

Encounter businesses offer high profit potential, but there are also some aspects that will not appeal to every entrepreneur. First, an encounter business must offer a service the public wants in a well-designed format that satisfies the customer. There is also a large cost to starting a successful encounter business. This book does not deal with financing, which must be worked out before anyone can get started in an encounter business.

The drawbacks of encounter businesses can be summarized:

- High initial cost
- Need for solid business skills (by the owner or professionals the owner hires)
- Work that is less challenging and less creative for providers
- Need to train workers and monitor the process (high management cost)
- Likelihood of high provider turnover

To set up an encounter business properly, the owner (or managers hired by the owner) must devise processes and jobs for the providers. While some businesses develop intuitively from the experience of the owner who begins as a provider (such as CDW and Massage Bar), others are planned out in detail from the beginning with an emphasis on doing the work in a new way that better meets customers' needs (such as Zoots and Calyx & Corolla).

A service business that begins or plans to become a publicly traded corporation will hire accounting expertise to plan methods for achieving high profit. It may begin with a concept of franchising or opening many locations as a way to maximize shareholder value. All of this requires a lot of business and financial expertise in addition to the skills involved in the actual service. Such companies must show potential stockholders how they plan to make profits, so the motivation is high to reduce costs wherever possible. The money raised by these companies goes into management and up-front costs of building attractive places (store, clinic, etc.) for providing a face-to-face service and/or for technology such as computer systems that may be crucial to the design of the service.

Conclusion

Encounter businesses will appeal to entrepreneurs who like to take a risk and enjoy the work of managing a company more than it will appeal to someone who wants to extend his skills to more people, although both kinds of owners end up with encounter businesses.

Points to remember:

1. Opportunities exist for starting encounter businesses in service areas where the cost to the customer is high and the skills needed are understood and can be taught to providers with less education than those at the high end of the profession.
2. An encounter service cannot be all things to all people; it must deliver a specified range of services, and owners, managers, and providers must understand and accept that.
3. Owners of encounter businesses need to offer customers an easy and painless experience that includes a way to complain if they feel mistreated. Customers rarely get angry because someone failed to smile or didn't call them "Bill," but they do get angry when the organization's negligence means they have a broken baby stroller and no one is willing to talk about it. Good processes and employees empowered to help are important in keeping customers satisfied.

Encounter businesses have made America (and the rest of the industrialized world as well) a land overflowing with goods and services that are affordable for the average person. Twenty years ago people wondered if we could really have a strong and healthy economy based on services. We now know the answer: Yes we can.

Notes

1. Ulin, David L. "Treated Shabbily, Like the Baggage," *Los Angeles Times*, January 5, 1999.
2. Bennett, Ralph Kinney. "Whatever Happened to Customer Service?" *Reader's Digest*, December 1998.
3. Donnelly, James A., Jr., *Close to the Customer* (Irwin, Ca.: Business One, 1992).
4. "Out of Focus: Contact Lens Policy in Texas," *Consumer's Union Report*, March 1997.
5. "Laws Regulate Lens Prescription," *Detroit Free Press*, December 30, 1998. (Letter from Harvey P. Hanlon, O.D.)
6. Lyke, M.L. "Layovers: People Who Knead People," *Washington Post*, January 11, 1998.
7. Thomas, Paulette. "Staples Executives Now Aim to Reinvent Dry Cleaning," *Wall Street Journal*, April 27, 1999.
8. Reidy, Chris. "Looking to Clean Up With Zoots, Duo That Helped Create Staples Aims to Be National Players in Dry-Cleaning Business," *Boston Globe*, March 31, 1999.
9. "Discounters Put the Press on Area Dry Cleaners," *Washington Post*, February 19, 1999.
10. "Ex-Advertising Man Moves on to High Tech Dry Cleaning," *St. Louis Post-Dispatch*, March 22, 1999.
11. Brokaw, Leslie. "Twenty-Eight Steps to a Strategic Alliance," *Inc.*, April 1993.
12. "Celebrated Jewelers Go National, but the Locals Won't Be Pushovers: Buyers of High-End Baubles Frequently Stay Loyal to Independent Stores," *Wall Street Journal*, August 5, 1999.
13. "But First, Call Your Drug Company," *American Demographics*, October 1998.
14. Marquis, Julie. "Doctors Who Lose Patience," *Los Angeles Times*, March 3, 1997.
15. Ibid.

16. Abbott, Andrew. *The System of Professions* (University of Chicago Press, 1988).
17. "But First, Call Your Drug Company," op. cit.
18. Relman, Arnold S. "Dr. Business," *The American Prospect,* 34, September-October 1997.

Chapter Five

Machine Providers: Managing the Automated Service Process

Advantages of Automated Service

In a highly-planned encounter business, the role played by service providers can be minimal. As already pointed out, workers who have little interest in the business and no source of motivation to provide good service can drive away customers. Finding good workers can be difficult, and training them is expensive. But technology makes possible another alternative: using machines to do the work.

Technology provides the means to do both mechanical functions that simulate human labor and more behind-the-scenes intellectual work that identifies likely customers and provides them with custom information or a custom product. Encounter businesses can bring to the service sector the same processes that unfolded during the Industrial Revolution, breaking down tasks into chunk-sized, simple processes, automating each step, then eliminating people entirely. Beginning with ATMs, machine-delivered service has been working its way into people's lives. ATMs at first simply automated the work of bank tellers, but this technology also opened the way for money machines in new places. Instead of having to go to a bank for cash during banking hours, people can now get money any time at their local convenience store, gas station, grocery store, airport, and many other locations. This is a technology that provided so much extra convenience that few ATM users would trade it for the personal touch they got when they went to the bank, stood in line, and were greeted by a teller. ATM use is a good example of how the meaning of "service" has changed.

There are some advantages to both provider companies and customers in automated service:

- It guarantees that the service is always uniform.
- It provides constant service with no shift changes or breaks.
- It brings service to more people at lower cost.
- It can create new service products through use of technology.
- It is a way to free humans from boring and unpleasant work.
- It solves the problem of not enough workers.

The Service Is Always Uniform

Encounter businesses are set up to provide uniform service to all customers, but both customers and providers sometimes try to deviate from the standard process. With a machine provider, that never happens. A customer who calls an automated information service is told to press number keys on his phone until he gets to the information he wants. If he still wants more information, there is nothing he can do about it.

The vending machine and juke box deliver the same product to each customer, and ATMs make no judgment about the person punching in numbers to get back cash. The automated recording gives out the same information to the weekly moviegoer as to the occasional moviegoer. These processes are totally democratic, functioning the same for billionaire and pauper alike. This can be an advantage but also a disadvantage. An automatic process with no flexibility does not let you give different treatment based on the value of the customer. Through use of the right technology, you could add some customization by having the customer input a card, a personal identification number (PIN), or password; or with hand- or eye-scanning, you get convenience for the customer and sales tracking for the organization.

The Machine Is Always There

One of the best features of machine service is that it is always available. The automatic teller machine (ATM), unlike the live teller, is available twenty-four hours a day. You can get a newspaper from a coin-operated box anytime the box contains papers, and the mail box is always there to receive your letter, as is the Federal Express box in many office buildings. These are familiar, unattended services that provide convenience around the clock.

Technology can bring that same convenience to customers for many kinds of services. Whether the information is available by phone, which allows a user to punch in a code, or through the Internet, the always-available format is a hit with customers. *The Forrester Report* quotes a financial company:

> We were skeptical about introducing [an automated system] with our senior citizen clients because they tend to be technology averse. But, customer satisfaction surveys indicate that they really appreciate it. They were concerned that they were interrupting the operator's job to ask about their accounts. Now, they feel free to call during the eleven o'clock news to find out how some world event affected their portfolios. The volume of calls is way up.[1]

This is the same kind of advantage that the fast food restaurant provides with a self-serve drink bar or the information phone number that provides movie times twenty-four hours a day. Paying bills online is another example. If customers want to do their accounting at 2 a.m., the online teller is available with never a complaint. In all of these cases, the customer does not have to "bother" a server. Providing a "serve yourself" option can be a way to eliminate a worker and please customers at the same time.

Serve-yourself music has a long history. Rowe International of Grand Rapids, Michigan, has been in business since 1909, primarily making juke boxes. Its first product was a player piano, an early example of automating a task that previously had required a skilled human.[2] Player pianos were limited to the "software"—paper tapes—that people created for them, so they were not exactly a substitute for real players, plus they never varied in the way they played. They lacked the custom touch of the musician, but they brought music to people who might not have had a chance to see live entertainment. People liked the player piano, just as they liked juke boxes— those shiny windowed boxes sitting next to the tables in family cafes across America that let diners listen to popular tunes by inserting a coin.

Bringing Service to More People at Lower Cost

Automated services can bring service to more people and lower the cost, although automation can also mean a big investment in equipment. Manufacturing companies that replaced people with machines spent a lot of money to do that. Services cannot always be replaced by just spending money on machines; in relationship businesses, the interaction between people is what's important.

One area where machines are being tried is in employment interviewing. InterActive makes a system called InTeleView for employers that screens job applicants. The company claims its system provides a competitive edge through use of technology. Applicants call a phone number anytime to hear recorded questions that can be answered "yes" or "no." The employer supplies the questions and how they should be answered. Another way employment interviews are being automated is through video interviews that headhunters supply to interested companies. Many companies also scan resumes and use software to pick out key words that they think will indicate the applicant is qualified. Human judgment might work better than these methods, but employing professionals to do this work is expensive.

Mass Customization: Machine Made but Customer Specified

Pure customization of a service requires customer and provider to collaborate as partners in a relationship in which they jointly develop the end result. An example is someone working with an architect to design and build a house. That kind of customization is expensive and available mainly to the wealthy. But along comes a new idea: mass customization. For example, a new way of serving music CD customers was reported by *USA Today* in its December 31, 1998, edition. It featured Electra Records, which offered a create-your-own CD to consumers who bought rap artist Busta Rhymes's new album online. Customers who purchased the album were sent an e-mail promotion that, for an additional $4.99, let them create a four-song CD from a group of ten Busta Rhymes singles. Nearly 30 percent of those who received the e-mail took advantage of the offer. It was inexpensive and customized within a range of limited choices. People who registered at the CDNOW Web site also received an offer to create a compilation. They received the following e-mail message:

> Select Your Own Songs! Hole. Green Day. Sugar Ray. Iggy Pop. Dead Kennedys. Monster Magnet. And more. Before they were big, they were struggling for a record deal, making demos and recording live. Now YOU can pick tracks from these rockers' early years and make your own Custom Compilation CD. You'll title it yourself and even write the liner notes!

These are custom CDs, but with a limited range of choices. Levi Strauss, with a long tradition of making sturdy denim jeans, will make its buyers a custom pair. For $55, consumers essentially can design jeans with the precise Levi's models, leg openings, colors, sizes, zippers, or buttons they want. Customers fill out a checklist at a computerized kiosk and receive their jeans in about two weeks. This process, too, has a list of choices, although not the unlimited choices someone would have if they went to a tailor. But then a tailor would charge more than fifty-five dollars.

In the apparel industry, "mass customization" means "the ability to customize products along a continuum of variables in quantities as small as one—while manufacturing at mass production speeds."[3] With military uniforms creating a demand for fast, customized clothing, current capability can take individual measurements and enter them via an order system that is capable of searching a data base of pattern pieces, determine if all the components are available, and make the pattern. If needed pattern parts are not in the system, the missing parts are flagged and automatically generated. The apparel industry uses software to build templates for cutting fabric and machines to do all the cutting. Going one step further, they are working on systems that can scan a person for the measurements, feed them into a computer system along with alteration rules specified by the customer for a style, and generate a pattern; the garment is then cut and sewn. This is mass customization—a garment made by machine but made to order.

These services involve the customer in creating a product, but do not require personal service by a provider. Unlike the craftsman of the past, companies using mass customization must produce large quantities of goods and deliver finished products in a timely manner. This is essentially an interaction between the customer and a process involving a machine. Customization no longer refers to a craftsman making up an item by hand. Now it means that machines and automatic processes, together with the customer, can create an individually specified product. Dell, the computer maker, produces "custom" computers for its customers, but, again, the "custom" part is limited to the options Dell offers.

Mass customization tries to be an analogy to the custom-made goods once available to ordinary people. But by using machinery to make the products, it takes what was a relationship process and turns it into an encounter process. The growth of custom products is reflective of a power shift that has been occurring over the last century as economic control has moved from manufacturer to distributor to retailer and, finally, to the customer. Retailers gained a lot of power over manufacturers when they built bigger stores like the huge Wal-Marts, Super K-Marts, and Home Depots. Then they compiled large data

bases of customers and their wants. Manufacturers had to produce what retailers wanted. And retailers are driven by customer preference.

Now customers can connect directly with manufacturers
and service providers and tell them what they want. Dell will
build a computer to order. Saturn will build a car to order. Levi-
Strauss will make jeans to order. Music publishers will create a
CD to order. And coming soon, even McDonald's, who wrote
the original gospel of uniformity, will make your burger to
order. But they'll do it without adding any time or cost to the
process. That's mass customization.

New Products Through Technology

Music has proven to be an area ripe for automation. Synthesizers store digital sound and can play back whole compositions
or just isolated sounds that are then put together in a new way.
The use of "sampling" to combine and mix previously recorded
sounds, along with the use of synthesizers, has eliminated the
need for recording artists to hire studio musicians. The pop recording business has come to depend on these techniques.

Sampling originated in 1980 when New York composer
Charles Dodge digitized the voice of opera great Enrico Caruso,
taken from old records, and used the resulting sounds to create
new recordings. Today's composers who use digitally stored
sounds and machines that recreate the sound of any instrument
can do what used to require a lot of people playing real instruments. Even live performances sometimes use a few musicians
and a synthesizer instead of an orchestra. Jeremy Rifkin discusses music automation in his book, *The End of Work*, mention-
ing an opera and a Broadway play that substituted synthesizers
for real instruments. He reports that a dispute with the musicians union in Long Beach, California, led to replacing all musicians with two synthesizers for a production of *Hello, Dolly*.[4]

Not just music, but making movies and commercials has
changed with the digital age. Technology has made it possible
to bring back dead movie stars. Companies can use digitized
clips from archives instead of hiring live actors. Digitized images of such famous film stars as Gene Kelly, Fred Astaire, and

Humphrey Bogart have been used in commercials. This process has only just begun, as technology will let movie-makers recreate famous persons and animate them. A young Gene Kelly could once again sing and dance in a new movie for a new generation of fans. A young, handsome and lean Elvis Presley could croon a new tune. The thin line between real and not real gets thinner.

Replacing Boring Jobs, Addressing the Worker Shortage

Some uses of automation replace what would be low-level, low-paying jobs. Substituting a machine can solve the problems of finding, hiring, and dealing with workers. Serving products through vending machines, use of smart cards for automatic purchases or debits, and using kiosks for information are examples.

Vending Machines

Vending machines, robot stores, have been serving up soft drinks and potato chips for most of the twentieth century. Modern vending machines may look similar to the classic 1950s' red Coke machines, but appearances are deceiving. By adding computer technology, these machines have been made more reliable, less likely to vend a cup with no coffee or spit out the wrong change. Machines that can identify a dollar bill or other types of currency and make change have helped build customer acceptance. Many vending machines can be programmed with different prices as products or prices change; some have built-in diagnostics capability for easier servicing; some can track data on which items sell the most, keeping historical records on all products sold; some can add a line of information about a product through a digital display, even using different languages. Companies specializing in building vending machine controllers can customize the electronics for whatever features a business wants.

Some machines can communicate with a remote location over a network, informing company headquarters when they are out of items. Rowe International's juke boxes come equipped with a modem that relates information back to the distributor. Their datalink module can report when the jukebox is out of service, if the bill acceptor box is full, the amount of cash in the machine, and the popularity rating of each tune. The distributor is automatically notified by datalink when a machine needs servicing, saving unnecessary trips to juke box locations. The information gathered on which plays are most popular lets these juke box businesses alert their customers to which songs to add to improve their profitability.

Instead of just being passive boxes accepting money and dispensing goods, vending machines, thanks to computer technology, have been made smarter. Federal Express has done the same thing with its drop boxes. During the 1996 Atlanta Olympic games, FedEx had to find a way to keep up with the increased number of packages. The company contracted with Skywire Corp. to create a new kind of drop box that continually monitors the status of its contents and lets the company know when it needs to be visited.

Smart Cards

Prepaid phone cards sold in convenience stores are another kind of service device that provides the customer with an easy way to make calls without dealing with the confusion of service providers. Europe and Asia are using "smart cards" for automated buying—a trend that hasn't become as common in the United States except for the growing use of phone cards.

A new use of the smart card is in laundromats. A newspaper article reported on a business in Madison Heights, Michigan, that will use prepaid debit cards to operate its Speed Queen washers and dryers. "Up to $300 in credit can be placed on the plastic, wallet-sized cards, each of which contains a computer chip," says the story. "Carrying a pocketful of quarters will be a thing of the past."[5] Universities, too, have adopted smart cards as a means of both identification and payment for items in campus stores. The University of Arizona issues "Cat Cards" (named for its sports team, the Wildcats).

Some supermarkets have introduced automated check-out shopping where customers paying with credit cards can scan all items themselves, slide their card through a machine, and leave the store without interacting with a clerk. Auto-checkout machines were in use in about 300 supermarkets nationwide in early 1999. They work like regular checkout scanners but with the addition of some anti-theft features. The devices made by Productivity Solutions, Inc, weigh each item, then weigh the total order at the end of the scanning to make sure the final package equals the sum of items scanned. Stores that are getting this system plan to mainly use it on unpopular shifts when they have problems hiring staff and to supplement busy times. Critic Jeremy Rifkin says it will eventually replace most cashiers. "The bottom line here is that the cheapest worker in the world will not be as cheap as the technology coming online to replace them."[6]

Beyond cards is something even more convenient and fool-proof: iris scanning. By early 1999, Bank United of Texas became the first U.S. financial institution to employ iris recognition equipment that "reads" the iris of the eye and matches that with stored pictures of each customer's eye. With this system, there is no card to carry, no number to remember. The customer presses a button at the ATM and initiates an eye scan. Each person's iris is unique, and this is a part of the eye that doesn't get diseased or change.[7]

Kiosks

Free-standing computer information systems called kiosks are replacing receptionists in many buildings. Users touch a menu on a computer screen to get the information they want. If the kiosk is a building directory located in a lobby, visitors might touch an alphabet letter for the first letter of a person's last name, or they might touch the function they want so someone who has come for a job interview might touch "Human Resources." The screen then changes to a listing for whatever was selected. Kiosks are often used with a phone that connects to internal phone numbers, so a visitor can connect to the person. Kiosks can also be used in stores to provide information. One use is bridal registries. The customer enters the bride's or groom's last name and gets a list of all items they have selected and which of those have been purchased already. A wine shop could have a kiosk that provides information on wine varieties and which to serve with different kinds of food. This is a value-added service that functions on its own.

Computer as Information Provider

Interacting With Non-Human Agents

The future as predicted by such pundits as John Naisbitt, Alvin Toffler, and Nicholas Negroponte is a digital age, a post-indus-trial age, and, if we believe Negroponte, a post-information age. In his celebrated book, *Being Digital*, Negroponte, who is head of MIT's Media Lab, paints a picture of a future in which we interact with "agents," digital assistants who know a lot about us. He sees this as essentially different from today's practice of keeping data about customers. He says, "A widely held assump-tion is that individualization is the extrapolation of narrowcast-ing—you go from a large to a small to a smaller group, ultimately to the individual. By the time you have my address, my marital status, my age, my income, my car brand, my pur-chases, my drinking habits, and my taxes, you have me—a de-mographic unit of one."

But he goes on to say:

> This line of reasoning completely misses the fundamental difference between narrowcasting and being digital. In being digital, I am *me*, not a statistical subset.
>
> The post information age is about acquaintance over time: machines [is] understanding individuals with the same degree of subtlety (or more than) we can expect from other human beings, including idiosyncrasies (like always wearing a blue-striped shirt) and totally random events, good and bad, in the unfolding narrative of our lives.
>
> For example, having heard from the liquor store's agent, a machine could call to your attention a sale on a particular Chardonnay or beer that it knows the guests you have coming to dinner tomorrow night liked last time. It could remind you to drop off the car at a garage near where

you are going because the car told it that it needs new tires."[8]

If machines could be created that would know customers as well as those in Negroponte's scenarios above, their interaction with customers would simulate a relationship. If a store had an intelligent agent that knew each customer's wine preference, the agent would be an excellent employee. It would know the customer but would not go off and start its own business and steal the customer. And it would not have to be paid a salary. From the customer's point of view, the agent would provide a service, but it would not be the same experience as interacting with a person. An agent—a computer program—could be efficient at what it was programmed to do, but it would not have any actual concern about customers or their desire to keep personal information private. Even Bill Gates does not think machines can act like people. He said in an interview in *MIT's Technology Review* magazine, ". . . technology will never replace the wonders of human interaction—no matter how good PCs get at recognizing voice or handwriting, they'll never read body language or smile back at you."[9] They certainly won't do it with the sincerity (or the insincerity, for that matter) of which humans are capable.

The move to use "bots" to guide users through some process is as close as we have gotten to Negroponte's vision. The Help Desk for Rocketmail, a free e-mail service, is staffed by "RocketBot," which (according to the Rocketmail Web site) "acts like a human customer support agent, to intelligently guide you through a question-and-answer session so they can resolve your problem fast and efficiently. You will quickly receive intelligent, consistent advice on how to resolve your problem yourself."[10]

Customers of Monsterboard.com, a job search site, can sign up to have an agent search for jobs for which they might qualify and send them e-mail when it finds suitable job offers.

Another service, Y2Klinks.com, uses "Millie" to search out answers to questions about the year 2000 bug. Its Web page explains, "Millie does not rely on simple keywords. Instead, she is based on a new Artificial Intelligence compiler . . . and many common words that search engines ignore can be important in helping Millie understand what you are saying." Millie is supposed to "learn" as more people ask her more questions. There is also this interesting and unexplained tidbit of information about Millie: "The good news is, Millie was designed by a woman."

In a variation of the agent idea, at the Sovereign Securities Web site (www.mydiscountbroker.com), an animated red ball with a big smile declares from the screen, "Hi, I'm Ric O' Chet, your personal assistant and resident site expert for mydiscountbroker.com." If you have the right plug-ins, you can hear Ric talk and watch him bounce around the screen as he guides you through opening an account. It's doubtful that users would perceive their interaction with Ric as "personal," but it makes what is essentially software seem friendly and nonthreatening.

Computers, whether through an agent or an online form or information page, dispense or gather information and provide the means of completing a transaction. Computerized knowledge bases, for example, are available to solve technical problems as a substitute for asking someone. When a customer calls and talks to a person, that service worker may be accessing the knowledge base and relating the answer. Customers seldom talk to an actual "expert" when they call for help. What they get is a person who has access to a lot of standard problems and solutions. Agents and "bots" are an interface between customers and the service. They are an interesting concept, but marketers need to remember that customers are less interested in cleverness and more interested in how fast they can open accounts and do transactions. Poor service is not forgiven because it is delivered with a smile or by a cute cartoon character.

Internet Health Care: Tapping a Huge Market

Health care sites on the Internet provide an example of how customers whose needs have gone unmet can be served. A report on online health care by research firm ING Baring Furman Selz in 1998 showed that many health problems go untreated.[11] For example, while 30 million Americans have genital herpes, only 10 million of them get any treatment.

A site like healthanswer.com, intended for use by the public rather than by medical professionals, lists symptoms, diseases, and treatments in a hyperlinked format that makes it easy to search for information. Someone with a rash, for instance, can see descriptions of different kinds of rashes listed along with other symptoms that indicate a possible cause. Each nicely formatted listing has a section called "Calling Your Health Care Provider," which helps people decide if what they have is serious enough to go to the doctor. The site describes probable treatments and tests for each disease. Healthanswer.com is linked to mothernature.com, a site selling vitamins and other health care products of interest to people who visit this type of site.

Responding to interest by the health care industry in using the Internet, Intel held a conference in October 1998 for health care companies interested in learning more about using the Internet. Intel CEO Andy Grove said, "E-mail and Internet technology have created an 'X-Factor' in productivity that has stimulated the U.S. economy through increased productivity and efficiency. It is time for an X-Factor in health care where Internet technology is used to keep costs in check while deepening doctor-to-patient relationships through increased communication and care."[12]

Grove may see the Internet as contributing to doctor-patient relationships, but given the high cost of health care, many customers of health care sites are probably trying to avoid a trip to the doctor. Indeed, Cyber Dialog, a market research firm, reports that doctors online spend most of their time talking to each other, not to their patients.[13] There are business opportunities in the communications gap between doctors and their customers, and online health care sites have appeared to fill that gap. These sites face a profitable future as pharmaceutical and other health care products find them an ideal location for ads touting their products and links to the companies' own Web pages.

As health care sites add more features of help to consumers, they will evolve into portals, according to research firm Jupiter Communications. One of the key drivers behind the rise of health portals, according to Jupiter, will be rapid growth in pharmaceutical direct-to-consumer (DTC) advertising online. Pharmaceutical and biotech companies can reach more people interested in solving a health problem through large health care portal sites than through other kinds of advertising. Jupiter has projected health and medical advertising online to grow from $12.3 million in 1997 to more than $265 million by 2002, with DTC representing about 50 percent of that figure.[14]

The Furman Selz report also discusses DTC. Showing its orientation toward customer encounters, it refers to a "disease market," which it says presents an "opportunity" for drug companies. To quote: "Because of high untreated populations in many disease markets and low compliance rates for those already on prescription medications, the pharmaceutical industry is presented with a unique market-expanding opportunity for approved and currently marketed drugs. In our opinion, DTC advertising is a key to unlocking this opportunity."[15]

The tenth annual (1998) Web survey by The Graphic, Visualization & Usability Center (GVU) shows that more than 80 percent of respondents accessed a medical information site at some time, with one in four checking sites monthly or more often.[16] Cyber Dialog reports that nearly 18 million Americans sought health care information over the Internet in 1998, about the same number who sought investment information. This is a huge market for health marketers.

Health care is a fertile area for self-help, a growing consumer trend. Using an Internet health site, a person can search through many possibilities and sometimes make an accurate self-diagnosis and learn more about the condition and possible treatments.

Popular consumer health Web sites in 1999 included the Mayo Clinic online (www.mayohealth.org), Dr. Koop Online (www.drkoop.com), and Betterhealth (www.betterhealth.com), with content mainly for women. Pharmaceutical companies maintain sites with information about the diseases for which they offer drugs. Consumers can do a search to find the growing number of sites with health information.

The pharmaceutical business once operated on a relationship basis, with salesmen visiting doctors to sell the benefits of their line of drugs. With the rise of managed care, they've had to shift their focus to HMOs and big institutions that act as gatekeepers over what doctors can prescribe. The legislative initiatives of 1997 that let drug companies advertise to the public have given them a way to go right to their customers with their messages, bypassing doctors and insurance companies. The use of the Internet to reach customers is the latest twist.

Insurance companies appear to be ambivalent about drug companies going right to the public with ads. An article in the Michigan Blue Cross/Blue Shield/Blue Care Network magazine about these ads expresses the concern that they create an "artificial demand" for a drug. They urge consumers to stick to their doctor's advice and to remember that advertised drugs may not be "the most cost-effective option."[17]

For the busy customer who may be unhappy with the fast and impersonal treatment at HMO clinics, a nicely designed Web site that provides both information and access to treatments that can be purchased can be very appealing. Winners in the online health care business will be those companies that offer customers convenience, support, and information— three things many people don't get at the doctor's office. Doctors themselves are generally not supportive of Internet medicine, perhaps fearing further loss of control over patient care. Many observers would say they have already lost control, as insurance companies force relationships to give way to encounters and people seek options that are either more satisfying and/or more affordable.

Some health care sites incorporate chat rooms and discussion areas, where people can help each other and interact with others who have similar interests. People with rare diseases, for example, can find each other and share information. As consumers become more educated through health care web sites, they may apply pressure on the government to make more drugs available over the counter, saving the cost of a doctor visit. Customers who don't have a trusted doctor with whom they have a relationship are more likely to resent the cost and inconvenience of a doctor visit when the main purpose is to get a prescription. The medical profession has brought this problem on itself by failing to take action against doctors who cooperate with web sites that sell popular drugs like Viagra to anyone, based only on a questionnaire. Doctors, who have not been supportive of their customers going online for medical information, may find themselves increasingly out of the loop as big pharmaceutical firms and other companies pushing vitamins and natural remedies take their pitch right to the customer. People who actually have a relationship with a doctor may not turn to these sources as readily as the growing numbers who do *not* have such a relationship.

Eliminate the Middleman?

Many Internet businesses are based on an old money-saving concept—eliminating the middleman (but called by the fancy new name, "disintermediation"). Toll-free phone and catalog services were all supposed to eliminate the middleman, but that hasn't happened in services in which enough people appreciate and want relationships. When relationships get too expensive, though, there is an incentive to bring a product directly to the public, as in the case of pharmaceuticals. Eliminating distributors, pharmacists, and even doctors would bring the price down, and most prescriptions are for chronic conditions and are a continuing expense.

Real estate agents who primarily locate and provide information that customers could find for themselves online are also at risk. Offering a Web real estate store, with lower costs than the usual agent's fee, could become a new model for selling homes. Insurance is also being "disintermediated." Companies have found TV and radio ads offering lower rates on car insurance and life insurance have swung customers away from agent-offered products. The home mortgage business has also discovered the Internet.

Buying and selling stocks has changed greatly, thanks to the Internet. Numerous sites offer discount trading. The big financial houses want to eliminate "star" stockbrokers and take advantage of the public's interest in investing. Many more people today own stocks than ever before, and many more engage in short-term buying and selling. Eliminating the middleman and taking even small fees for online trading can be very profitable.

Sometimes the Web service, instead of replacing the middleman, becomes the middleman. Examples are Priceline.com, which will find the best price for an airline ticket or hotel room, and E-Loan, Homeshark, QuickenMortgage.com, and GetSmart.com, Web sites that promise to find the best mortgage price for home buyers. These services help people find low prices and take a fee for doing so (just as a middleman would). They compete with relationship providers who work with customers to find the best deal. Auction sites like eBay.com are pure middlemen. They bring together buyer and seller.

Music distribution also has changed. The newest way to acquire music is over the Internet where the new MP3 format delivers quality sound in a compressed file users can download. The music industry is becoming a battleground as the Internet shifts power from recording companies to musicians and music consumers. A coalition called the Secure Digital Music Initiative, according to MSNBC, is trying to "find a way for the entrenched powers of the recording industry to survive as the popularity of downloading music from the Internet explodes."[18] This is no small trend. When a track from a Tom Petty release was made available in MP3 in 1999, 157,000 people downloaded it in just two days. And, at the same time, "MP3" was running neck-in-neck with "sex" as the most popular Internet search term. The research firm Forrester is predicting the market for digital music delivery will reach $1 billion by 2003.[19] This appears to be a classic elimination of the oft-maligned middleman, but look again.

Companies like MP3.com that host the music files take a cut, but it appears to be a much smaller cut based on their reduced costs. Because customers can listen to the music before buying and can get information on the artists online, the Web site reduces the need to get hearings on radio stations and MTV, all of which costs money to send free demo CDs and do promotion. Artists can sign up to have MP3.com make their CDs and split the price, which must be under $10. These CDs are sold as "DAM CDs." This is Digital Automatic Music, and the CD the customer gets contains both audio and MP3 files.

The artist gets a login ID that lets him check on his sales, and he can cancel the arrangement at any time. MP3.com was claiming six million visitors per month as of early 1999.

In a *Wired* interview, rapper Chuck D said the major record labels were fighting the digital format because "they won't be able to pimp MP3." Asked if the Secure Digital Music Initiative had a chance against MP3, he replied, "No. The dam has burst and the chunks are in the water." He explained the economics this way: "Today a major label makes a CD for as little as 80 cents, then sells it to a wholesaler for $10.50 so the retailer can charge $14—that's highway robbery."[20] But MP3.com makes money selling CDs for five dollars, and artists who might not get a hearing otherwise can find fans and make money.

It would seem that the good old middleman is here to stay. In some cases, he's just gone digital.

Shopping on the Internet

Online shopping is one of the fastest growing types of e-commerce. Christmas 1998 saw shoppers tote up $2.3 billion in sales on America Online (AOL) alone, accounting for about half of all online shopping. Book giant Amazon.com sold $250 million worth of product (books and music) in its fourth quarter, a 279 percent increase over 1997.[21] Internet research firm Jupiter Communications estimates 1998 holiday sales totaled $3.14 billion.[22]

Not everyone was happy. More than 270 Christmas shoppers filed complaints with the Better Business Bureau over Shopping.com, charging that an online store didn't fulfill orders or provide proper customer service. Web stores, like walk-in stores, need to turn shoppers into repeat customers. Research firm Bizrate.com, based on a survey of 67,000 shoppers in 1998 fourth-quarter, found that 96 percent of those who bought online and got their merchandise on time said they will buy again online, but only 46 percent of those who encountered delivery problems said they will consider making another purchase.[23] Web stores are a new way to shop, and customers who have bad experiences may not be back. Like other encounter businesses,

Web sites need to provide reliable service to retain their customers.

E-mail: It's Huge

The most common kind of Internet service is not shopping, it's e-mail. By 1999, about 41 percent of Americans had computers and were online; and almost all of them used e-mail. Getting an Internet e-mail account is as easy as signing up for America Online (AOL) or going to www.hotmail.com, www.rocketmail.com, or www.juno.com, or numerous other sites to get a free account. These services make money by selling information about their users to marketers. Hotmail and Rocketmail are Web-based services, while Juno lets users connect by phone and retrieve their messages and read them using Juno's easy-to-use mail software, which runs on their PC.

Popular portal sites like Lycos also offer free e-mail accounts. Portals are popular sites with a search feature and links to news, shopping, and categories of information. Other big sites, such as publishing giant Ziff-Davis through its ZDNet site, are also offering free e-mail (as well as "v-mail"—video e-mail). These services make money by building traffic at their sites, which makes them attractive to marketers. Netscape's Netcenter portal site is adding mail and other features as well, such as an appointment calendar that can remind users of upcoming events.

Internet mail services can be used by people who don't even have computers. By going to a library, community center, senior center, Net Café, or any other place where the Internet is available to the public, anyone can log on and, using their assigned ID and password, receive and send e-mail. Hotmail, the first and most popular of these services, went live in 1996 and by 1998 had more than 10 million subscribers.

E-mail has big potential for marketers. Microsoft bought Hotmail, along with its user list, in 1998. Not to be outdone in the business of building a huge subscriber base, Yahoo bought Rocketmail the same year. Coupling free e-mail with the many features of a portal site encourages users to adopt that site as their Web "home page." The more people visit a portal, the more attractive it becomes for advertisers who want to use the Internet to reach potential buyers.

E-mail facilitates both relationships and encounters. People can carry on a close relationship through e-mail (as in the movie "You've Got Mail"), and they can read ads and receive sales offers through e-mail. While relationships almost always eventually involve face-to-face meetings or at least phone calls, e-mail makes it easy to keep in touch in between. Many Web businesses include an e-mail address for customers to send questions. When the customer gets a personal reply back from a real person, it can build confidence in the company and the integrity of ordering over the Web. But companies that list an e-mail address and then send back a canned message by autoresponder are accomplishing nothing and hurting their credibility.

E-mail also works for many business-to-business or provider-to-business relationships, as people in different locations send messages and files back and forth between meetings. E-mail has made possible collaborations between people who are widely separated geographically, giving rise to many more opportunities for providers and more options for customers.

Unwanted E-mail

Customers of the large e-mail providers often find their mail boxes loaded with electronic trash, solicitations to use pornographic sites, get-rich-quick schemes, offers for credit cards, and other unwanted messages. Early Web users coined the term "spam" to describe these unsolicited e-mails and leveled heavy criticism at the perpetrators. But no amount of complaining has stopped the barrage of junk e-mail. Marketers using e-mail buy millions of e-mail addresses from people who use their technical skills to "vacuum" up addresses from Internet sites. One such service selling e-mail addresses sent a pitch that says, "We can send up to 200,000 e-mails out for you with your own sales letter. The e-mail addresses that we use are freshly extracted daily from people actually online either chatting or surfing!" People who are busy "chatting" and "surfing" don't know their e-mail addresses are being "extracted." Often those who use these services give a fake return address to keep from getting millions of "replies" back from recipients who didn't want the message and might hit the "reply" button and type some unflattering descriptions of the sender. Legislation is in the works to make using a fake return address illegal.

In the manner of yesterday's mass marketing techniques, e-mail spammers are looking for only a small percentage of responses—2 percent or less might make a big profit. The fact that the other 98 percent don't like getting the message in their mail box doesn't concern them. Perhaps it is only because the first use of the Internet was communication among scientific and technical organizations that users object to getting unwanted mail. In the world of "snail mail," everyone gets lots of "junk mail" delivered by the U.S. Post Office. This paper mail must be tossed in a trash can whereas getting rid of an unwanted e-mail is as simple as hitting the "delete" key.

Anonymous Information Gathering

People who surf the Web often encounter sites that ask for registration in return for access to information. The Electronic Privacy Information Center (EPIC) surveyed the top one hundred Web sites in 1997 and found that forty-nine of them solicit user information.[24]

EPIC's Web site notes that almost all sites allow at least some anonymous browsing. "By avoiding the collection of personal information, Web sites encourage users to visit sites. In the physical world, we note that very few stores require the collection of personal information before allowing someone to enter." In this way, shopping on the Internet is less private than going to a store.

Many Web sites leave a small file called a "cookie" on the user's hard drive. The Web site's server reads the file on subsequent visits and stores information about visitors completely in the background, which is passed on to the site's server. The visitor never knows. The more sophisticated user understands she can set her Web browser to inform her when a site leaves a cookie, giving the user the chance to reject it.

EPIC's survey showed twenty-four of the one hundred top

sites use cookies. Some use the cookie strictly for their own use, such as storing passwords, but others could use the information for marketing. Depending on how the programmer designed the cookie, hackers could access the cookie information, which is stored in unencrypted form on the user's hard drive. Some new marketing services retrieve and merge cookie data and collate it with information from census, motor vehicle, and credit data to put together profiles of users. This detailed kind of data on customers is then sold to companies that want such data.

Other businesses track which sites users visit. For example, www.did-it.com, is a digital advertising service that will optimize a customer's Web site to be picked up by search engines; it also sells banner ads on groups of related Web sites to customers who pay only for the actual "clicks" that connect users to their site.

Can organizations harm themselves with customers by parading their knowledge of the customer's online behavior? Yes, say analysts at Zona Research. In a research report, Zona says the need for online marketers to increase revenues by selling information and databases about their customer lists to any and all bidders outweighs the importance of protecting privacy. The Zona report states, "Marketers and vendors that honor and acknowledge consumer privacy concerns will add considerable cachet to their brands. Just as obnoxious and pushy sales people can damage brand, considerate and helpful sales people can build brand loyalty. Shocking customers with invasive, detailed knowledge of online behavior could go a long way to damaging brand."[25]

If customers get angry enough about unwanted data collections and marketing pitches, they may push for legislation against it, the same way consumers fought for and got legislation against automated phone calls.

Building "Relationships" vs. Invasion of Privacy

What some companies see as building relationships, many customers see as an invasion of their privacy. The key to customer comfort seems to be to limit the information requested and explain why it is needed. Excite.com, for example, tells customers it needs their zip code so it can personalize weather information and their birth date so it can supply horoscopes. The hope is that this will keep users from simply lying when they complete these forms.

The Graphic, Visualization, & Usability Center's (GVU) tenth Web user survey (run during 1998) reveals that over half of those responding say they have entered false information on registration forms at least some of the time, although only 6 percent routinely provide false information (i.e., 75 percent of the time or more), while 57 percent of females reported that they *never* falsify information, compared with 45 percent of males.[26]

In an article in *MIT's Technology Review* magazine called "Data Smog," David Shenk echoes the concern of many computer users about giving out personal information:

> Indeed, the ability to gather and analyze information conveniently and cheaply means that our personal privacy has replaced censorship as our primary civil liberties concern. What once might have been considered harmless personal trivia—which videos you rented this week, whether you like starch in your laundered shirts, whether you buy name-brand or generic aspirin—can today all be turned into useful intelligence by powerful cross-referencing data bases.[27]

Despite obvious signs that customers don't like supplying personal information, many companies continue to think of data-gathering as building relationships when what they are really looking for is what one article euphemistically called a "revenue opportunity."

Remote Diagnosing

Remote diagnosing seems like a good idea—someone having a problem with her computer calls a help desk, where a technician remotely operates the malfunctioning computer in order to diagnose and fix the problem. This saves time and money because it eliminates the need for an onsite visit. However, this capability also lets the remote operator look into all the remote computer's directories and files, add and delete files, and perform many other tasks. Some of the software now available lets a remote operator "see" what's on any computer connected to a network, without the computer user knowing. Used benignly, it might be of benefit. But it poses problems regarding privacy. Like the cookie that the user doesn't know is there, a remote probe of his computer can let someone snoop on a lot of private documents.

So Why Don't People Use Automated Service?

While many automated services are popular with customers, some are not.

Forcing Customers to Use an Automated Service

Delta Airlines, in January 1999, tried to force customers to order tickets over the Internet by adding an extra two-dollar charge for *not* ordering from Delta's Web site. No other airlines followed Delta with such a charge, and travel agents were incensed since they receive no commission on booking through the Internet. They also felt Delta was trying to keep passengers from gaining comparative prices by making them buy from Delta's site rather than through a booking service. Delta had so many complaints it had to withdraw the charge after only a few weeks.

Customers don't like having their options cut off, and Delta's customers who use travel agents could easily see the surcharge as a move to discourage people from using a relationship type of service. While ordering tickets over the Internet is popular, *forcing* customers to order this way is not. One wonders why Delta didn't just raise ticket prices by $2 and then offer a discount to customers who used its Web site. Customers like discounts but hate surcharges.

Some hotel chains have put in an automatic check-in process for their frequent customers, but it has not been popular.

Customers have not seen it as a convenience, and most continue to go to the check-in desk and talk to a clerk. People simply prefer dealing with a live person in most situations, so automated service must offer something extra. It must be seen by customers as adding value such as the convenience of always having the service, the ability to get exactly the right information without having to wait for an available person, free refills from self-serve drink dispensers, or the ease of swiping a card through a machine.

Intelligent Processes: Think Like a Customer

Designing workable processes is vitally important when automating a service. The process needs to make sense from the customer's point of view, not just support the flow of work. Customers get really upset when they order something, then find there is no way to cancel or change the order. Don Crabb, a columnist for ZDNet, received many complaints about the service from CompUSA, including the following story from a reader:

> I purchased a CompUSA-branded computer from Comp-USA mail order. Less than 12 hours later, I called to cancel the order. I was informed that once it was ordered it had to be shipped. I said I didn't need the computer and to save shipping it to me. They said there was nothing they could do about it (ironic for a store based on computers). Some two-and-a-half weeks later, they shipped it to me. Let me get this straight: It is more efficient for CompUSA to build a computer, ship it to me, and pay for its return shipping than it would be to somehow get ahold of the people who build the computers and cancel the order. Anyway, I left at least six phone calls asking for a [Return Merchandise Authorization] RMA—none were answered. Finally, I stayed on hold for ten minutes or more until I got a human voice. The RMA was issued. I waited a week and a half for the return authorization from UPS to show. It didn't, and no one returned my calls to CompUSA asking for assistance. In the end, my wife took the computer to Kansas City (during a planned vacation) where they have a CompUSA store

and returned it to them. This was to avoid the 30-day limit on returns. They would not refund the $24 shipping even though I was assured multiple times that we wouldn't have to pay anything, including shipping. I'm done with Comp-USA mail order and I won't recommend it to the many physicians I tutor on the computers.

Another company that provided no way to cancel or change a Web order during Christmas 1998 was Lillian Vernon, a well-known catalog company. A customer who found the Web site had swallowed the address to which she wanted a gift sent, immediately called to report that her "confirmation notice" did not have the right "ship to" address. No one knew anything about the order. She sent numerous e-mails that only returned back a canned message, even when she put "someone please read this" as the message subject. Finally, when she called for the third time, the person answering said the order did not exist and to reorder, so she did. Later, she called again, only to find they now knew about the Web order, and it had been shipped to her. She was told to refuse the package when it came so it would go back, and charges to her credit card would be removed. But since it was a personalized item, it would be useless for resale.[28]

Like the CompUSA story, apparently whoever devises Lillian Vernon's Web process thought it better to have an order made up and shipped, then sent back, rather than devising a way for a customer to alter the order.

The *Indianapolis Star* reported a horror story about a customer who tried to order airline tickets to Las Vegas over Priceline.com. He had placed a $300 bid for a pair of tickets, but Priceline got no takers at that price. Instead of that being the end of it, a few days later the customer received a $634 credit card charge and an itinerary for the trip. When he went to his card company to get the charge removed, his bank interceded with Priceline, but added $98 in bounced check fees.[29] The customer says he will never use Priceline again after that experience.

The above problems happen only with encounter type service. If a customer has a personal representative, she is more likely to communicate the wanted service correctly in the first place, and if there is a change, the customer will be talking to the same person she talked to before, who naturally will know what she is talking about. In a relationship business, processes do not always need to be spelled out as providers learn how to work with customers and share information. In an encounter environment in which providers and customers don't know each other and provider time with a customer is limited, processes must be made clear to both providers and customers. Customers must have a way of knowing what is happening with their order.

The company that probably serves as the best role model for direct ordering is Dell Computer, the number one direct sales company anywhere. Dell customers can configure their own PC and track their order through assembly and shipping. Could this be part of the reason Dell sales are over $18 billion a year?

Conclusion

Automating the service process is a logical outcome of the encounter format. Organizations must be aware of the ambivalent feelings customers are likely to have toward automated services. Will these services, and the organizations that offer them, be perceived as inflexible and unfriendly, or will they be welcomed as a new kind of convenience? It depends on how organizations implement unattended services.

The Internet and the services it brings to the public are changing the way a lot of businesses operate. Internet services are basically encounter services but with the potential to offer lots of information and choices to the public.

Marketers are using technology to learn about their customers but face the challenge of not offending customers with invasive data collecting. No amount of collecting data in and of itself turns an encounter business into a relationship business, but mass customization and the ability to offer customers choices within limits, is both feasible and a growing trend.

Points to consider:

- To what extent can you automate your business? If you are in a service area that is changing from relationships to encounters, you should look at ways to automate.
- Companies that sell over the Internet are basically encounter businesses; they must offer value over in-person sales.
- Should you use a Web site for information only, or can you make sales over the Internet? Don't try to make sales unless you have a process that accommodates all the functions you provide over the phone or in person, such as a way for customers to track (and cancel or change) their order.
- Are you a relationship provider who can make use of an informational Web site and/or e-mail to keep in touch with customers? Any relationship business that must compete with automated encounter services should look for ways to service customers more efficiently too.

Notes

1. "Computing Strategies," *The Forrester Report*, 11:11 (September 1994).
2. Rowe International Web site (http://www.roweami.com/juke/data.htm).
3. Bobbin Live Web site (http://www.bobbin.com/media/97sept/mc.htm) January 18, 1999.
4. Rifkin, Jeremy. *The End of Work* (Tarcher-Putnam, 1995).
5. Tom Willard, "Couple's Bright, High-Tech Store Cleans Up Image," *Daily Tribune* (Royal Oak, Michigan), February 19, 1999.
6. Jennifer Brown, "Self-Serve Supermarkets Let Customers Replace Cashiers," Associated Press, as reported in *Detroit News*, May 11, 1999.
7. Associated Press, "Eye Scanning ATM Goes Online," as reported on MSNBC, May 13, 1999.

8. Negroponte, Nicholas. *Being Digital* (Vintage Books, 1995).
9. "Titans Talk Tech: Bill G. and Michael D.," *Technology: MIT's Technology Review,* May/June 1999.
10. From "Frequently Asked Questions" on the Rocketmail Web site (www.rocketmail.com).
11. Miller, Thomas E. "The Health Care Industry in Transition: The Online Mandate to Change," *Cyber Dialog,* presented at the Intel Internet Health Day, October 27, 1998.
12. Newsbytes News Network, "Intel's Grove Pushes for Health Care on Internet," (www.newsbytes.com), October 27, 1998.
13. Miller, Thomas E. op. cit.
14. Jupiter Communications press release, "Market Conditions Ripe for Rise of Health Portals: User & Investment Momentum Strong; Hurdles Remain," October 27, 1998.
15. DeNelsky, Stephen J. and Max B. Haspel. "E-Health: Getting Connected in the Digital Age," part of the Health Care Information Series from ING Baring Furman Selz presented at the Intel Internet Health Day, October 27, 1998.
16. The Graphic, Visualization, and Usability Center's WWW User Surveys, tenth survey, run from October 10, 1998 through December 15, 1998. Results available online (http://www.gvu.gatech.edu/user_surveys/survey-1998-10/).
17. "An Ad for All Reasons," *Living Healthy,* Spring 1999.
18. Bowermaster, David. "The Music Industry Seeks Harmony with the Net," MSNBC Web site (www.msnbc.com), April 8, 1999.
19. Broersma, Matthew. "How Digital Music Could Change Your Life," ZDNet News (www.zdnet.com), April 30, 1999.
20. Freund, Jesse. "Listen Up: Chuck D Has Some Choice Words for the Pimps in the Music Industry," *Wired,* March 1999.
21. "Online Holiday Shopping Sets Record Sales," *USA Today,* January 6, 1999.
22. Beck, Rachel. "Sales Soar, but Not All Shoppers Are Pleased With Their Internet," Associated Press, as reported in *Detroit News,* January 18, 1999.
23. Ibid.
24. "Surfer Beware: Personal Privacy and the Internet," June 1997, report from the Electronic Privacy Information Center. (http://www.epic.org/reports/surfer-beware.html).
25. "Everyone is Talking about Privacy on the Net, but Who Actually Is Doing Something about It?" Reported by ZDNet, September 25, 1998.
26. The Graphics, Visualization, and Usability Center at the Georgia Institute of Technology in Atlanta, Georgia. op. cit.

27. Shenk, David. "Data Smog: Surviving the Info Glut," *MIT's Technology Review*, May/June 1997.
28. The customer in this story was one of the authors of this book, Theresa Welsh.
29. O'Malley, Chris. "Netting the Best Fares: Buying Airline Tickets and Other Travel Features Online Increased Threefold Last Year," *Indianapolis Star*, March 29, 1999.

Chapter Six

From Pseudo-Relationships to Enhanced Encounters: Forging the Customer-Organization Link

What Is an Enhanced Encounter?

Encounter businesses that deliver what customers want—fast, convenient, low-cost service in a familiar and uniform process—are providing what we call an "enhanced encounter." This usually takes the form of a chain business, but it can apply to any service that concentrates on the strengths of encounters and doesn't mistake serving customers in an encounter format with having a relationship. When companies say they have a relationship with their customers, often what they really mean is they have loyal customers who come back or who recommend the service to others, exactly the situation most businesses want. But this is not what a customer thinks of as a relationship. The customer is pleased because she gets the service she expected, not because she thinks she has a relationship.

Enhanced encounters use the same service models as pseudo-relationships and are characterized by a loose C-P link and a tight C-O link, as shown in Figure 6-1. But they don't have to offer "pseudo" anything; they can offer genuine excellent service. The difference between pseudo-relationships and enhanced encounters is in the way the business tries to build the tight C-O link, as suggested by Table 6-1 on page 162.

Figure 6-1 Enhanced Encounter Models

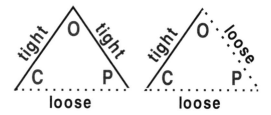

Shouldice Hospital: Encounter Strategy, Satisfied Customers

An example of an enhanced encounter is the Shouldice Hospital in Ontario Canada, founded by Dr. Earle Shouldice in the 1940s. Dr. Shouldice developed a method of doing hernia operations that let patients recover much more quickly. When his reputation spread and there was more demand for his services than he could fill, he set up his specialized hospital and trained other doctors to use his method. This brought the value of his techniques to many more people. Interestingly, Dr. Shouldice always felt the surgical technique itself was not the only important part of the "Shouldice Method." Patient recovery in a pleasant environment with patients helping each other was also part of the method. The Shouldice Hospital Web site explains:

> Most importantly, you will find other patients eager to compare notes, discuss any concerns and ultimately alleviate any anxieties. In fact, many years ago a group of patients so thoroughly enjoyed their stay that they approached Dr. Shouldice and asked if he would sponsor an annual reunion.

Table 6-1 Pseudo-Relationships vs. Enhanced Encounters

What	Pseudo-Relationship	Enhanced Encounter
Provider behavior	Provider acts according to a script	Provider acts from his training, experience, and product knowledge
Method of getting customers	Making assumptions from data; "personalized" pitches based on data	Advertising convenience, low price; customized pitches based on data
Advertising emphasis	Claiming to establish a relationship with customers	Claiming knowledgeable, dependable service at low prices
Organization attitude toward providers	They are interchangeable; de-skill work as much as possible	It is worthwhile to try to keep providers via pay, training, incentives
Providers' ability to deal with customer problems	Little to none—customer complaints handled by Customer Service	Some leeway for providers to deal with problems on the spot; manager available if customer is abusive
Type of experience for customers	Fast, cheap, convenient location; length of time spent waiting varies; customer may feel rushed once he sees/talks to the provider; process has familiar look and feel, but price/process can vary with time/place or other conditions	Convenient hours and location; dependable, uniform price and process; staffing and process reduces wait time as much as possible; exciting ambience; unique way of presenting the service or product
Type of experience for providers	Strict work rules; provider expected to "be nice" to all customers, even abusive ones	Flexible work rules; providers can personalize their work space; providers not expected to deal with abusive customers; manager intervenes and backs worker
Role of managers	Design and enforce a total process that requires little training for providers, who know only their part	Provide leadership, design and explain the process to providers and help them understand how their part fits in and its value to the company; back up workers if disputes arise
Training	No training, minimal training, or focusing more on smile training than substantive training	Training in how to do the job well, how to suggest process improvements and answer customer questions and how to avoid stereotyping customers
Method of judging quality	Tracking numbers—how many customers served in what amount of time	Looking at the total time it takes from the customer's point of view, and whether the customer got what he expected

He agreed, providing that all those who came to the dinner used the occasion for a medical check-up. Since 1947, an annual reunion has been held at the Royal York Hotel where a group of doctors examine as many as 1,400 former patients before they all enjoy a banquet and a floor show.

The Shouldice Hospital offers a highly specialized medical treatment for one specific kind of problem. The patients who come know they are not getting Dr. Shouldice, but they are getting his method which has been used for more than 250,000 hernia operations with a greater than 99 percent success rate. A pretty good selling point. Shouldice Hospital represents a triangle with tight C-O and O-P links. The customer may not spend much time with the actual doctor who performs the operation, but he gets excellent service.

Shouldice Hospital is an encounter-format service that uses a standardized procedure where it really counts with the customer—the hernia operation is done by a doctor who specializes and uses a highly successful technique. Having the customers go through the procedure together so they can exchange information and sympathize with each other beforehand, then discuss their progress afterwards, substitutes for having a personal relationship with the doctor. It serves the same purpose as the Internet health sites discussed in Chapter Five which facilitate people helping each other. Having pleasant surroundings and encouraging the patients to interact with each other is a part of the Shouldice method that contributes to the positive feelings of those who use the service. For anyone facing such surgery, knowing you will have a skilled surgeon is far more important than actually knowing the doctor. The information and attention you need before and after can be handled in other ways, as they do at Shouldice.

Building a Tight Link Between Organizations and Customers

Chain businesses are here to stay, so what can an encounter organization do to get and keep customers? Instead of providers forming relationships with customers, an organization offering service in encounters needs to build a tight C-O link. This effort can take one of two courses:

1. It can build a pseudo-relationship by trying to duplicate qualities of a relationship that cannot actually occur in encounters, like trying to create the familiarity of a relationship by having employees smile at customers or call customers by their first name. This strategy focuses on having people act as if they had a real relationship.
2. It can build an enhanced encounter first, by working on the inherent strengths of encounters, such as convenient hours, no appointment needed, and low cost, and making these advantages known to customers; and second, by delivering service in a unique environment and/ or process known to be effective with its target customers, building up brand loyalty.

The first method is not an effective way to get and keep customers. While there is certainly nothing wrong with providers who smile and act friendly with customers, these actions work only when they are part of the provider's normal way of behaving. Some businesses put out "Help Wanted" signs that say "now hiring smiling faces" or "hiring friendly people" or the like. To the extent that they can find such people, it's a great idea. Internal motivation is the best kind. But hanging your whole strategy on the hope that your providers are friendly or forcing them to act friendly is not a smart approach.

Instead, service businesses should focus on building enhanced encounters with their customers. Let's look at some of the differences between a pseudo-relationship and an enhanced encounter.

Enhanced encounters, like pseudo-relationships, can take one of two forms (or be a combination of the two):

1. The customer is familiar with the organization through previous interactions, advertising, or the reputation of the business.
2. The organization keeps data on what its customers purchased and uses the data to make the service experience

faster and more convenient and to offer reward programs to frequent customers.

So-called "relationship marketing" and the popularity of the ideas in *The One-to-One Future* by Don Peppers and Martha Rogers have led many organizations to try to build relationships with customers based on data. Organizations may keep data on what a customer purchased, when the purchases were made, and how the customer paid; the customer's address, home and work phone numbers, number of family members, and income category; whether the person is a home owner, and so on. Big-time data gathering is exemplified by Wal-Mart, which has a 24-terabyte database on its customers that is second in size only to that of the federal government. Wal-Mart can analyze data down to individual shopping carts. Using data to determine trends and analyze customer likes and dislikes can clearly be helpful.[1] This is not the same thing as using the data to make assumptions about what a specific customer might buy.

Most organizations do not have the data-gathering ability of Wal-Mart, but they can help their customers by keeping track of what they purchase each time and not asking for data or information they already have. A catalog coffee business can ask customers, "Do you want the same order as before?" A medical clinic worker can say, "We already have your medical history. Are there any changes?" instead of making customers supply that information over and over.

Responding to Customers' Preference for Relationships

Studies at the University of Arizona[2] and at the University of New South Wales in Sydney Australia[3] have shown that customers having a service relationship with a specific provider have more service interactions within a twelve-month period and are more satisfied than those who received services in encounters. Encounter customers also reported more negative emotions. Much of the dissatisfaction with service is because service organizations give the public poorly-designed encounters.

Organizations have sought to improve customer satisfaction by trying to build "relationships" with customers to keep them coming back but without understanding that the encounter strategy does not—and cannot—provide a real relationship. By definition, an encounter is service from whichever provider is available, exactly the strategy used at Shouldice Hospital, where customers are very satisfied. But many businesses don't use the techniques employed at Shouldice; instead, they have employees wear name tags and smile at each customer, thinking this will build customer loyalty. Methods such as having bank tellers call each customer by their first name does not make the service more personal and can actually offend some customers who feel such familiarity should be reserved for their friends. All of these practices focus on things that are not important to most customers and doing them will not make encounter businesses competitive with relationship providers. Encounter businesses need to compete on their strengths—efficient, inexpensive, convenient, uniform service that can also be friendly and take place in a pleasant atmosphere. Customers may generally prefer relationships, but they can be satisfied with a well-designed and well-executed enhanced encounter.

Managing Providers in Enhanced Encounters

Encounter employees who work in pseudo-relationships do not mistake managed behavior for a relationship any more than do customers. Providers are likely to feel a loss of control over the conditions of their work when forced to conform to rules on how they should act in front of customers. Lack of control over work is a cause of high turnover, and high turnover means less-experienced employees and more unfamiliar faces for customers who do return.

Some encounter businesses require little of the people they hire and make no effort to keep employees for the long-term. This type of business needs to work hard at building a tight link between the organization and the customer so the customer feels a loyalty to McDonald's, for instance. Building a strong brand identity and reminding customers of the dependability and uniformity of the product are helpful in keeping customers. Encounter businesses can try to reduce worker turnover by providing incentives for employees to stay long-term. Home Depot, Marriott, and Sears are examples of the kind of business where employees feel a sense of belonging. These organizations begin with a loyalty from their employees that helps them get and keep loyal customers. The customers value the genuine helpfulness of the staff at these places. This is supported by the findings of Benjamin Schneider and David E. Bowen that having satisfied employees leads to satisfied customers.[4]

Frederick F. Reichheld and his consulting firm, Bain & Company, also discovered a connection between employee retention and customer satisfaction:

> In the course of consulting work at one leading national chain [of auto service shops], we discovered that the service outlets with the highest customer retention also had the best employee retention. We then surveyed competitors by type and found the local garages had the best employee retention, followed by regional chains, national chains, and auto dealers, in that order.

Bain & Company then interviewed customers to try to find why they were more loyal to the local nonchain shops. Here's what Reichheld says they concluded: "On the one hand, people believed the mechanics at chain outlets and auto dealers had better training and more sophisticated equipment. On the other hand, they put more faith in the local mechanic's judgment and believed he'd give them better service."[5]

What the Bain consultants found was the important characteristic of trust that exists in a real relationship. People who use a neighborhood mechanic trust that person, and that is more important to them than the superior equipment and training that exists at the chain shops. Does it make sense to think it would make any difference whether the employees at the chain shop smiled or called customers by their first name?

Successful Enhanced Encounters

The news in service businesses in the coming decades will be the continued rise of pseudo-relationships and enhanced encounters, along with a steady decline in the percentage of service delivered through real relationships.

The University of Arizona study[6] showed that in most cases those customers who had a relationship with a service provider also received some service from other providers, suggesting that encounters play an important supplementary role for customers who have a regular relationship provider. These results held across seven different service areas, three diverse samples, and two different ways of measuring a service relationship. This shows encounter businesses can attract customers who don't have another provider as well as those who do.

Building on Strengths

The University of Arizona research indicates some characteristics of relationships important to customers can also apply in the encounter format. Combined with the strengths inherent in encounters (fast, convenient, low cost), emphasis on these qualities can help businesses build effective enhanced encounters.[7]

Trust

Research indicates customers can come to trust an organization that delivers service in an encounter format. While trust develops naturally in relationships, encounter organizations must build trust based on the customer having repeated positive experiences.

Customer experiences with chain drugstores offer plenty of horror stories about long waits for prescriptions and lack of access to a pharmacist. But what if the customer has only good experiences? What if he can conveniently call in his prescription, and the time he is told to come and pick it up is always accurate and there are no long waits? What if the customer finds the printed information about his drug supplied by the chain's computerized data base helpful? What if the store is clean, attractive, and well-stocked with items the customer wants to buy when he comes in to pick up his prescription? When the encounter service works according to a well-designed plan, it can lead to trust. The advantage to the organization is that the trust will extend to all the locations of that particular chain. The chain drugstore may have a location near the customer's place of employment and another near his home. He will tend to patronize both locations as a result of his positive experience.

This same scenario can apply to any service business. If the customer goes to a Jiffy Lube near her house and likes the service, she will look for a Jiffy Lube when she moves to a new neighborhood. A customer who likes the food at the Big Boy restaurant near his house will go to Big Boy when he's shopping at the mall.

But it can work the other way, too. A customer who got the wrong prescription once at the chain drugstore may not visit any of their locations, attributing the poor performance to the chain. A customer who thinks she was overcharged at Jiffy Lube will not go back to any Jiffy Lube. If a customer thinks the salad bar at the Big Boy near his home was too skimpy on quality ingredients, he may skip Big Boy next time he's at the mall.

The Bain consultants who found trust in auto dealership service was lacking may have been seeing the results of previous bad experiences on the part of customers. Overcoming these perceptions, once they exist, can be very difficult. Such businesses may lose some of their customers, but others will come back because they don't know where else to go or figure another shop won't be any better. David L. Ulin, the man who had his baby stroller damaged by an airline, continues to fly with that airline because he says the others aren't any better.[8] But the poor quality experience customers have at some encounter businesses provides a market for relationship businesses, at least for those customers persistent enough to find an independent provider.

Convenience

Businesses wanting customers to become regular patrons can compete with relationship businesses on convenience. An enhanced encounter service should be available the maximum number of hours, and processes should minimize any wait time.

Customers can be encouraged to "stop by any time." This is a real advantage the relationship provider cannot offer, and the pseudo-relationship business may offer it but not get it right. Do customers have to talk to more than one person, and is there a wait in between? What is the total time from the customers' point of view? If a customer spends twenty minutes on hold waiting for a service representative, it hardly matters that the conversation took only two minutes. If the fast food place has a line all the way out the door, the customer will not think it was "fast food," even though it took the counter clerk only thirty seconds to take the order. Look at the total time for the customer and do what you can to minimize it: Hire more workers, add another check-out line, or automate the process.

Customized, Not "Personalized"

Customize a service when you can, but don't get hung up on personalizing it. Encounter services are not personal, and concentrating on using customers' names or trying to pitch them products making assumptions from limited and incomplete data is not going to build customer loyalty. Relationship providers can potentially take any type of customer and provide the specialized service some people need, but encounter businesses can't and shouldn't try. Burger King's customized element is limited to "hold the pickle, hold the lettuce." The company says you can "have it your way," but they will not cook a burger rare or provide a whole wheat bun if a customer requests it. Likewise, Levi-Strauss might say it will make customized jeans but not for someone who weighs 400 lbs or wants flannel instead of denim. H&R Block will do anyone's taxes, but not for someone who's been indicted for tax fraud and is looking for help. Don't claim what you can't deliver.

Uniform but Unique

Successful encounter businesses establish a theme, often one with universal appeal. Their business model is unique and different from that of their competitors. When they see the model working, they duplicate the business in many locations. A business theme does not have to have a counterpart in reality;

it just has to have appeal to customers. Some businesses imitate a romanticized past, recreating mythical images of times and places that don't exist.

PetSmart, a chain of pet supply stores, uses a small-town analogy with its veterinary service, adoption service, and grooming service in separate little village shops inside a huge store with aisles full of pet supplies. Each PetSmart store is the same, but with their unique design and service concept, these stores are different from any other chain selling pet supplies.

Hard Rock Cafes reinvent Hollywood. All Hard Rock Cafes are the same, but their implementation of the Hollywood theme is unlike any other chain of restaurants. Mexican restaurant chain Don Pablo rewrites history with pictures of Pancho Villa and other historical figures on the walls and the decor of a quintessential but nonexistent cantina. They have created an environment pleasing to their customers that distinguishes them from other Mexican restaurants.

Even the future can be exploited by using a Star Wars theme or building on the image of a future that never happened, like the Jetsons, where kids go to school in little flying machines and the household robot cooks the food. These all draw on familiar cultural icons, needing no reference in the real world. The important thing is that each location duplicates the model, and the model is unlike any of the business's competitors.

The uniformity of chain offerings is important in building loyalty, along with the uniqueness built into the service model. The familiarity with the service experience builds a comfort level for the customer and sets expectations. For example, when a hungry family pulls off the I-75 expressway that connects Michigan to Florida to eat at one of the numerous Cracker Barrel restaurants along the route, they expect to walk across a wooden porch with rocking chairs, enter a little country store with fun items, and leave their name at a desk by the door leading into the wood-paneled restaurant. They know they can browse among the sweat shirts, jams, dolls, and country kitchen plates and utensils until their name is called. Then they know the menu will feature home-made biscuits and corn muffins and lots of good country cooking, and their table will have a wooden peg game they can play while their food is being prepared. If any of these elements were to be missing, this family would be disappointed. They could get biscuits and hash browns somewhere else, but it wouldn't be the same experience as going to Cracker Barrel. The *expectation* of a known experience—knowing there will be the porch with the rockers, the country store, the peg game, the biscuits, etc., draws customers back. Cracker Barrel's loyal customers don't know the providers who will serve them, but they know what to expect when they come, and they are satisfied when they get what they expected. Make your service theme unique, then be sure it is implemented exactly the same way at all locations.

Some service themes and processes have wider appeal than others. The Cracker Barrel service model, with its country theme, is perfect for the I-75 corridor that winds through "hillbilly" territory, but might not be as popular in sophisticated New York or trendy Southern California. The more universal the theme and method, the more the business could be exported anywhere.

Quality

The encounter structure doesn't have to mean inferior quality. Chain businesses sometimes succeed because they offer something better than independent businesses. Take Starbucks, for example. A place that sells you a cup of coffee would seem to be a poor idea, given the many restaurants, snack bars and even gas stations that sell a fresh cup of coffee. But Starbucks offered a superb cup of coffee with many variations in a pleasant setting and appealed to customers who wanted something more than ordinary coffee in a Styrofoam™ cup that you drink standing up at a convenience store. Other examples are Godiva Chocolates and Mrs. Fields' Cookies, each of which specializes in one kind of product they do really well.

Wal-Mart earned plenty of criticism that it was killing Main Street merchants in small town America, but was that ever fair? There might be good reasons why customers prefer Wal-Mart. James F. Moore, in *The Death of Competition*, relates a story of visiting his grandparents in Mattoon, Illinois. His grandparents were ages 98 and 99, and he was faced with how to spend a hot summer afternoon with them. They decided to visit the new Wal-Mart store. Here's his impression:

> The Mattoon Wal-Mart, like many others, is open 24 hours a day, 365 days a year. This time of year, it is deliciously air-conditioned. Much to my surprise, the Mattoon Wal-Mart proved a revelation. It was then the largest Wal-Mart in North America. At 225,000 square feet, it seemed like a covered football field. But its size was not as impressive as its upscale appearance, when considered from the perspective of what is normally available in a small Midwestern farm town. I remembered my childhood of white bread and last year's fashions sold by Main Street merchants who held virtual monopolies with indifference toward customers. In contrast, this Wal-Mart sold live lobsters and several types of gourmet cheese. It offered well-made, stylish clothing. Toys were bright, clean, and stressed farming, construction, and auto-racing themes, not weaponry. Specially designed, full-spectrum lighting cast a warm glow over the entire scene. We had entered a little bit of nirvana only a short drive from home.[9]

Moore obviously thought Wal-Mart a good addition to the town. Even if his family knew the downtown merchants, familiarity did not make up for the lack of variety and higher prices of the independent stores. The total package offered by Wal-Mart added up to a better experience than shopping on Main Street.

Another voice defending "big box" stores is Sam Staley, a policy analyst with The Buckeye Institute for Public Policy Solutions in Dayton, Ohio. Writing in the *Dayton Daily News*, Staley says communities benefit by a turnover in businesses, with the less efficient ones going under. "Customers," he writes, "will leave [mom-and-pop] stores permanently" if they get bigger selection or more value in the big box stores. But existing businesses can respond by improving what they offer. He describes a grocery store called Dots that increased its space and products while building community ties. It survived and prospered, despite competition from bigger stores. He says groups like Sprawl Busters that are fighting what they call "the Wal-

Martization of America" are not helping communities. He concludes that "rather than focusing on the relatively small benefits of insulating antiquated businesses from competition, local citizens and public officials should recognize and embrace the community-wide benefits that come from new business growth."[10] Staley, like Moore, believed that the big chain stores bring benefits to customers through their variety and quantity of products and through the pressure they exert on older businesses to examine and improve what they offer customers.

Think Like a Customer, but Support Your Staff

Enhanced encounter businesses are customer-oriented. That means they design their processes with the customer in mind. They measure their results in customer satisfaction, not in time-based metrics. They maintain convenient hours, have a consistent process, and make sure their staff can answer questions.

Try to reduce uncertainty for your customers by keeping the experience as uniform as you can. Customers won't like it if they don't have any idea how long they'll have to wait. Phone services should not play a message that says, "Your call is important to us," then keep people on hold for a half hour. If you can, work out a system to let them know how long they'll have to wait. A message saying, "The wait will be about ten minutes," would be appreciated by most customers. Don't capriciously change prices and conditions for the service. If the customer comes and finds the price is twice as much as last time, she won't care to hear "That's what you paid before? You must have been here on Monday."

Managers at enhanced encounter businesses train and support their staff by giving them as much flexibility as they can in their hours, dress, and appearance of their work area. If it makes no difference to customers that the phone representatives wear jeans to work and that's what workers want, then let them. Encourage staffers to make suggestions on how they can serve their customers better. Managers should also let their workers know they do not have to take abuse from customers. Be ready to step in if a customer threatens a worker. In an encounter business, any worker is more valuable than one abusive customer. Do not expect low-paid providers to know how to deal with that kind of situation.[11]

What's Wrong With Pseudo-Relationships?

The essential weakness of a pseudo-relationship is its "pseudo" quality, the fact that customers interact with an organization, not a person. Pseudo-relationships try to fix this problem by emphasizing the wrong things. They try to recreate the elements of a relationship that simply cannot exist in an encounter structure.

Real Passion vs. "Smile Training"

Employees in encounter businesses generally do not feel the same kind of passion for their work as relationship providers. They are there doing a job, usually on a regular shift, and often for low pay. It's a job, not a profession requiring a commitment. The work itself may hold little meaning for them, especially if they work for a company that regards workers as easily replaced, interchangeable parts.

To combat worker apathy, companies sometimes turn to training sessions to fire up workers to be more "customer-oriented." These sessions concentrate on acting, getting workers to act as if they care about customers, whether they actually do or not. Often employee resistance to these methods is strong and they accomplish little or nothing.

Research suggests that customers rank small talk and smiles well below actually getting the service. Rafaeli and Sutton, in studying convenience stores, found that when customers were in a rush and/or the store was crowded, they didn't care at all whether the clerk smiled and chatted with them. When they had plenty of time and/or the store was almost empty, customers rated the service better (or were more satisfied with the service) when the provider smiled and engaged in small talk.[12]

Relationship providers, more than encounter providers, are free to use a different style with each customer as they try to find what works. Encounter providers, trained to treat all customers the same, may have more difficulty dealing with the actual differences in customers' behavior and style, which they cannot control. Providers are more likely to be "customer-oriented" if their customers have no problems using the service. If the customer is cranky because he had to wait in a long line, or was given forms to complete that made little sense, or thinks he was overcharged, he is not going to present a smiling, happy face to the provider, who, in turn, may forget everything he was told about being "customer-oriented."

Rather than offering pep rallies for good service, companies may fare better offering their employees some real incentives to value their employment in the form of good pay and benefits. By providing such desirable extras as child care and transportation—often a problem for low-paid workers—they can build more goodwill than any amount of "smile training." If they do provide training, they'll get more mileage out of training workers how to do their job better and giving them access to the information they need to better serve customers. Companies should also share the business's mission, its history, and its goals and show employees how their efforts make a difference. This will infuse the work with some meaning.

Carole Presley, senior vice president for marketing at Federal Express, believes you cannot force extra effort from employees. You can only make them like where they work. She says:

> Each employee obligates himself or herself to a certain level of mandatory effort as part of accepting the job. That's what the employer can expect in return for the wages paid. But if the employee is involved—turned on, committed, and feeling part of something important, then he or she adds a certain amount of discretionary effort to the job. This is the something extra that comes from belonging and believing.[13]

Disconnects Between the Organization's Intent and What Actually Happens

The biggest problem for encounter businesses is when what the organization intends to happen and what the customer expects to happen does not happen. Some customers may become so angry they will never return and will tell their friends not to patronize the business. In the worst scenarios, these lapses end up on the evening news or in court.

A good example is what happened to a group of Northwest Airlines passengers at Detroit Metro Airport on January 3, 1999. A heavy snowstorm had struck and the airport crews had been slow to clear runways, taxiways, and ramps. Northwest did not have enough workers to cope with all the problems since half of their employees weren't able to get to Metro Airport because of the storm. Northwest did not cancel flights; instead, the airline loaded passengers and queued up planes that could not take off because of the snow problem. Some planes then sat on runways for six, seven, even eight hours. The same thing happened to some flights that had landed and couldn't move to the terminals because of the snow. At least 4,000 passengers were stranded on about 30 Northwest Airlines jets. There was no food, bathrooms became unusable and smelly, and the stench of unbathed people, some of whom had slept on the floor at the airport before boarding, was unpleasant.

Airline personnel were not helpful, and one lady said she was threatened by an attendant when she stood up to stretch. She was told to stay seated. Passengers said no one told them what was happening, as they waited and waited, stuck in uncomfortable airline seats with children wailing, babies without their formula, and everyone's temper frayed to the breaking point.

A few angry passengers called the media on cell phones to relate what was happening to them on those planes, and the story hit the six o'clock news in Detroit. Already reeling from previous bad publicity over a pilots' strike, Northwest was once again on the defensive in its hub city (see the comments of *Detroit News* columnist Laura Berman in Chapter One).

While Northwest offered free flights to everyone who went through this ordeal, that did not satisfy most. In January 1999, a class action lawsuit was filed on behalf of those who were stuck on those planes, citing "false imprisonment."

In addition, Northwest may lose its dominance at the Detroit airport. As a result of this incident, U.S. Congressman John Dingell wants legislation that would discourage one-carrier dominance. "When thousands of airline passengers are left in airplanes for up to eight hours without any sign of relief or some way to get off the plane," he told the *Detroit News*, "there's a big problem."[14]

But the fallout didn't end there. Others in Congress have proposed legislation guaranteeing some rights to passengers, and the American Society of Travel Agents has proposed an Air Traveler's Bill of Rights. They are responding to an increasing number of airline passenger complaints —25 percent more filed with the Department of Transportation in 1998 than in 1997, and airlines were at the top of the list of industries with the most customer complaints in 1999.

Northwest Airlines surely does not intend to abuse passengers and has responded with a number of initiatives to improve service, but its employees are dealing with customers who are mostly strangers. It is up to the organization, not the workers, to have a process for dealing with emergencies. Passengers can find plenty of scapegoats. They can point their fingers at the hostile attendants, the pilots who didn't explain why they weren't going anywhere, or whoever made the decision to board those planes, but their ultimate revenge in the guise of the lawsuit must be against the organization—Northwest Airlines.

The same disconnect can happen in small ways with many other businesses. A chain drugstore advertises a low price on film, but when the customer gets there the store is out of the sale film and has only the more expensive kind. A customer walks into a roast beef fast food restaurant and is told they are out of beef. A customer shopping at a women's clothing store finds the clerks all talking on the phone and no one to help her. A customer at a chain hair salon finds the beautician cut her hair too short when she asked for a trim. They both had different definitions of "trim." The drugstore misspells the customer's last name so when she comes to get her prescription, they don't have one for Joan Trayner. Only after Ms. Trayner insists they must have it and that she needs it right now do they discover a prescription for Joan *Traner*. The clerk who took the order spelled the name wrong, and the customer is now talking to a different clerk. The drugstore could have avoided this problem by using multiple keys to search for a customer—for example, by phone number or address in addition to a name.

Providers will make these kinds of mistakes; a good encounter process builds in redundancy and avoids irritations that can be the reason the customer does not come back.

Stereotyping Customers

In the typical encounter business, providers know nothing about any particular customer and use the same scripted approach to all customers. When people know nothing about someone other than what they can see, they usually fall back on stereotypes based on the person's appearance. This is a perfectly normal and natural process, well-studied by social psychologists. Everyone does it because we all want to live in a predictable world. With no prior experience and no information about the person, we rely on what is commonly believed about people based on their appearance, and we continue to hold those beliefs until we have enough information or experience to form a more accurate impression. If the person in front of the provider is different from him, the person goes into a mental category of "outgroup." People think of outgroups as being more homogenous than their "ingroup." To put it another way, a white person is more likely to think all African-Americans share group characteristics than she is to think all white people share group characteristics, and vice versa. This leads to slight variations in the provider's demeanor and actions towards customers, depending on how those customers are quickly sized up and mentally classified.

Two researchers[15] found that waitpersons tended to be more formal and less open with people who were different from themselves. They also reported that women servers tended to be friendlier than male servers with male diners, due, apparently to assumptions that men expect women to be friendly. Older customers who have hearing problems may get treated in a condescending way. Pretty young girls may get faster service from male providers than middle-aged women. Older white employees may have a fear of young black males and be slow to serve them. Providers may be quicker to help members of their own ethnic group than members of the perceived outgroup.

Providers in service jobs use these superficial judgments to come up with slang terms for their customers, such as restaurant workers calling people who eat a lot "pigs" and those who don't tip much "cheapskates." Those in management are called "suits," and accountants are "bean counters." Cab drivers call their customers "fares." Ethnic groups are frequent victims of stereotypes. Unflattering words and stereotypical attitudes can come into play when people do not know each other.

At its worst, these superficial judgments of others can be full-blown discrimination that can lead to lawsuits. Denny's restaurants paid dearly for its employees who treated black patrons differently from white patrons. A service worker who insults a customer, either intentionally or inadvertently, could cause the organization to be hit with a lawsuit or just a business-crippling story on the evening news. Diversity training may help, but some of the problem is systemic. When a service transaction is very short, there isn't any basis for knowing much about the other person, who could be an ax-murderer or psychopath (but probably isn't).

Dr. Leonard Berry, director of the Center for Retailing Studies at Texas A&M University, says, "Our country suffers from a growing customer respect deficit. Technologically, we are getting better at serving customers, but attitudinally we are getting worse. Respect for customers is revealed through the company's sincerity, sensitivity, language, and trust."[16] The company can only manifest these qualities through its employees. This growing customer respect deficit is an unintended outcome of encounter businesses; providers and customers don't know each other, making it easy to blame the other when things don't go as planned . . . easier than it would be to blame someone you know well.

In a relationship business, stereotypes quickly dissipate once provider and customer get to know each other. That doesn't mean that relationship providers don't have prejudices or fall back on stereotypes. It just means that when people have repeated contact with one another, they begin to develop an opinion of the other based on their experience with that person rather than relying on a stereotype. In a relationship business, providers have more leeway in accepting or rejecting clients, so they may simply find excuses to avoid taking clients from their outgroup. But encounter businesses cannot do that. They are based on the interchangeability of customers and providers. Service is designed to be egalitarian, but all people are not the same. Providers will be less comfortable with some customers than with others even though they must try to treat all the same. Organizations are responsible for seeing that they do.

Winning Customer Loyalty

Reward Programs

Encounters are set up to treat all customers the same, but by keeping track of customers' purchases, an organization can provide special offers or rewards to customers who spend more money or are frequent patrons. This can be something as simple as giving coupons for free items when someone spends a certain amount or giving customers a card that gets punched each time they use the service with a free product for a given number of visits. Reward programs are a way of ranking customers by the amount of business they do, and they provide data on which customers are price sensitive. Some people buy things regardless of price (more or less) while others will buy only when they get a discount or free gift.

Reward programs can work across all economic strata. Budget hotel chain Travelodge launched Travelodge Miles in June 1997. The program thanks frequent Travelodge customers for their patronage with frequent-flyer miles, free hotel nights, free rental cars, and other travel perks. Customers earn one "Travelodge Mile" for each qualified lodging dollar spent at participating Travelodge and Thriftlodge motels. Members who use a magnetic member card that keeps track of their miles when they check in can redeem them once they have 250 miles (for a Sleepy Bear doll, T-shirt, or road atlas), or they can keep saving them for other rewards at higher mile levels. In its first five months, Travelodge Miles attracted 30,000 new members, and was adding approximately 200 members daily in late 1998.[17]

Reward programs like these need to deliver. Frequent flyer programs that put too many restrictions on how customers can use their miles can backfire. Customers feel gypped if they find they can't fly when they want to or can't go to the destination they wanted or that it will take them fifteen hours and three stops to get there.

In other reward programs, people are paid for becoming customers. A customer might accept a check for changing to a new long-distance phone service, for example, but this does not create any real loyalty. A long-distance phone service customer interviewed for a *Harvard Business Review* article on relationship marketing put it this way:

> The flood of advances from companies undermines any one overture so that it doesn't matter which company you end up doing business with. I got some reward from the second company for switching; I don't remember what. Then company A paid me to come back. It was like I was hunted prey—$50 here, $50 there, $100 to leave company A a second time. I was a college student at the time, and the money was great. But it was crazy. The salespeople on both sides kept telling me how important a customer I was to them, but who pays you to be their customer? I wasn't developing a relationship with either company. I was just taking the money.[18]

Where does making offers the organization thinks the customer might want shade into unwanted intrusion or just become all-out war between competitors with customers opportunistically picking up whatever goodies they can?

The One-to-One Future suggested that a way of dealing honestly with customers is to simply pay them for considering an offer or listening to a commercial. Such schemes are now appearing, one in the guise of free long-distance service for customers willing to listen to commercials first. This service, offered by BroadPoint Communications, offers callers two free minutes of domestic long-distance service for every ten- to fifteen-second ad they listen to. To use BroadPoint's FreeWay service, customers must register at the company's Web site and provide personal information, such as household income, number of children, and ethnic background. Members dial a toll-free line from any telephone and then plug in an identification number and the phone number they wish to reach. They may listen to as many ads as they choose and can stop listening at any time. Then their call will be connected. Most people listen to seven or eight ads.

Results for the advertisers have been mixed. A hefty 27 percent of FreeWay users who heard promotions for Eagle Eye Sportswear called the company's 800 number after hearing its ad, which promised a free turtleneck to respondents. But less than one tenth of one percent of those who listened to ads for Vermont Teddy Bear's BearGram, a service that sends teddy bears for special occasions, called to place an order. BroadPoint plans to make it easier for customers to call advertisers on the spot, then return to their own call.[19]

BroadPoint Chief Executive Perry Kamel, a former McKinsey consultant and MCI executive, said the company spends only about one dollar to acquire each new user, compared with between $50 and $150 that major long-distance companies spend to steal customers from each other.[20] It costs so little because their main way of getting customers is word of mouth.

Even schools are being solicited to trade exposure to ads for freebies. A program called ZapMe! offers a free computer lab (15 PCs with a server and high-speed Internet access via a satellite dish on the roof) to schools that are willing to expose their students to ads that appear on the PCs' customized Web browser. ZapMe! is similar to cable TV's Channel One, which provides free content to schools but also carries ads. Billboard ads continuously rotate on the screen while students surf the Web. ZapMe! gets the right to monitor students' browsing habits, breaking the data down by age, sex, and zip code. It delivers the aggregated information to advertisers and marketers, who use it to try to get at the interests and present and future buying habits of the huge Echo Boomer generation, the teen-age children of the Baby Boomers. ZapMe! tries to be a responsible medium by running public service announcements, such as those from Mothers Against Drunk Driving or from universities, and will not run ads selling tobacco or alcohol.[21]

Not everyone thinks ZapMe! is a great idea. "Corporate predators like ZapMe! should get out of schools and let children alone," said Ralph Nader through Commercial Alert, an activist group he founded. "Parents, not corporations, should raise children."[22] But in economically depressed districts, ZapMe! has supporters. At Mt. Diablo High School in Concord, Calif., technology coordinator Ted Maddock says ZapMe! has been a good fit for his school, which has a predominantly minority student body. "I think it is a good way for schools like mine that are strapped for resources," he said.[23]

Data have become a valuable commodity, which some marketers pursue relentlessly. The very terminology used in the ad business reveals an aggressive mindset. They "target" various groups, "aim" their ads at some segment, and try to "capture" a market. Perhaps the poor consumer feels "bombarded" by all the attention.

Embracing Causes That Matter to Customers

Another way organizations attract customers is by embracing a social cause that is important to their customers and potential customers. For example, Ford Motor Company supports activities that benefit breast cancer research because it would like to attract more women car buyers and knows breast cancer matters to women. Frito-Lay built a playground in a Hispanic neighborhood of Houston as a way of appealing to Hispanic customers who tend to be very brand-loyal. Hardee's, a fast food chain, gave $1 million to the Duke Children's Hospital in Durham, North Carolina. Families with children are prime customers. Pillsbury donates food in five cities to Second Harvest food banks, a cause with appeal to its customers. McDonald's franchisees support Ronald McDonald Houses, which provide temporary housing for parents with hospitalized children.

The Chronicle of Philanthropy reports that "America's business leaders say they remain committed to the concept of philanthropy, but they are more and more likely to ask how a gift will contribute to their company's goals before reaching for their checkbook." Supporting a "good cause" that also happens to appeal to potential customers is called "Cause-Related Marketing."[24]

Judith E. Nichols, in her book, *By the Numbers*, suggests

businesses take giving seriously as a marketing method by partnering with a charity that can help win customers. "Ask your
potential partners to provide clear examples of how their organizations are perceived positively by the target groups," she
writes, "and evaluate carefully what the organization wants and
can do." She gives examples of appealing to baby boomers, suggesting ". . . isn't there a logic in sponsoring quality public tele-
vision broadcasting—at-home, upscale entertainment? Or
addressing boomers' fitness needs by funding medical research
on back pain and furniture at a school of medicine? Or working
with boomer concerns by providing furniture for a day care or
elder care center?"[25]

A 1998 survey by a marketing firm that helps companies
set up marketing programs showed 63 percent of the respondents said they were very likely or somewhat likely to consider
a company's reputation for charitable donations, up from 56
percent the previous year. "Our survey confirms that consumers
expect the businesses they patronize to be responsive to social
issues," said Carol Cone, chief executive officer of Cone Communications, a Boston-based marketing firm.[26]

Another important trend that companies shouldn't ignore
is the growing interest in a clean environment, the so-called
"green" movement. Companies with environmentally friendly
products and services can win customers away from companies
whose practices are suspect. A phone survey conducted in
Michigan by the Lansing firm EPIC/MRA found 60 percent favored tighter air quality regulations by the federal government
and were willing to pay more for "clean" products—a startling
result in a state dependent on the auto industry. The survey
also showed 44 percent think air pollution is causing global
warming.[27]

Another "green" phenomenon is interest in vegetarianism
(a trend among young people), alternative medical practices,
and spiritual renewal. In the American West, a new breed of
"eco-farmers" tries to raise their cattle without killing wolves,
then market their product as "predator-friendly" beef. Once the
province of radical fringe groups and New Age adherents, these
concerns are going mainstream. Just look at the image of Vermont ice cream maker Ben & Jerry's, whose founders built their

business partly on being an environmentally responsible company and partly by giving away 7.5 percent of their pre-tax earnings to charity, including their own employee-managed foundation (they have a position called Director of Social Mission Development). Then think of the bad press garnered by Tyson Foods, the Arkansas chicken-raising company, that was hit with allegations of trying to influence a Secretary of Agriculture and of despoiling land and polluting water through agricultural run-off.[28]

Letting customers know about your good deeds and responsible corporate citizenship can be a powerful way to influence their buying choices. When customers dealt with local merchants in earlier times, they would feel good about the grocery store that sponsored a little league team or a clothing store that donated mittens to a shelter. Today's corporations can get closer to customers by supporting causes important to them, including charities in the communities where they are located.

Conclusion

As a business owner, you want customers who come back. You can accomplish that by capitalizing on the strengths of encounters. Consider the reasons most entrepreneurs opt for the encounter structure:

- Encounters can provide the service at less cost to the customer and more profit to the owner.
- Encounters do not bind customers to the provider but may bind them to the organization.
- Many business owners have simply not thought about the difference between encounters and relationships and organize their business along currently accepted management practices, which is basically the encounter strategy.

Like the plot of the movie "You've Got Mail," in which the big box book store drives out the little neighborhood book store, chains win because they offer customers real advantages. But organizations that market nationally and/or globally have

kept the model of the small local business and looked for ways
to have a relationship with their customers, just as the village
shopkeeper once had. They fall into the trap of mistaking having data about someone for "knowing" someone. Providers in
encounter businesses do not have relationships with their customers, but when organizations design an enhanced encounter—service that builds a tight C-O link—they can have
customers who are satisfied and loyal.

Notes

1. "America's Best Technology Users; Retail Winners: Wal-Mart,
   Gap, the Home Depot, Wimp, J.C. Penney," *Forbes*, August 24,
   1998.
2. Gutek, B.A., A.D. Bhappu, M.A. Liao-Troth, and B. Cherry.
   "Distinguishing Between Service Relationships and Encounters,"
   Journal of Applied Psychology, Vol. 84, No. 3.
3. Woolf, Loren A. "The Psychology of Customer Expectations,"
   University of New South Wales in Australia, 1998. Secondary
   analysis of data collected by Woolf for undergraduate thesis.
4. Schneider, Benjamin and David E. Bowen. *Winning the Service
   Game* (Harvard Business School Press, 1995).
5. Reichheld, Frederick F. *The Loyalty Effect* (Harvard Business
   School Press, 1996).
6. Gutek, B.A., A.D. Bhappu, M.A. Liao-Troth, and B. Cherry. op.
   cit.
7. Ibid.
8. Personal communication with David L. Ulin.
9. Moore, James. *The Death of Competition* (Harper Business, 1996).
10. Staley, Stan. "Big Box Retailers Bring Important Regional Benefits:
    Competition Can Cause Existing Businesses to Improve," *Dayton
    Daily News*, July 9, 1999.
11. Bowen, David E. and Benjamin Schneider. op. cit.
12. Rafaeli, A. and R.I. Sutton, "Expression of Emotion as Part of the
    Work Rule," *Academy of Management Review*, 12 (1): 23–37.
13. Quoted in Karl Albrecht. *The Only Thing That Matters: Bringing the
    Power of the Customer Into the Center of Your Business* (Harper Busi-
    ness, 1992).
14. Cole, Kenneth. "U.S. Will Investigate Storm Delays at Metro,"
    Detroit News, January 14, 1999.

15. Mars and Nicad, quoted in Gutek. *The Dynamics of Service* (Jossey-Bass, 1995).
16. Texas A&M Center for Retailing Studies (http://www.crstamu. org/).
17. Dowling, Dorothy. "Frequent Perks Keep Travelers Loyal," *American Demographics*, September 1998.
18. Fournier, Susan, Susan Dobscha, and David Glen Mick. "Preventing the Premature Death of Relationship Marketing," *Harvard Business Review*, January/February 1998.
19. Emert, Carol. "Ad Strategy Offers Callers Free Long-Distance," *San Francisco Chronicle*, October 13, 1998.
20. Ibid.
21. "Free PCs, Net Access Tempt Schools," MSNBC Web site (www.msnbc.com), December 6, 1998
22. Ibid.
23. Ibid.
24. Quoted in Judith E. Nichols. *By The Numbers: Using Demographics and Psychographics for Business Growth in the '90s* (Chicago: Bonus Books, 1990).
25. Ibid.
26. "Customers Value Donations Made by Retailers," *Philanthropy Journal Online*, December 1998 (http://www.pj.org/corporate_giving/corpsurvey1201.cfm).
27. Askari, Emily. "Earth Rates Near Top in State Poll," *Detroit Free Press*, November 21, 1998.
28. See U.S. government Web site (www.usdoj.gov/opa/pr/1998/May/ 213) Department of Justice press release on settlement of a federal lawsuit, resulting in fine of $6 million against Tyson Foods for polluting Chesapeake Bay, May 8, 1998.

Chapter Seven

Relationship Businesses: Using the Original Service Model

What Are Relationship Businesses?

Everyone likes relationships. Personal relationships with family and friends give life its meaning, and business relationships are very much like them. Relationships are the model for every type of service, and the personal and trusting nature of relationships is what service businesses try to imitate. However, as life becomes too hectic and busy to maintain numerous relationships, the percentage of real relationships people have is decreasing as more services come from encounters rather than a personal provider.

But there are still types of service that are primarily delivered in relationships and opportunities will continue to exist for people who want to start a relationship business. Because service in a relationship is usually more expensive, these businesses tend to have higher-income customers or offer their services to companies rather than to individuals. Service is often in areas requiring special skills, training, or education, involves a skill the customer does not have or simply is a convenience for someone who doesn't want to or doesn't have time to do her own gardening, cooking, child care, or whatever.

Relationship businesses can be classified as follows:

1. Traditional professional services to individuals or businesses, offered by providers with specialized education and experience such as lawyers, accountants, stockbrokers, doctors, and business consultants
2. Personal services offered to individuals, such as hairdressers, massage therapists, maids, and personal trainers
3. Services involving special skills and special tools or equipment such as the work of graphic artists, photographers, printers, plumbers, landscapers, and musical instrument tutors (some of these providers work with businesses rather than with individuals)
4. Micro businesses that are one-person or family-operated where regular customers get to know the owner who is also the provider; examples are handymen, small café owners, and small shop owners. These providers may also do business in encounters with infrequent customers.

In addition, some relationship providers are employed by the same company as their customers. Secretaries or personal assistants are examples, but we will deal here only with providers offering services outside their own company.

Relationship businesses are generally not organized as corporations, although some (such as CDW, which assigns a specific provider to a customer) may be. More likely, these businesses are partnerships or sole proprietorships. Because the corporation form of business offers some protections, wealthy people sometimes incorporate even if they are the only employee of the corporation. Well-known entertainers or sports figures might incorporate (if you're Wayne Newton or Michael Jordan, this makes sense).

Can You Offer Both Relationships and Encounters?

Some businesses offer encounters to most customers and relationships to a smaller number of more valuable customers. Textbook companies, for example, have a mechanism for ordering books in encounters but also send sales representatives around to universities to talk with professors who might be potential authors. Utility companies may have encounters for residential customers, but personal representatives for larger commercial customers.

Organizations already set up for encounters could consider offering relationship service to some customers. Not only would this please those customers it would also provide a promotion path for the best encounter providers. Those providers who had their own customers could also serve as support people and possibly trainers for those who serviced customers in encounters.

The Relationship Models

Relationships have a tight C-P link, and the other links in the triangle can be any other configuration, as shown in figure 7-1.

Figure 7-1   Relationship Models

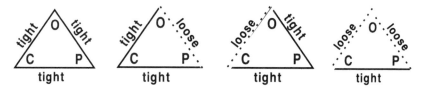

The model with all tight links is probably rare and might be unstable as the organization and the provider are in competition for the customer's ultimate loyalty. At the other end, the organization is very loose, perhaps just a sharing of resources among a group of professionals. This could be a situation that shifts around as providers split off and go their own way, taking customers with them, while new providers move in, bringing their customers and contacts. The two middle models are probably the most common. The second (tight C-O and loose O-P) describes a company with a tight link to customers but which assigns customers a specific provider. Computer supplier CDW, where customers always talk to the same account representative, fits here, as does telecommunications provider Coast to Coast, which advertises that customers always deal with "Larry" (presumably a composite stand-in for its assigned account representatives).

The third model (loose C-O and tight O-P) could be a prominent firm in which the providers are well known and identified with the firm (like Joseph H. Johnson and Lewis S. Goldman of Johnson and Goldman Associates). It could also be a multi-level marketing organization like Amway, in which the provider is tied to the company through financial arrangements and has a steady list of customers.

When There Is No Organization

A provider with no organization, the oldest kind of relationship business, does not fit our models. People who do work "on the side" usually use this method, but so do many full-time providers. Many providers, such as people who massage your tired muscles, teach you to play guitar, do your bookkeeping, paint your walls, or refinish your wood floors, get by without an organization. They make contact with customers in a personal way or through ads in local newspapers that say "Call Tim" (or "Bob" or "Jane"). They get work because they perform a service that others need or want. Money goes right from the customer to the provider, with no middleman. There is no corporate culture to conform to or leadership vision to guide each day's activities. There is no manager setting rates and handling bookings. This is the oldest kind of one-to-one and probably began with the world's oldest profession, where one woman provides a personal and intimate service to one man. This primitive and basic format worked quite well before there were government regulations, taxes, competition from professionally managed firms with deep pockets, and the mobility to move around in a world of strangers. As society grew more complex, this basic one-to-one service model grew less effective for both customers and providers, and gradually most work moved to the auspices of an organization.

What Organizations Mean to Workers

Organizations provide a context for life that goes beyond what they produce or sell. Sometime before the 1950s, corporations began to substitute for many of the social institutions upon which people had depended. Churches, community activities, and even families were replaced by the employing firm, which supplied the philosophy and goals to vast numbers of middle-class Americans, besides laying out their daily tasks. These were the people who, William H. Whyte wrote in 1956, "have left home, spiritually as well as physically, to take the vows of organization life, and it is they who are the mind and soul of our great self-perpetuating institutions."[1]

But the 1950s was also the decade that saw the shift from manufacturing to service, and the "organization man" (the title of Whyte's best-seller) began to disappear, eventually culminating in an explosion of entrepreneurism in the 1990s. Now a little upstart group of visionaries can build up an Amazon.com to challenge giant Barnes & Noble. Cyber businesses, many with dispersed employees and no steel and brick headquarters, are the antithesis of the culture that created the Organization Man. New ideas, new technologies, and indifference to the nuances of status characterize this new age of business.

Again looking back to the middle of the twentieth century, to another 1950s social prophet, Vance Packard, who wrote in 1959 in his best-selling book, *The Status Seekers*, "In the hierarchy of the big corporation, stratification is being carried to exquisite extremes." Packard went on to say, "Employees in big offices, as well as big plants, are finding their work roles fragmentized and impersonalized. There has been, perhaps unwittingly, a sealing-off of contact between big and little people on the job. And there has been a startling rise in the number of people who are bored with their work and feel no pride of initiative or creativity."[2] Forty years later, large numbers of people still work in organizations. Despite the decay noted by Packard and the downsizing and layoffs of the 1980s and 1990s, corporate life remains attractive to many. But organizations no longer want many of the workers they once would have hired. Lean and efficient, today's organization has pared itself down to "core competencies," a phrase that excludes many service providers. Programmers, writers, artists, food service workers, maintenance and support people may work *at* a big company but not *for* it. Far from the paternalistic embrace of the organization, these workers are employed by agencies that rent them out to other companies; some, denied a spot in the corporate hierarchy, rent themselves out to the highest bidder. Unlike the status seekers of yesterday, many of today's workers believe they don't need an organization.

The high tech entrepreneurs whose success came not from staying forever with an old-line organization but from their vision of the digital future are also the new American heroes. Jeff Bezos, the visionary behind Amazon.com, smiles from the March 1999 cover of *Wired* magazine. The caption reads: "Why him? (and not you?)"

Selling Services to Organizations

Some individual providers sell their services, not to another individual, but to a company. Companies have more money to spend on services than individuals, so they make good customers. Consultants make up a lot of this group. Some retired executives come back to their old companies as consultants, or they use their contacts to get other customers.

Providers who work on temporary contracts for companies are a growing segment of the working public. Estimates are that two million people each day are working on temporary contracts. These are generally relationship services, but they are a little different because company policy and funding are involved. Providers may have a contract limited by time or money, or the work could be episodic, occurring only when there is a need.

Not all contract work is to the workers' benefit, and this is not lost on the workers. Many companies use temporary workers to fill what are essentially permanent jobs (sometimes called "permatemps"). They do it to maintain flexibility and reduce labor costs. In May 1999, contract workers at Microsoft sued claiming they were really employees, and won a lawsuit against the giant software company that required Microsoft to offer these contractors the same stock options they offer their regular employees. It was clearly in the best interest of these workers to gain employee status at Microsoft where, incredibly, the average employee made $300,000 in 1998, mainly in stock options.[3]

Relationship Businesses—Personal and Steady

Customers are generally more comfortable doing business in a relationship than in an encounter, partly because the service is delivered in a personal way. As provider and customer get to know one another, the service becomes more reliable and familiar for both, and a sense of trust and loyalty develops. Customers can depend on a relationship provider, who either is the owner or has a stake in the business. If a hairstylist gets a frantic call from a good customer who needs her hair done fast, that provider will try to fit her in. But the Supercuts shop down the street can't do that. The providers who work there must take the customers as they come through the door.

Why are customers generally more satisfied with relationship services?

1. The provider and the customer get to know each other through repeated interaction, and this helps the provider tailor his service to the customer's exact needs.
2. The provider is directly dependent on customers for her income; if she fails to perform as the customer wants, she will lose a continuing source of money, so she tends to work hard to please each customer. Each steady customer is also an important source of referrals for getting new customers.
3. The provider may get to like the customer as a friend; a sense of personal duty as well as the satisfaction of contributing to the quality of someone else's life leads her to do her best for that customer.
4. The provider working in a partnership or sole proprietorship has a legal obligation to deliver the service he offered.

The flip side of this familiarity of service experience for the customer is the steadiness and continuity of business for the provider. Unlike the encounter business that is constantly engaged in strategies to steal competitors' customers or get new customers, a relationship business can operate with a limited number of customers and may get all its business from word-of-mouth recommendations. This frees the provider from the constant need to market her service and lets her concentrate on building skills and satisfying customers.

Relationship customers are basically people who are not concerned about "getting a good deal"; they place value on the quality of the service itself, and are willing to pay the going price. They are not like the fickle college student who changed phone companies each time a new incentive was offered. In real relationships, there is no need to offer discount deals, coupons, or take out expensive ads. Customers are attracted to the quality of the service and the loyalty inherent in a relationship, not the price.

Real One-to-One

Relationships are prized by customers because they deliver real one-to-one service, based on real knowledge (not data) of one another that leads to genuine concern about each other. Unlike numbers in a data base, knowledge of the customer's character, personal qualities, and preferences can help a relationship provider deliver exactly the right service. Repeated contacts can build motivation to "get it right" and bring the provider real satisfaction for a job well done.

Banks and pharmacies provide examples of businesses in which customers prefer relationships but have increasingly had to settle for encounters.

Banks

Small town banks traditionally provided business loans based on knowing the people to whom they loaned the money. Both provider and customer had a stake in the community and an incentive to see that the loan was paid back, for the sake of both. The customer would need the bank in the future. The bank wanted to retain the customer.

But more than 5,000 community banks have disappeared in the 1990s.[4] "The CBS Evening News" reported January 11, 1999, on the small town of Henniker, New Hampshire, whose community bank was bought by Bank of New Hampshire, which was owned by People's Heritage Financial Group, a $10 billion corporation. One Henniker business owner was quoted as saying the community bank was not afraid to loan money to local business people because the officers knew them. When the owner's third year in business was tough and he couldn't make his payments, the bank helped him manage and he got through it. But all that changed with the coming of the giant bank.

Another local businessperson said the bank's practices have hurt him to such an extent that he may have to close down. The bank had lost his checks on more than one occasion and caused him embarrassment and loss of goodwill. Angered by his treatment, one day this man demanded a receipt from a bank clerk. When he looked at the receipt, he found an insult scrawled on it. He sued. The bank manager expressed surprise, saying he couldn't imagine that his employees would do such a thing. But the old trust between bankers and business people was gone, victims of the giant, distant corporation that no longer put a face to the names on loans.

Banking has been making the shift from relationship to encounter, with customers having little choice if there are no independent banks left in their community. Like HMO customers who joined because it was the only plan offered, business owners in small towns that lose their locally controlled bank have little choice but to deal with the big bank that doesn't know them. Big banks may claim to have personal service or talk about customers having access to a "personal banker," but unless the customer sees the same person each time, it is not a relationship.

Pharmacies

In a relationship, the incentive to serve the customer is obvious. Relationship providers know all their customers and generally want to keep them. In many businesses that have been targets of takeover by chains, customer service is the main way a relationship business can survive. Pharmacies are a good example. *Detroit Free Press* columnist Bob Talbert talked to about fifty owners of independent drugstores in the Detroit area in 1998 for a series of columns on chain drugstores. Each owner stressed the importance of taking care of customers.

Talbert found the independent drugstore owners he inter-viewed believed they kept their loyal customers because those customers valued the personal service they received. Whatever convenience or price advantage these customers might have gotten at a chain did not make up for slow and impersonal ser-vice. But lots of potential customers are required by their health plan to get their prescription filled at the chain drugstore, which is a continuing problem for the independents. The same thing has happened to small shops catering to women who have had mastectomies. The *Detroit Free Press* ran a front-page article on February 15, 1999, in which several women who own small shops that custom-fit undergarments and prostheses for women who have had surgery were quoted. They had all lost business when the major managed health plans in the area signed con-tracts with large medical equipment chains to exclusively ser-vice their members. Customers of the small shops got personal service in a friendly and feminine setting that they preferred to the medical atmosphere of the big supply chain stores. One customer said of the small shop, "They made me feel like I was female again. At the medical supply stores, I felt like I was hand-icapped."[5]

Talbert noted that the more successful independent drug-store owners market their personal service as an advantage. Some provide personal instruction on use of drugs or medical appliances. Customers can count on seeing the same pharma-cist and staff each time, whereas the chains move pharmacists around to different stores, and clerks come and go. The chain stores are arranged so customers do not talk to the pharmacist, while independents encourage interaction between customer and pharmacist. The successful independent drugstores, like the small shops catering to women with mastectomies, worked on building relationships with customers.

Overcoming the advantages of the chains is not easy for independent drugstores. *Preservation* magazine carried a story about a pharmacist who opened a drugstore in Sioux Falls, South Dakota, competing with eleven chain drugstores nearby. But the article stated the independent was "doing something the chain-store pharmacists don't do—are all but prevented from doing—and that is cultivating a relationship with the customer." This pharmacy added value by delivering prescriptions to home or office with, as the article states "an almost maniacal speed and enthusiasm. A lawyer or banker who calls in a prescription from his office in the morning sometimes finds it sitting on his desk a few minutes later."[6]

The chains have less incentive to care whether their prescription service is personal. Talbert said he found that independent drugstores rely on their prescription business for about 80 percent of their revenue, but for chains, prescription services account for only 25 percent since they also sell a lot of other merchandise.

The chain drugstores, true to the egalitarian encounter format, have a system of filling prescriptions in the order in which they are received. If a customer calls in a prescription, and twenty other people are ahead of that customer, then that prescription will not be given any priority no matter how great the need. In an independent pharmacy, the pharmacist can use her judgment in deciding which to fill first. If someone has a cab waiting, for instance, the pharmacist can do him the courtesy of quickly getting the prescription ready. Or if someone urgently needs a pain killer, an independent pharmacist can serve that person first. The chain store pharmacist must follow the procedure set up by management while independent drugstores are usually owned by pharmacists.

Thomas Petzinger, in *The New Pioneers: The Men and Women Who Are Transforming the Workplace and Marketplace,* tells the story of Richard Ost, who opened a small pharmacy in an older ethnic neighborhood in Philadelpia. By really listening to his employees and customers, he tailored his services to the needs of the community and built it into a $5 million-a-year operation. One day early in his business life, Ost noticed one of his clerks writing out a prescription label instead of using his computer-generated label system. He discovered the reason: The customer did not speak English, and the clerk was writing the directions in Spanish. Ost responded by adding Spanish labels to his computerized setup. Later, as newer immigrants moved into the area, he added Vietnamese labels. The author says of Ost, "He grew his business not by planning but by adapting, not with business-school knowledge but with real-life experience. His employment policies, his use of technology, and even his pricing wove his business into the fabric of the surrounding community." However, Ost eventually became a consultant to other drugstore owners and sold his pharmacies (which had grown to three) to giant Rite Aid.[7]

Drugstore owners feel the pressure to sell out to chains, but customer satisfaction remains higher at the independents. The trade journal *Drug Topics* reported in April 1998 survey results that showed 80 percent of customers of independent drugstores but only 51 percent of chain customers said they were "very satisfied."[8]

What Works

The kinds of businesses where relationships work are mainly offering services to high-income customers. One of the reasons customers choose a relationship provider is wanting someone with a reputation for exceptional skills. Obviously, in an encounter, this is not relevant. Encounter customers may feel the organization provides a good service, but they do not have any control over which provider they get. Customers who want a provider with known professional skills will pay more for a relationship. For example, if they need a lawyer, they want the best. They will seek advice on who is highly regarded in the legal service they require. If they move to a new location and are seeking a hairdresser, they will ask around to find the best hairdresser, regardless of what that person charges. The same is true for gardening services, an architect to build or remodel a home, or a medical specialist. There are a large number of potential customers who care more about reputation than about price. If they can't get a recommendation, they may seek out "the best" by reputation.

Just as someone seeking out a new provider will get advice from others, so, too, will they become a source of referrals if they are satisfied with their choice of provider. This informal network of referrals is important to the relationship provider. It may be his sole method of getting customers. Because of this, relationship providers have a really large stake in providing good service. Their business literally will not grow if they don't get referrals from satisfied customers.

Once considered unprofessional, advertising is a method some relationship providers use for getting customers. This probably works best when the provider charges a fairly high fee and where the service is intense but not ongoing. For example, a lawyer who handles accident cases or malpractice cases might advertise his services since once he litigates a case, he's done with that customer and needs another one. Providers who don't come from a well-connected family and don't have enough experience to have built contacts might use advertising to get started.

As they build their business, providers may get into a situation where they cannot handle any more customers. At that point, they have four choices:

1. Raise their rates and keep the customers willing to pay more
2. Turn down new customers
3. Turn over some of the tasks they do to an employee or associate and/or give the less lucrative clients to an associate
4. Turn their business into an encounter business by training other providers to do what they do

Most businesses would opt for the first choice and raise their rates. But some, who are attached to their current customers, may take the second choice. If the provider is not insistent on working alone or keeping the business very small, he might choose number three. He could hire someone to take calls, book jobs, and do some clerical work. He could also hire an associate with similar skills and take a cut of that person's billings. Others, who are driven by a desire to earn more money or who feel the service is important and want to make it available to more people, might choose option number four. Like Dr. Shouldice, they could teach others their technique and reach many more people.

Built on Trust

Relationships are built on trust. Just as people trust their friends and family, they also come to trust a relationship provider.

While the familiarity a customer feels when patronizing a chain business is based on the uniformity of each location, the familiarity in a relationship business is personal, based on the people involved knowing each other. The dynamic is exactly the same as when neighbors talk over the back fence, or parents exchange stories at a meeting at their kids' school. These are people who know each other and expect to see each other again.

Relationship providers are less likely to push a sale that doesn't really benefit the customer. *PC World* magazine ran an article called "Where to Get the Best PC Deals Online" that checked out a number of popular resellers, including CDW, the company profiled in Chapter Three that assigns personal representatiVes to customers. Under the heading "Most Refreshingly Honest Advice," the article states "When we e-mailed CDW to ask whether it could preinstall FrontPage on a PC, a sales rep replied that it could, for $60—but he advised against it since installation was too easy to justify paying CDW to do the job. It takes a human being to be so candid."[9]

Trust builds business but carries with it personal responsibility. A relationship built on trust suffers shock waves when the provider does not deal honestly with the customer. One example that pops up in the news frequently is an investment adviser who loses the money of his clients, either through criminal intent or through incompetence. Business relationships, like personal relationships, happen because of what people have in common. An investment advisor builds her clientele by getting to know customers and winning their trust. But sometimes that trust is based on what they have in common, not on any objective information the customer has about the provider's abilities.

The *Wall Street Journal* of January 27, 1999, reported on a case of ex-football player Brian Smith who was working for Dean Witter Reynolds and made friends with a number of National Football League players, talking each of them into giving him large amounts of money to invest. Smith had an amazing amount in common with his first NFL customer, Larry Roberts. Both had played for southern colleges, both played in the NFL, and both suffered similar knee injuries that shortened their careers. Common backgrounds and interests like this can quickly build a relationship.

Smith and Roberts' relationship began in 1995 with Smith making many promises of big investment returns. It ended the following year with the 6-foot-6-inch, 280-pound Roberts attempting to throw the 6-foot-6-inch 265-pound Smith out a thirtieth floor window in the Atlanta office of Dean Witter Reynolds. Smith apparently had lost $140,000 of Roberts's money, and Roberts was demanding its return. Roberts was one of about twenty NFL player, to lose money by dealing with Smith.

The *Wall Street Journal* notes that there is a lesson in this story. Normally cautious people might feel comfortable giving money to someone with whom they have a lot in common. They quote Robert Bontempo, a Columbia Business School professor trained as a social psychologist: "When someone has markers of similarity—the same religious group, the same way of dressing—or shared historical experiences like pro football, there is assumed to be a bond there and a feeling they're less likely to be taken advantage of. But the only predictor of future behavior is past behavior."[10]

Relationship providers need to be sensitive to their legal responsibilities. The cashier who overcharged a customer will not go to jail, but a relationship provider who defrauds a customer may. When there is liability for some action carried out in the name of a corporate entity, it is normally the corporation, not any individual, that is held responsible. But providers working in partnerships or sole proprietorships are responsible for their actions in a way mere employees are not. Such workers have a legal obligation to deliver the service they offered to the very best of their ability. But providers who lack deep pockets are less likely to be sued than corporations, which are viewed as bottomless pools of money by much of the litigious public.

In the case of Brian Smith, it was unclear whether he intended to defraud the athletes he dealt with. What is known is that he went from Dean Witter to Merrill Lynch & Co., where he signed up more football players. Willie Anderson, a young Bengals lineman who invested his entire bonus check of about $2.8 million with Smith, complained to Merrill that his account had losses of $1 million and that $500,000 was missing. Finally, after having his brokerage license revoked, Brian Smith disappeared. Investigators hired by Roberts, Dean Witter, and Merrill Lynch were still trying to find him in early 1999.

Providers can abuse or be dishonest with customers, but it can work the other way around, too. Customers can also abuse providers by not paying the bill or lying about their circumstances. Picture a defendant in a legal case telling his lawyer he's innocent when he's not or leaving out important details. Customers can conceal income from their accountants or solicit the accountant to hide income to avoid paying taxes. Customers can "pay under the table" when they have handyman work done in their house to help the provider avoid taxes. Working couples needing a nanny can do what Attorney General candidate Zoe Baird did and not send the social security tax to the government. That lets them give more money to the nanny but shortchanges her long-term interests (and is illegal and can have consequences, as Baird so sadly discovered). Trust is the foundation of a relationship business and both parties—customer and provider—need to deal honestly with one another for this strategy to work.

Behavior of Relationship Providers

From the point of view of providers, working in relationships is more satisfying. How a service worker relates to customers could be visualized as a continuum, going from a totally scripted performance that is always the same to a highly personalized and flexible approach to each customer. At the far left is the fast food worker and at the far right end is the investment advisor. One has no leeway in how to do the job, and the other has substantial control of his actions toward customers. People generally like to have control over their work. High degrees of stress are associated with work that is routine, not work that is highly skilled. The investment advisor gets to exercise creativity and judgment in his work, and this builds a sense of self as a competent and worthwhile person and adds to his enjoyment of life. Relationship providers often work many extra hours because they are engaged in work they love doing and feel a sense of ownership of their work. It is analogous to the pride in craftsmanship felt by the shoemaker or the cooper of times gone by.

The provider in a relationship is not likely to stereotype customers or behave in inappropriate ways. The provider needs her customers to make a living and will therefore be polite and friendly, without requiring any training program on how to be customer-oriented or rules that she must smile. Even providers employed by organizations that work in relationships are likely to maintain cordial behavior toward customers. In some cases, they may get a commission for each sale, so maintaining good relations is in their financial interest. In other cases, they know they'll be seeing that person again, and that provides an incentive. This is in strong contrast to the perception of poor service in encounter businesses. The clerk who shrugs away questions or who is not empowered to fix the problem is the picture of uncaring service to the complaining public. Relationship providers are not all perfect, but they have a big advantage in delivering good customer service: They see the same customer over and over. This helps them learn how to please the customer, and it gives them an incentive to behave in a way appropriate to their service provider role.

Like the preindustrial craftsman, a relationship business depends on the provider's skill and time. There is only so much of the provider to go around, only so many hours in the day. Relationship businesses are not as lucrative as encounter businesses because the owner cannot leverage the work of the provider. The chain drugstore can have the pharmacist do only the work that she must do by law and parcel out other parts of the work to lower paid people. That's leverage. Relationships work against this. The customer wants "his" provider, not someone else. The longer they have been doing business together, the tighter the bond becomes as the provider develops expertise at meeting the customer's needs, and their times together become more familiar and closer to the customer's ideal service transaction. The customer depends on the provider and will not accept a substitute. A provider in this situation cannot leverage her skill over greater numbers of customers. An attempt to do so may result in loss of any sense of relationship. Like the gynecologist with six examining rooms who rushes into each room, poking each patient with icy instruments, then rushes to the next room to do the same—diluting one's service too much just alienates customers who feel the personal touch is lost.

Relationship providers often work in fields that require specific education or training, which they are likely to get on their own. The doctor goes to medical school, the lawyer to law school, the hairstylist to beauty school. The plumber goes through a union apprenticeship, the accountant goes to graduate school, and the consultant goes to business school. In truth, a lot of provider expertise comes only through work experience, but more opportunities exist for working in relationships when providers bring their education with them than for those who are trained on the job. On-the-job training usually means the organization has a certain way it wants things done, and that means working in encounters.

When the qualifications for the work take time and money to acquire, providers generally feel their first loyalty is to their profession. This may at times clash with their commitment to their employer. A clinic hiring doctors, then trying to dictate every aspect of the work, may find that doctors, with their long years of education and internship, are likely to feel such control is an infringement on their professional judgment, and some will quit. An unemployed doctor is still a doctor. An unemployed McDonald's counter clerk is just unemployed.

The loyalty to and identification with the profession is a plus for the customer, who assumes he is getting the benefit of the provider's personal expertise, which comes from education and experience and is not just doing what the company told him to say or do. Professionals who worked hard to get their credentials often display them in their place of business or list them on their business card. You might hire a consultant because she went to the Harvard Business School, for example, not just because she is with McKinsey.

Relationship providers are concerned with getting and keeping customers but not with efficiency in the same way as encounter businesses. Efficiency does not necessarily equate to good customer service. The man with the broken baby stroller, for example, found the airline was quite efficient at deflecting customer complaints. By having no process for customers to be heard, the airline eliminated a lot of work, but it may also have driven away a lot of customers. Relationship providers make their customers a priority and are highly motivated to listen to any suggestions a customer might make. This is clearly one of the reasons customers like relationships. The provider actually listens because it is in her best interests to do so.

Family Businesses

Many businesses start small, with family members the main employees. These businesses may begin as relationship businesses and grow into large encounter or pseudo-relationship organizations. The Marriott Corporation, for example, was started by John Willard Marriott in 1927 with one A & W root beer stand in Washington, D.C. He and his wife, Alice, worked together to build a string of "Hot Shoppes" featuring Alice's recipes. His sons worked in the business from the time they were old enough to do chores. The family went on to own Big Boy and Roy Rogers restaurants and only later, under John Willard's son, got into hotels. John Willard was personally involved in the business until he died in 1985, leaving a son in charge.

In family businesses, there is often an emotional attachment to the work and a paternalistic concern for the employees. Sometimes this translates into a caring environment in which to work. For example, John Willard Marriott is said to have always told his managers if you don't have happy employees, you won't have happy customers. Over the years, Marriott has paid attention to the needs of its hourly employees, and they have responded with loyalty to Marriott, which has a very low employee turnover rate. Marriott employs many recent immigrants, for whom it offers onsite citizenship classes, and former welfare recipients, for whom it offers a class in basic work skills. A Marriott International's senior vice-president for human resources noted that the supervisors spend 15 percent of their time "doing social work," helping employees with personal problems. Marriott also offers stock options to all employees, which has helped make employees feel they are part of a company family.[11]

Ford Motor Company also began as a family business, founded by Henry Ford in 1903, with his son, Edsel, an active manager and Edsel's son, Henry Ford II, the chairman from 1943 until 1980. Henry Ford was famous for paying his workers five dollars a day, high wages in those days (the prevailing wage was three dollars a day), and believing that cars should be affordable for the average person. Ford Motor Company did not become a public company until 1956 and the Ford family still owns 40 percent of the stock. William Clay Ford, Jr., a great grandson of the founder, became chairman in 1999. When a tragic explosion at a power station at the Ford Rouge plant killed and injured a number of workers in early 1999, Chairman Ford rushed to the scene and told reporters, "Our employees are like extended members of our family." He made a point of visiting all the injured workers and their families and personally asking if there was anything he could do. He made sure relatives had free parking at the hospital and provided a refrigerator for the visitors' waiting room. He picked up the tab for motel rooms near the hospital. His concern for his injured employees seemed genuine and unusual to the workers' families and to the reporters who covered this tragedy. Chairman Ford was heard on local radio saying it was "the worst day of my life."

At the time of his appointment as chairman, William Clay Ford, Jr., only 41 years old, described his vision for the company as "product leadership, the highest quality and customer satisfaction, environmental leadership, and corporate citizenship."[12] He showed everyone what he meant by corporate citizenship on that unfortunate day at the Rouge power station when he reacted like the owner of a family business.

But neither Marriott Corporation nor Ford Motor Company are actually family to their employees. On the contrary, as public corporations, their interests lie in whatever pleases Wall Street and causes their stock price to rise. This is not to suggest that Marriott managers don't care about their employees or that the Ford chairman only hurried to the accident site to gain good press, but to point out that public corporations are not family businesses.

The description of an enterprise as a "family business" seems to have an aura of good feeling about it, though, and many organizations proudly advertise that they are "family-owned and operated," perhaps a way of implying that customers can expect to deal with people who have a commitment to the business, who make customers a priority. It is useful to keep in mind that family businesses are not all relationship businesses. If they are publicly traded corporations, they are more beholden to Wall Street than to their workers, many of whom are not even employees.

By contrast, a family business that is privately owned can make its own rules, without consulting Wall Street or taking the advice of high-priced consultants pushing the latest business fad or management strategy. The Jiffy Mix company of Chelsea, Michigan, sells 1.4 million little blue boxes of muffin mix every day. Like Alice Marriott who created recipes for the business she shared with her husband, Mabel Holmes, the wife of Jiffy Mix's founder, devised the recipe for their first product back in 1930. Today, a third generation of the family still owns and operates the business. Jiffy has *never* advertised its products! It has no marketing department and has never laid off anyone in its entire history. CEO Howdy Holmes knows his workers personally. Private companies like Jiffy can take a long view and concentrate on having great products and on pleasing customers rather than fixating on earnings.

Frederick F. Reichheld writes in his book, *The Loyalty Effect*, that publicly traded companies are limited by the need for profits:

> . . . the pinch will come the minute short-term earnings hit a bump, or the instant your industry enters a period of great change. Pressure on quarterly earnings is guaranteed to bring out the worst in public investors and to underscore their lack of concern for the company's future. Their demands for short-term earnings improvement will sharply increase the danger of shortchanging customers and employees, and of initiating a downward spiral into mediocrity.[13]

Businesses that are truly family owned and operated can concentrate on satisfying customers and building tight links with their employees.

Starting a Relationship Business

People start relationship businesses for a variety of reasons. They may want to practice a profession for which they have spent years preparing, or they may be refugees from the corporate world seeking to escape their Dilbert-like existence. Whatever their reasons, doing business in relationships is different from setting up an encounter business.

How is it different? When you begin, you don't need a management team. You don't need an organization chart. You don't need a human resources department. You don't have to design jobs and determine the minutia of the daily work. The people who work with you will be associates who will have their own pool of clients or customers, and they must have the personal and professional skills to satisfy those customers. You may hire some support people to answer the phone or help with billing, but you—the owner—will be personally involved with each of your customers. You will build a relationship with those customers, and you may deal with them over a number of years and get to know them quite well. In many cases, they become indistinguishable from personal friends. Even the U.S. Congress had a problem with this when they tried to reform lobbying. They had to allow Congressmen to have dinners with their friends, even if those friends were lobbyists. But if the lobbyist was a stranger, then the restrictions would apply. The essence of a relationship is that it occurs over time, it is between two people (not one person and an organization), and it is voluntary. People stay in relationships because they want to. This is true of personal as well as business relationships.

What You Need

What are the ingredients for a successful relationship business?

1. The ability to provide a service people want and will pay for
2. A way to get initial customers
3. Business skills

Any business must provide something people will buy. A relationship provider has to deliver a service people want or need. An accountant can provide tax advice and complete tax forms that people don't want to do themselves. An architect can advise and draw up plans for home remodeling and additions. In both of these cases, helping the customer decide what's best is part of the service and may be a reason people use these providers. The more people are seeking advice or help in making decisions, the more they are likely to use a relationship provider—and the more they expect as well. Someone who knows exactly how she wants her hair cut may go to Supercuts and tell the hairstylist how to cut her hair. But another person may feel she needs a new look but doesn't know what would be best. She seeks out a hairstylist recommended by a friend and begins a relationship where she will get continuing advice on how to style her hair to her best advantage. Relationship providers must add value in terms of their time and expertise. Most importantly, each provider must get to know the best way to work with each customer. Unlike encounter businesses, relationship providers can tailor the service to what an individual customer prefers.

Starting up may be the most difficult part of a relationship business, for both provider and customer. Many providers begin their business with one good customer and branch out. Relationship providers can begin by asking their circle of friends and acquaintances to refer likely customers. People who are already well-connected have an advantage. Once lawyers simply "hung out their shingle" and sat in their office waiting for customers, but this is not a good model in the digital age. The "shingle" you hang out today may be on the Internet, and your customers could be anywhere. Your network of contacts could extend for many geographic miles but be quickly accessible via your e-mail distribution list. Relationship businesses need to promote their services, but do not need to do it in the same aggressive, public way as encounter businesses. Like the lobbyist whose friends and clients tend to be the same people, a relationship provider's business can just grow from contacts made through notes, phone calls, former business associates, and personal contacts.

Relationship services become more efficient over time but may be awkward in the beginning. The provider may not deliver everything the customer wants at first, but the payoff comes from staying with the relationship. Just like married couples get to know each other so well they can complete each others' sentences, relationship provider and customer become more familiar with each other over time.

Everyone has heard about high rates of business failure, and nothing contributes more to that than lack of basic business skills: the mom-and-pop café that fails to figure its real costs, for example; the hairstylist whose customers love her but who forgets to pay her taxes; the lawyer with a talent for taking clients who don't pay the bill. Service professionals need to have great skills at what they do, but they also have to mind the business. That means knowing their fixed costs, hiring help only when they can afford it, and sending Uncle Sam his money when it is due. Some providers try to go into business with no financing, and that may be unrealistic. Others might "keep their day job" and moonlight as an independent provider, waiting until they build a small clientele before going full time and adding associates. One of the advantages of a relationship business is not needing massive financing, but that doesn't mean no financing.

Drawbacks to Relationships

Relationship businesses can have some significant drawbacks:

- No matter how many people need your service, you can only reach a small number of customers. This may be fine, or you may feel dissatisfied with the limitations on the number of customers you can serve when many more people would probably be interested in what you have to offer.
- Many customers may not be able to afford your service, and you may not be able to treat all customers equally as encounter businesses do; you may have to cater more to those who provide you with more income. Again, that may be fine with you, or it may bother you to have to

give less than your best to some so you can give more time and energy to your biggest spenders.

- It may be difficult to find people with the needed skills to work as providers; you may have to share profits with those you hire. If you work alone, this won't be a problem, but if you add associates and grow, you'll have to find others who have good skills and share your basic philosophy.
- If you plan to do all the work yourself, you must also have business skills and plan to spend time on administrative work. Sole proprietors have to keep up with taxes and insurance on their own or work with other professionals who have these skills. In any case, it will take up time you might rather devote to your real work.
- Your profits will be limited by the available time of providers; some of your providers may be more skilled than others and may become demanding, even quit and "steal" your customers. There's not much you can do about it except pick your associates carefully.
- You will have to deal with the difficulties of establishing relationships with customers and of ending them. Relationships are more emotionally demanding than giving service in encounters, and ending a relationship can be an unhappy experience.

Star Providers

Providers who work in relationships can find themselves becoming celebrities. Lawyers who handle famous cases (like Johnny Cochran, who defended O.J. Simpson) may be in big demand, both to handle legal work and to give speeches or appear at seminars. A hairstylist to the stars may have many more potential new customers than he can handle. Consultants who write books that are widely read may find their phone ringing steadily with new business and requests for interviews. These providers can pretty much dictate the terms of their work. They can pick and choose clients, taking only the work that really interests them. Obviously, this is a great situation for the provider. If they are with a professional firm, such providers can leave the firm, taking their clients with them. Wall Street analysts with wildly successful track records can become stars as can managers who build a reputation for turning around troubled companies, or consultants who put together big merger deals.

Large professional firms may discourage anyone from becoming a star as star providers can be difficult to manage. They make demands and sometimes expect preferential treatment. A star performer can help bring in a lot of business for a firm, though, as well as build the reputation of the entire firm that rides on his coattails. Some providers may like the ancillary services and camaraderie of the firm rather than going out on their own. Is it wise to encourage or discourage star status? For a one-person operation, it is obviously a plus to be a star. Taking on high-visibility work, even pro bono work, can be a good move. Lawyer Geoffrey Fieger made a name for himself as Dr. Jack Kevorkian's lawyer and later ran for governor of Michigan (he lost—the public apparently did not think defending "Dr. Death" a good qualification). Although Kevorkian didn't pay for the services, Fieger got lots of other business out of being in the news all the time. In 1999, he turned up as the lawyer for one of the families who lost a son in the Columbine High School killings.

For providers just starting out, becoming the protégé of a star provider is another good way to build business. Star providers, by definition, have more business than they can handle, and many are open to mentoring a junior associate. A chance to learn from someone well known and well regarded would jumpstart any career.

Being a star performer is the very antithesis of the encounter model, in which providers are interchangeable. Customers are not supposed to build any relationships with providers and are specifically discouraged from doing so. Fast food workers, for instance, could not get their work done if each customer engaged them in chit chat. Store clerks are supposed to help customers, but not engage in long conversations. However, customers value time with star performers. To a great extent, all relationship providers are selling their time. And with star performers, customers understand that the provider's time is valuable. Customers who would be furious about having to wait around at McDonald's because the counter person was chatting with them instead of getting their food are willing to shell out the money to get time to talk with a famous lawyer or discuss theory with a famous consultant.

Star performers do not have to cater to clients and some may be difficult to deal with on a personal level. Like the opera diva who expects everyone's adoration, star lawyers, doctors, and consultants may behave arrogantly without damaging their business. They are, after all, stars.

Conclusion

Customers like relationships because they are not encounters. A relationship feels different, as research done at University of Arizona shows. Responses of people surveyed in areas of trust, relating, and knowledge were markedly different for those in relationships from the responses of those in encounters and pseudo-relationships. Relationships go against the trend toward impersonal service. While the perception of service going downhill is strong, customers who regularly visit "their" provider, a person they know and trust, report high levels of satisfaction.

Not everyone can afford service in relationships and sometimes there is no relationship business available. If a town's only cheap eatery is Burger King, then people wanting a cheap restaurant meal will have to eat there and will also have to accept the process. And into the void left by the chaining of America can come fresh new entrepreneurs who offer something different, their own unique kind of personal service.

Starting and operating a relationship business is different from starting and operating an encounter business. A relationship business can start small—and it can remain small if the founder wishes. Or it can expand by taking in partners or by hiring assistants and clerks to relieve the service provider of tasks that can be delegated to others. Some tasks, like payroll or tax preparation, can be farmed out to other firms.

Relationship businesses allow the owner to concentrate on providing the service for which she is trained. Relationship providers often love their work. The success of their enterprise is, however, also dependent upon business skills. An owner who lacks the needed skills must hire someone else to handle the business side of the enterprise. Encounter businesses will continue to expand into new territory, making it harder all the time for relationship businesses to flourish except in niche markets.

New technologies, the topic of the next chapter, may help some relationship businesses to be more competitive but may accelerate the demise of other kinds of relationship businesses.

Notes

1. Whyte, William H. *The Organization Man* (New York: Doubleday, 1956). Quoted from the University of Pennsylvania's 1950s' Web site (http://www.english.upenn.edu/~afilreis/50s/home.html).
2. Packard, Vance. *The Status Seekers* (New York: Pocket Books, 1961). Quoted from the University of Pennsylvania's 1950s' Web site (http://www.english.upenn.edu/~afilreis/50s/home.html).
3. Helm, Leslie. "Temp Workers Stand to Gain in Microsoft Ruling," *Los Angeles Times*, May 14, 1999.
4. "CBS Evening News With Dan Rather," January 11, 1999.
5. Anstett, Patricia. "Women Lose Choice for Health Products," *Detroit Free Press*, February 15, 1999.
6. Ehrenhalt, Alan. "Philips Avenue Wants to be Your Friend," *Preservation*, July/August 1999.
7. Petzinger, Thomas. *The New Pioneers: The Men and Women Who Are Transforming the Workplace and Marketplace* (New York: Simon & Schuster, 1999). Excerpted in the *Wall Street Journal*, March 5, 1999.
8. Herzog, Boaz. "Big Business Plagues Small Pharmacies: Independents Disappear as Chain Stores Move in," graph on customer satisfaction using data from *Drug Topics*, April 20, 1999.
9. McCracken, Harry. "Where to Get the Best PC Deals Online," *PC World*, September 1999.
10. "Old NFL Man Trusts His Money To Another One, Now Regrets It," *Wall Street Journal*, January 27, 1999.

11. "Low-Wage Lessons: How Marriott Keeps Good Help—Even at $7.40 an Hour," *Business Week*, November 11, 1996.
12. "Young Ford to be Chairman," *Detroit Free Press*, September 12, 1998.
13. Reichheld, Frederick F. *The Loyalty Effect* (Boston: Harvard Business School Press, 1996).

Chapter Eight

Using Technology: Building Profits and Pleasing Customers

Using Technology to Create Efficient Service

One of the ways chain businesses come into being is when an entrepreneur recognizes that a service many people use is delivered in an inefficient way. It may be a personal service provided mainly by mom-and-pop businesses; but mom and pop are often slow to see their market changing or to adopt new technology. Even if they see the need to change, they probably lack the capital needed to make a big shift in the way they operate.

Let's look at the dry cleaning business, which has traditionally been offered by small, individually owned shops. What have they been doing wrong that might allow a chain like Zoots to steal their customers?

1. Not open enough hours for busy people, offending their best customers—career people who need business attire every day
2. Pricing women's items higher than men's items, offending a major segment of their market and leaving themselves open to charges of discrimination and sexism

3. Making it inconvenient for customers to check if their clothes are ready, offending everyone
4. Using an environmentally harmful chemical to clean clothes, offending the growing number of customers who care about "green" issues (and young customers, their future market, who often care a great deal about this)

Can technology solve any of these problems? Yes, along with some new ways of doing things. Zoots' solution minimizes contact between customer and provider, which makes the service less personal. Personal was the selling point for mom-and-pop businesses. But look at what the customer gains! She puts her clothes in her Zoots-supplied bar-coded garment bag and hands it through a window. Her credit card number is on file, and she pays the same rates as men pay. She goes to a Web site to check whether her clothes are ready, then she can pick them up any time, including late at night, from a locker. She also has the option of having Zoots pick up and deliver her dry cleaning for no extra charge. In addition, she has the satisfaction of knowing her clothes were cleaned with a chemical more environmentally friendly than the one commonly used by other dry cleaners. All of these conveniences and benefits seem like a good trade-off for the loss of contact with the store owner. Of course, the process has to work, and the clothes have to look great, or the customer may go back to the small friendly shop.

When a business is thoroughly planned based on what customers want, it can examine every aspect from a customer point of view. For instance, Zoots' management found the employees liked using rubber bands to hold hangers together because they could put them around their wrists, but the customers didn't like them.[1] So the organization switched to twisty ties. It is easier for professional managers to implement these kinds of changes than for the mom-and-pop business, which tends to keep on doing whatever it has been doing. Its lack of foresight about changing customer needs creates opportunities for encounter businesses.

Encounter Businesses and the New Blue Collar Work

Encounter businesses and technology go together like bread and butter. Chain businesses use computer systems to tie together their locations and networks and use intranets to distribute information and move data. In many cases, their front-line workers sit at computers all day retrieving information about customers or entering new information and product orders. Service workers use computerized cash registers that instantly look up an item's price and debit the item from inventory. Fast food workers can press a button with a picture of the item the customer wants and punch up the five-dollar bill the customer hands them while the processor figures the change and displays it on a screen in front of them. These workers don't have to know the basics of adding and subtracting involved in making change.

The new kinds of technology-enabled jobs do not pose the same kinds of physical dangers to workers as going into mines, tending a blast furnace, or working with huge presses that can cut off a hand. But there are new maladies associated with the work: carpal tunnel syndrome from running a keyboard and mouse for hours, eye strain from looking at the monitor, muscle aches from long hours of sitting, and the kind of isolation from reality that comes from spending days alone in a windowless cubicle, or speaking the same words over and over to fast food customers. The narrow focus reduces the worker's ability to understand the process, and this makes the work less satisfying. When the pay is small and the work repetitive, workers tend to become unhappy and quit.

Langdon Winner, who teaches political theory at Rensselaer Polytechnic Institute, has observed, in his insightful essay on Silicon Valley workers, the contrast between "ordinary workers" and the well-paid high tech workers. Those workers who are not part of the well-paid and much-ballyhooed high tech workforce "typically face a much different set of possibilities":

> As they enter an electronic office or factory, they become the objects of top-down managerial control, required to take

orders, complete finite tasks, and perform according to a set of standard productivity measures. Facing them is a structure that incorporates the authoritarianism of the industrial workplace and augments its power in ingenious ways. No longer are the Taylorite time and motion measurements limited by an awkward stopwatch carried from place to place by a wandering manager. Now workers' motions can be ubiquitously monitored in units calculable to the nearest microsecond. For telephone operators handling calls, doing data entry, rates of performance are recorded by a centralized computer and continuously compared to established norms. Failure to meet one's quota of phone calls, insurance claims, or keystrokes is grounds for reprimand or, eventually, dismissal.[2]

The work once available in factories was not easy or enjoyable either, but the increasing efficiencies gained by automation contributed to high pay for workers (along with unionization), and many stayed in the same job their entire lives. This has not happened for encounter service workers, who suffer from low pay and low prestige. They are the new blue collar workers, and business owners need to be aware that technology can make work more efficient but, depending on how you use it, can also make for less satisfied workers.

Call Centers: Encounters Made Possible by Technology

The modern call center—those beehives of identical cubicles, each with a worker talking into a headset, keying in data or reading information on a computer screen—is typical of the new blue collar environment. No longer wearing blue shirts with their first name embroidered on a patch, these workers nonetheless are in an environment that dictates and constrains their activities in the same way Henry Ford and his managers prescribed every motion of his assembly line workers. These centers take calls from people trying to book flights or hotel rooms, order from a catalog, or who have a problem with a product or a service they've paid for. The customer who uses these services, like the consumer who buys the output of factory production, does not see the provider of the service. The anonymous provider talking into his headset is part of a process that is part human and part machinery. Like the fast food worker who moves quickly from one customer to the next, the call center worker's contact with each customer—aided by the technology of telephony—is brief.

Computer support is one activity mainly handled by call centers. Customers who buy software, then need help using it, are offered either a free hotline to call or some kind of paid support. If a company offers free service, it obviously can lose money on people who call too often (i.e., use too much of the service). People who have a problem with their computer or with the software they are using, or who want to order an upgrade, are usually required to call a phone number that connects them to the call distributing equipment that routes their call to a call center worker.

Do tech-support call centers provide good service? The *Wall Street Journal* reported on a survey conducted by market research firm Service Intelligence using fifteen "mystery shoppers" who called tech support lines at six major software firms. In one-fourth of the ninety calls made, the support people either gave the wrong answer or said the problem could not be solved, even though all the questions were taken from the companies' Frequently Asked Questions (FAQs) on its Web site. Some of the problems the callers encountered: getting wrong answers before getting the right one, long waits while the support person looked for the answer, waiting on hold for more than a half hour before getting a person, and not getting through at all. In one case, the caller made thirty attempts over five days to reach the support line, all unsuccessful. Another caller had to push eighteen numbers on the phone keypad to get through to a live person. A spokesman for Service Intelligence said they had expected to find a "high level of knowledge in answering questions" but found the opposite.[3]

What can computer companies do about this poor service to the public? While a company makes no money from a support call, answering the customer's questions keeps that customer a user of the product and makes it more likely he will purchase upgrades or buy other products from the company. Businesses should decide if they want to provide good support on the theory that it helps them keep that customer or if their business is not hurt by offering a minimal service. Some possible solutions:

1. Charge for support, as some companies have done, either as part of the cost of buying the product or as an optional extra charge.
2. Take a good look at how the call center is performing, and make adjustments. Why are the tech support people unable to answer questions, and what can you do about it? More training? Better pay? Bringing the service in-house?
3. Move support to the Web, offering answers to common questions in a FAQ page or provide a knowledge base like Microsoft has and let users know they must use it. This would be more accurate but less convenient for some users who prefer talking to a service representative.
4. Sponsor a Web chat room or news group so users can help each other.
5. Offer service in relationships instead of encounters so each user has an assigned support person to call when she needs help; let the support people know they own each problem that comes to them, and they must get back to each customer with an answer.

Relationship Computer Support

Where the customer base is of a known size and the customers call frequently, it may be feasible to assign a specific support person for a group of users. This would save the cost of operating a call center. Users would have no assurance of always reaching their provider, but organizations could implement a system like CDW's; when the customer's provider was unavailable, another provider on the same "street" could take the call. When providers get calls they cannot answer, they can refer that problem to someone else who has the expertise needed, then follow up with the customer. This is the same process the medical profession uses when a general practitioner refers his patient to a specialist, but remains that patient's primary doctor. Support workers, by taking ownership of their customers' problems, would accept responsibility for providing accurate answers.

Table 8-1   Benefits/Drawbacks to Relationship Computer Support

	Call Center Encounter	*Relationship*
Cost	Low labor costs, but high cost for equipment	Higher labor costs, but lower cost for equipment
Contact	Customer deals with whoever takes the call or is available; many problems dealt with on the phone; if the problem can't be solved, the provider tries to find the answer and calls the customer back	Customer deals each time with the same contact person, who takes ownership of the problem. When the provider lacks the expertise needed, he consults with someone else, then gets back to the customer
Customer confidence	Customer has little confidence of actually getting a call back when he deals with an overworked stranger each time; if the customer calls again about the problem, he may have to explain it all over again to a new provider	Customers have high confidence of getting a call back because they know the provider; the provider knows customer will call him again (not just call the organization again) if he doesn't get an answer in a timely fashion
Customer behavior	Customers may try to contact a support person directly in hopes of getting that person assigned to their problem	Customers deal only with their contact person; they are not as likely to "circumvent the system"
Provider behavior	Provider does not know the level of knowledge of the customer and may either talk over the customer's head or appear patronizing	Provider knows the customer's level of expertise and discusses the problem at a level the customer understands
Technology	Large investment in equipment and software to operate in a call center environment	Could be operated with just a phone and desktop software for tracking calls
Determining customer satisfaction	Use of monitoring and metrics to determine if customers were properly served	Providers get direct feedback, but management must rely on reports from providers or customer surveys

Table 8-1 compares relationship support with a call center environment. Providing support in relationships is a radical solution that goes against the tide; but knowing that people prefer relationship service to encounter service, a company that does this could build a loyal following of customers and providers.

Using Technology to Measure Worker Performance

The same technology that created their job can compile data on how workers do it, such as how many customers they waited on or the number of calls they took, how long each call lasted, how many keystrokes they entered, how many sales they made, and other items that technology can capture.

Michael Cusack, in *Online Customer Care,* notes:

> . . . many call centers find it more satisfactory (and cost jus-
> tifying) to measure their effectiveness based solely on met-
> rics such as the quantity of calls answered, calls abandoned,
> and the average speed of answer, rather than on more in-
> volved factors, such as the number of calls resolved on the
> first contact versus average talk time, levels of customer sat-
> isfaction, cost/benefit and root cause analysis, integrity of
> online information, average percentage of customer base
> contacting customer care, and the timeliness of customer
> callbacks.[4]

Help-desk workers may be quick to close calls when their performance is measured by numbers alone. When calls are monitored for length of time, workers try to end each call quickly. New Century Energies in Denver, Colorado, found this to be true. New Centuries operates in western states, with 1.4 million residential customers and 900,000 business customers. It has two call centers: Denver and Amarillo. Partly in response to coming deregulation, New Century has recently decided to change some of its procedures. Its call center workers were monitored for length of time and number of calls, but as Director of Market Research and Evaluation Suzette Tucker-Welch relates, "We were measuring efficiency, not how the customer sees service." She says with competition coming to their markets, the company must be ready to compete on customer service. "Energy is a difficult sell," she says. "You can't see energy. But customers can experience service."[5]

Call centers can be linked to Web sites where customers can look for answers, and, if needed, talk to a support person via Web phone. Call center agents in this arrangement take calls that come from both regular phone calls and from Web phones; the same agents can also handle requests coming from e-mail and chat rooms.[6] This may help integrate the call center into the company's other operations and create a technically rich environment in which all workers can participate and learn.

Use of Web phones and even e-mail does not solve the problem of too many calls. Someone still has to answer each call and waiting on hold for a half hour with a Web phone is no less frustrating than waiting on a regular phone. Companies that cannot add extra people to answer Web phones should do without them and concentrate on adding content to their Web pages that provides answers and reduces the need for customers to talk to a live human.

Effect of Technology on Providers

Rigid employment practices may antagonize and stress workers to the point where they care little about the company or the customers. New Century Energy's Tucker-Welch says, in explaining their move away from metrics, "We need to have happy workers too, to reduce the turnover." She favors giving workers more leeway in doing their job and empowering them so they can solve more customer problems.

There is no evidence that tightly-controlled workers actually do more work than those given more autonomy. The main justification for close control is twofold:

1. Where you have high turnover of employees, it is too expensive to train everyone, so making narrow jobs with tight control can substitute.
2. It is less likely that an employee will insult a customer and cause a lawsuit if his behavior is monitored.

Each of these reasons has some merit in some situations, but companies that want a tight O-P link, with the goal of reducing turnover and getting employee buy-in for the company's values, should understand that these goals are incompatible with heavy-handed measures of control.

Some service providers come to feel hostility toward their equipment and make remarks like "When I go home, I don't want to use a computer." They've had enough of the computer during their working day and do not see using a computer as enjoyable activity. People who want to know how the computer works, who enjoy investigating and using new technology would be very frustrated working at a call center. People can be quickly trained to do such work, but they learn very little that would help them move up to a more fulfilling and better-paying job. The same is true of many encounter service jobs where workers learn only how to use the specific software needed for their job.

Technology also eliminates some kinds of work and often creates new jobs to do the same function as the jobs it took away. The entertainment industry offers many examples. New technologies will let movie fans download movies to their TV via cable. This could be the death knell of video rental stores and their jobs. Movie theaters too are about to go digital as the necessary quality has finally been achieved to show digital movies on the big screen. This will mean movies can be sent electronically to theaters that can make copies for multiple screens. It will totally change movie distribution and eliminate jobs for projectionists. Musicians are in less demand as music is created electronically. George Lucas has created animated characters for his *Star Wars* movie, *The Phantom Menace*, that have major parts. Claymation characters are popular on cable channels and ZDTV has its "Dash" and "Tilde" animated characters that present tips between regular programs. Sometimes these animated characters even do interviews (with real people!).

Museums sometimes give visitors a recorded tour using an imaginary guide. Visitors are given a tape player and headphones and listen to spoken commentary that guides them through the rooms and exhibits. This eliminates jobs for live tour guides, but makes work for people who design and create the tapes. Visitors like it because they can move at their own pace and stop the tour anytime.

Peer-to-peer support facilitated by technology also represents a way for companies to reduce the use of paid workers. In an article titled "The Best Things in Cyberspace Are Free," Paul Wallich argues in the pages of *Scientific American* that free computer support via Usenet and Web pages is very effective. Discussing the popularity of the shareware operating system, Linux, he says "archives of Usenet articles about Linux contain about 200,000 postings, with 1000 or more added every day." [7] The sheer quantity of information about Linux has encouraged companies to use it even though it is "unsupported" shareware. The phenomenon that Linux illustrates is the new customer-driven economy, where grass roots support for a piece of shareware and the power of the Internet have pushed this upstart UNIX look-alike to where it has giant Microsoft worried.

Effect of Technology on Customers

It is not just the role of provider that has changed because of technology. Being a customer is also different. While the concept of "segmented" markets has been around for a long time, the idea of "relationship marketing" owes its existence to technology. Garth Hallberg, in a book titled *All Consumers Are Not Created Equal*, discusses brand loyalty and frequent buyer programs.[8] In order to know who is a frequent buyer, companies have to have a way to keep track of customers and their purchases. Computers and database software have made this fairly easy, and the cost of storing data gets cheaper all the time. Hallberg says the airlines' frequent flyer programs were the first loyalty programs and these led to an insight on the part of marketers that free tickets were not the only kind of reward. They found customers also were influenced by nonmonetary perks such as "upgrades, special reservation lines, and early boarding as well as less tangible benefits, like being greeted by name or 'being in the know' through advance information delivered by program newsletters."

Hallberg goes on to describe a program he worked on through Ogilvy & Mather Advertising for Kimberly-Clark, initiated in 1983, that he calls the "first nontransactional, nonreward-based brand loyalty program." The product was Huggies Disposable Diapers. The key element was a series of newsletters called *The Beginning Years* sent every three months to customers with babies. He says this provided the customer with "unexpected recognition from the marketer" as well as "information that was highly relevant and useful to the target audience." The program was rolled out nationally in 1985, reaching a large majority of the 3 million families with new babies.

This kind of campaign falls nicely into the category of enhanced encounter, with Kimberly-Clark wanting families with babies to think of them when they needed diapers; Moms got useful information and their appreciation helped build their loyalty to Huggies. What it did *not* do was build a database of who was actually buying Huggies, but Kimberly-Clark felt the newsletter was one of the reasons Huggies surpassed Pampers, becoming number one in sales of disposable diapers. Kimberly-Clark did maintain a database of families with babies, but did not track purchases. As computing power grew and loyalty programs proved their worth, the idea of tracking purchases and looking for meaning in data burst on the marketing scene.

The *One-to-One Future* by Peppers and Rogers was published in 1993, proclaiming that marketers should go for "share of customer," not share of market.[9] When Ogilvie and Mather built Huggies into the number one brand, they were still looking at share of market. They knew they had a lot of customers and they had a lot of names in a database, but which of those names actually bought Huggies? And how many boxes of Huggies did the buyers buy? Peppers and Rogers came along and told companies they should stop bothering with nonbuyers. Technology could let them know who the buyers were and what they bought. Using that data, you could sell good customers more of the same. You could reward those who bought lots of products and treat them differently from people who only occasionally bought your products. You could, they proclaimed, build a "relationship" with your best customers.

What is wrong with this picture? Consider high-income consumers who actually spend money on a variety of goods and services. Now the companies whose products they buy use the relationship marketing concept to store data on what they buy and send them offers to get them to buy more. If they order jazz music CDs, they get offers to buy more jazz. If they buy wine by the case, they get wine newsletters and offers from wineries to buy more wine. If they buy books online, they get e-mail about more books they might enjoy. Telemarketers call them with offers. Companies they buy from sell their customer lists, so if Winery A sells its customer list to Winery B, the customer gets notices from both. Information gathered from Web sites gets sold to marketers who send out more offers to customers based on which sites they visited or personal information left at sites requiring registration. The end result is a customer getting many more offers than she wants or can respond to, as Figure 8-1 shows.

Highly desirable customers—those who spend a lot—can find themselves with so many messages from sellers that they may just stop listening to any of them or demand that the government put a stop to some of the channels marketers use.

Figure 8-1   Too Many Offers

How many ways can you divide up the $100,000-a-year customer? And how many offers will that person even listen to or read? As more companies adopt relationship marketing, the more likely it becomes that there will be a backlash against it. The customer—whose connection with these companies is more like the connection of the hunted to the hunter than like a relationship—has only so much time and money to give to these marketers and their products.

What about customers who are not high income? They may get many fewer offers and find fewer opportunities for special buys. As marketers abandon customers who are not brand-loyal and who don't spend a lot, these consumers may find no one wants their business. The "share of customer" for someone earning $30,000 a year is going to be less than "share of customer" for someone earning $100,000 a year, and some marketers will decide these low spenders are not worth bothering with. However, others may see an opportunity for providing these lower-income customers with services they need and will pay for in affordable encounters.

An article that appeared in *Business Week* in April 1999 referred to this differential marketing as "a sophisticated kind of discrimination."[10] The article alleged that customers found not to be big spenders could be left on hold when they call, not informed of discount deals, and even cut off. The tone of the article warns the public about this new threat to privacy, that the service they receive (or lack of service) could be the result of data that businesses have collected about them. Organizations like the Electronic Frontier Foundation track threats to privacy. Its executive director, Tara Lemmey, is quoted in *Business Week* saying, "There's a fine line between good service and stalking."[11]

Businesses also are using data mining to reduce "churn" (the number of customers who leave). Software identifies customers who may be prone to sign up for someone else's service, then the software can automatically configure a customer retention program. Customers of US West, for example, whom such software identifies, are offered a special package of services at reduced rates, according to its Vice President of Relationships and Databases, Dennis DeGregor. He says data mining is proving more effective and less expensive than untargeted mass mailings and has lowered their churn rate.[12]

What could result from too much relationship marketing? Some possibilities:

1. Customers throw away all unsolicited mail.
2. Customers sign up for services that screen out telemarketers.
3. Customers delete e-mail from unknown sources or buy blocking software that filters out e-mail from unknown sources.
4. New Web privacy policies are mandated for all sites with something to sell; these policies let surfers deny or limit data to marketers or limit how it is used.
5. Consumers pressure the government to pass laws

against selling data or sending offers without first getting the customer's permission.

6. People pushing "simple living" ideas find many receptive listeners as well-heeled potential buyers turn against excessive marketing and reduce their consumption of goods and services.

Too much solicitation of choice customers is like the "tragedy of the commons" that Garret Hardin wrote about in a famous 1968 essay.[13] The customer, in this case, is the "commons" that all the marketers want; their time and attention have become a valuable resource. A "commons" always begins by being of benefit to those who use it. The idea goes back to the New England "commons" areas, land set aside for everyone's cows to graze. If everyone has the same number of cows and the number of cows doesn't exceed what the land can feed, this works out. But if a few people get more cows, then these people benefit more. If everyone else gets more cows so there are more cows than the land can support, then no one benefits, and eventually the land is ruined. A commons dilemma occurs when it is in any person's best interest to overuse a resource that everyone uses. Marketers' relentless pursuit of high-income customers will result in many feeling overwhelmed and offended by a bombardment of unsolicited and unwanted sales pitches. Relationship marketing, far from building relationships, may end up as a tragedy of the commons scenario.

In businesses that offer service in real relationships, the tragedy of the commons never occurs because the provider eventually has enough customers, and other relationship providers tend not to be so aggressive and steal from each other. Each can only service a limited number of customers and generally seeks unserviced customers—people moving to the area, young consumers just getting started, or the newly wealthy.

A Short History of Machine Service

If machines are not making business owners rich by waiting on customers and doing most of society's work, it's not because people haven't tried to make it happen. The vision of machines taking over work has long been part of our literature and culture. Its appeal to business owners is in eliminating the cost and problems associated with workers. It also has an appeal to workers, many of whom would be happy to let machines do their work if they could continue to have an income.

Machines that can perform automatic operations originated with the clockwork figures of medieval churches and eighteenth-century watchmakers. These automata were built mainly for entertainment, notable for their movements, not their capacity to interact with humans, but they must have given people the idea that machines could do useful work.

Computers added the important element of intelligence to machines. British mathematician Charles Babbage is credited with inventing the first true computer in the 1820s. He was never able to see if the machine he conceived would work because he could not raise the funds to build it. In 1991, British scientists, following Babbage's detailed drawings and specifications, constructed his "Difference Engine." The machine worked flawlessly, calculating up to a precision of thirty-one digits.[14]

Babbage, perhaps using his insights into the way a computing machine would operate, is as well known for his observations on the cost of labor. He realized that when the labor of building a product is separated into its component parts, each part done by a separate worker, the cost of production goes down because each worker can be paid less than a single worker who performed the entire task. Babbage's vision was remarkably predictive of our own time and, in a capitalist system, is the insight needed to wrest more profit from human labor and point the way to machine labor. It anticipates the ideas of Frederick Taylor.

Before the personal computer revolution of the late 1970s, computers were the province of specialists and were employed mainly to do tedious calculations, spawning the data processing industry. But computers could do much more than calculate missile trajectories and issue pay checks, and new roles appeared with the coming of small, inexpensive personal computers, beginning with the Altair in 1975, based on the Intel 8080 microprocessor. The Altair was sold as a kit and had to be programmed by pulling switches on the machine's front panel, but it was an immediate success. More advanced computers soon appeared as hobbyists wrote programs for TRS-80s, Ataris, Commodore PETs and Apple IIes.

One of the most popular of these early programs was called ELIZA, programmed by Joseph Weizenbaum way back in 1966. Versions of ELIZA were a favorite of early personal computer users, one of a small selection of off-the-shelf programs. Imitating a Rogerian therapist, ELIZA analyzed words the user typed and reflected back words that seemed to indicate it understood. For example, the user types, "My mother doesn't understand me." ELIZA answers, "Why do you say that?" The user replies, "She doesn't like my boyfriend and he's really a great person." ELIZA replies, "Who else thinks he's a great person?" The user types, "My father likes him." ELIZA replies, "What comes to mind when you think of your father?" And so on.

While early computer hobbyists just had fun with ELIZA, some people saw the superficial exchanges between user and computer as real therapy. When ELIZA first appeared, an article in *The Journal of Nervous and Mental Disease* hailed it as a way to make therapy more efficient.[15] The article suggested ELIZA be used in mental hospitals and said, "Several hundred patients an hour could be handled by a computer system designed for this purpose." Although ELIZA is considered a forerunner of Artificial Intelligence (AI), its inventor, Weizenbaum, thought it "understood" very little. He was distressed by some users' positive emotional response to it since he knew it relied on rules to make its responses. But something that looks like a relationship can feel like one—for a while. This is the same as mistaking looking good for being good. It brings to mind an old comedy routine that begins, "I'm not a doctor, but I do look like one . . ."

Appropriate and genuine emotion is needed for some kinds of service. A human counselor can empathize with someone suffering a tragedy like the death of a family member, while a machine cannot. Therapy requires a human connection and ELIZA, just a computer program, could not feel human emotion. Marketers today fall into a similar trap when they mistake encounters for relationships. The encounter provider, like ELIZA, follows a set of rules in her interactions with customers, regardless of how she actually feels. Of course, a human provider does have actual feelings; she is simply not free to express them. A machine will always follow the rules while a human may not.

In the popular culture, computers that mimic human feelings have tended to run amok. One was the psychopathic HAL in Arthur C. Clarke's masterpiece *2001: A Space Odyssey.* HAL's softly patronizing voice uttering the words, "I can't do that, Dave," as he tried to deal with conflicting goals, are memorable.

Another favorite of computer buffs is a *Star Trek* episode featuring the original cast. In this episode, "The Ultimate Computer," Captain Kirk must watch as the M5 computer, on its initial tryout, runs his ship. He learns the earlier models, M1 to M4, were "not entirely successful." But M5, which its inventor says "thinks," screws up, and torpedoes a harmless freighter. Later it fails to distinguish between war games and the real thing and fires on other Federation star ships. When the M5 computer, which has absorbed the values of its human creator, realizes what it has done, it "commits suicide" and turns itself off. Captain Kirk is relieved to learn that human judgment and intuition are still superior to that of the machine. M5's fictional creator, Dr. Richard Daystrom, wanted computers to run starships so man would not have to be exposed to dangers and would be free to do other things. This TV episode was made during the 1960s when there was a lot of fear about automation replacing people, so the story reflected the times and concluded that the human qualities of judgment and leadership could not be duplicated in a machine.

Many science fiction writers saw robots as the way machines would serve us. Isaac Asimov, who was responsible for "the three laws of robotics," popularized this idea.[16] Asimov's Robby was an early robot that the story says was built in 1996—another missed prediction. But Asimov also predicted a human backlash against robots. In his collection of robot stories, robots are eventually banished from earth for any purpose but scientific research.

Another fictional robot named Robby starred in the 1956

movie classic, *Forbidden Planet*. Although he was a mere movie prop, Robby cost $125,000 to build and appeared in other movies and TV shows as well. Robby could synthesize any substance and make clothes for his eccentric master's lovely daughter, but later robots performed more heroic feats. In *Star Wars*, lovable little R2D2 saves the galaxy by storing the plans for the empire's Death Star and delivering them to Obi Wan Kenobe; even the whiny "droid" C3PO does his best to carry out the orders of his boss, Luke Skywalker, including confrontation with the evil Jabba the Hut. These machines exemplify the tradition of robots as personal servants, an idealized view of machine as friend and helper.

The year 1996 came and went without any faithful "Robby the Robot" offered for sale, despite some working models that appeared in the early 1980s Heathkit and Androbot, a company founded by the legendary Nolan Bushnell, father of Pong, the first successful computer game, offered robot models to the public. One of Androbot's robots was called "BOB" (Brains On Board), perhaps a foreshadowing of Microsoft Bob, an "agent" who appeared some years later to teach us how to use Microsoft Office. Androbot's BOB was the highlight of the Winter 1983 Consumer Electronics Show in Las Vegas where it fetched cans of Budweiser for fascinated onlookers. The buzz over the new "robot revolution" dominated the news in the high-tech community throughout that year, as experts predicted a multibillion dollar industry. Bushnell himself expected these robots would become part of everyday life by the year 2000. He was wrong.[17] Consumers did not buy BOB, just as they later rejected Microsoft Bob.

NASA has added to robotics, creating machines that can move on the most inhospitable of terrains, including the rover that cruised around the surface of Mars and thrilled millions of visitors to NASA's Web site in 1998. Duplicates of Rover did well on the toy market. NASA, with no budget for manned missions, has had to rely on its robots and computers to explore our solar system and beyond. They've proved that robots can go out in space and send back useful information, but the robot, unlike a human, can never feel the thrill of going "where no one has gone before."

During the 1980s, Americans often found themselves answering the phone and listening to a robot whose pitch was anything but personal. Telemarketers were making use of new machines that could dial a block of phone numbers and spiel out a message as the phone was answered. People found they could not even hang up on these robots. The Telephone Consumer Protection Act of 1991 made it illegal to use an autodialing phone machine to make calls using a prerecorded voice. This illustrates the kind of backlash that can develop against unpleasant and intrusive automated processes.

Computers have become ubiquitous. They hide in all kinds of appliances: cash registers, medical diagnostic equipment, hand-held car diagnostic devices, even microwave ovens. As these devices get smarter, they can provide service in a way that emulates the clerk who calls the customer by name or the mail-order catalog representative who knows the customer's sweater size. Web sites that are interactive and greet users by name would seem to be the successors to all this. Mechanical robots never made the grade with the public, but animated characters and agents on TV and the Internet are becoming common.

Mechanical robots have been more successful in factories. In 1995, about 700,000 industrial robots were in use throughout the world—only 60,000 of these in the United States although many more could be employed.[18] The industrial smokestack industries, particularly the auto industry, have been quietly employing robots to do work once done by people. Now it's the service sector's turn to find ways to use machines instead of people.

How Relationship Providers Use Technology

If encounter jobs are the new blue collar work, what about relationship providers? How do they use technology? Relationship providers tend to use computers in a more generic way, selecting and learning to use the tools that help them serve their customers. They may use a number of different kinds of software, each for a different purpose, such as word processing for correspondence, spreadsheets for bookkeeping, desktop publishing for brochures and newsletters, a Web browser for research, and e-mail to keep in touch with customers and colleagues.

Empowered by Technology

In relationship work, technology is empowering, giving workers tools to accomplish more and to absorb and understand information of use to their customers. Doctors can take the output of imaging technologies to locate a tumor more quickly, lawyers can search databases and quickly find citations important to a case, an accountant can try different ways to take a deduction to determine which is of most benefit, and stockbrokers can check the rise and fall of various funds and quickly sell shares without leaving their chairs.

Creative work gets new dimensions from technology. Although actors and musicians are being replaced by animation and synthesizers, other artists who use the technology are finding a source of creative liberation. Graphic designers can lay out brochures without expensive film-stripping, photographers can modify and enhance pictures easily, musicians can morph sounds and sample words into new musical forms, animators can create fanciful landscapes and amazing creatures, and artists can use the techniques of both painting and drawing in one work using sophisticated software. Technology mainly replaces routine work while offering incredible new tools for those who learn to use them and new levels of experience for the customers of these exciting forms of artistic expression.

Technical work has leaped forward using the tools of technology. Products can be designed in 3D and viewed from all angles on a computer screen, materials can be tested without building the product, cars can be crashed in the computer instead of the test track, and consumer products can be prototyped in a solid form in minutes with instructions from design software. Engineers can be more productive using powerful computers and software that they control and use to produce more with fewer people.

Monitoring the Work of Professionals

While encounter workers are often monitored by the computers they use, the same thing can happen to professionals. Where professionals work for an organization rather than as independent practitioners, pressures for cost-savings and efficiency lead to monitoring. HMOs decide how many patients doctors should see in one day, and computers spit out data showing when tests should be ordered, when certain treatments are warranted, and when they are not. Pharmacists, too, have been under pressure to fill more prescriptions, leading at least one state (North Carolina) to introduce a bill to limit the number of prescriptions they can fill in a day as a protection for consumers.

Doctors don't like what they see as interference with their professional judgment, but data turn up interesting facts that managers naturally feel justified in using to set standards. Why, for example, are rates for Caesarian section births at 24 percent in this country when experts say the rate should not exceed 15 percent? Why should rates be higher for women who have private medical insurance, are private rather than public clinic patients, are older, are married, have higher levels of education, and are in a higher socioeconomic bracket?[19] Or why should GM employees get cardiac-bypass surgery at twice the rate of comparable groups?[20] Could it have to do with their full-coverage health insurance and the profit in these operations? GM's executive director for health plans, Jim Cubbin, thinks so. "We are convinced that there is a very high percentage of very low-quality care provided across the country," he says.[21] These are the kinds of questions raised when managers begin looking at numbers. These questions are legitimate and provide a chance for doctors to look at their own practices.

If it's OK to monitor the time it takes an auto mechanic to replace brake pads, why not the time it takes a physician to perform a hernia operation? Exactly what is it that separates professionals from other service workers? David Maister, in his book *True Professionalism*, points out that the opposite of "professional" is not "unprofessional" but "technician." Technicians have specialized skills, but they do not take initiative or engage in the kind of independent judgment that is expected of professionals. "Professionalism," concludes Maister, "is predominantly an attitude, not a set of competencies."[22]

Clashing Cultures Interfere With Intelligent Use of Technology

Technology is too important for any service business to ignore. Even relationship providers will be at a severe disadvantage if they try to do business with just a phone and a Rolodex. Customers expect providers to have fax, e-mail, and a Web site and be able to receive computer files. In encounter businesses, computer technology plays a crucial role, and using it correctly can be the difference between success or failure. Unfortunately, differing views about use of technology plagues some companies.

James Martin writes in *Cybercorp* about the clash of culture between technophobes and technophiles.[23] The MBA in his gray flannel suit who talks about Return on Investment (ROI) and shareholder value does not trust the long-haired computer guy in scruffy clothes who wants to talk about megabytes and bandwidth. The techie types often do not think much about the effect of technology on business, and the business types do not think much about use of new technology to obtain an advantage. Martin tells of one company that referred to its computer people as "Martians" because they spoke a strange language no one understood. He tells us about a 1995 survey of 250 senior executives, conducted by *Computerworld*, who were asked, "To what future position would you consider appointing your senior information technology manager?" An astounding 48 percent said they would not consider appointing their information technology (IT) chief to *any* senior business position.

This antagonism is illustrated in a story that's making the rounds of the Internet. It goes like this:

> A man is flying in a hot air balloon and realizes he is lost. He reduces altitude and spots a man down below. He lowers the balloon further and shouts, "Excuse me, can you tell me where I am?" The man below says, "Yes you're in a hot air balloon, hovering thirty feet above this field."

"You must work in Information Technology," says the balloonist.
"I do," replies the man. "How did you know?" "Well," says the balloonist, "everything you have told me is technically correct, but it's of no use." The man below says, "You must work in business." "I do," replies the balloonist, "but how did you know?" "Well", says the man, "you don't know where you are, or where you're going, but you expect me to be able to help. You're in the same position you were before we met, but now it's my fault."

But, Martin tells us, business people need to understand technology to succeed. "To implement the cybercorp mechanisms and opportunities that are necessary across all our institutions today," says Martin, "a high level of technical knowhow is needed; a chief executive needs to be fully in control of how technology is used."[24]

Organizations need to use technology to do things in new ways. This is not just the automation of the past but adopting new paradigms. Online stores are a new way of selling. Digital cameras are a new way to think about making pictures. Gene therapy is a new way to think about disease. Technology can sweep away entire businesses that don't see change happening under their noses. Martin mentions the Encyclopedia Britannica company that continued putting out giant sets of books, oblivious to the fact that its real competition was not from other producers of giant sets of books but from a new place: Microsoft simply rolled over them with its multimedia CD-ROM encyclopedia, *Encarta*. Britannica has survived by moving online with a subscription service.

Network hardware maker Cisco System, whose motto is "empowering the Internet generation," is selling products that will bring about the convergence of data, voice, and video. Your PC will also be your telephone, your TV, your radio, your mail box, and your music player. This has many implications for business, which must use these new channels for reaching and selling to customers.

New Technology and How to Use It

Computer support people have been, as expected, early adopters of new technology. Training is often conducted in many locations simultaneously by use of remote conferencing equipment consisting of video cameras and networked computers running shared software in multiple locations. Business meetings can be conducted this way to save travel time and costs, and even medical diagnoses can be made remotely. There will undoubtedly be more applications of remote conferencing in the future.

Cable TV is another new source for training and support, as pioneered by publisher Ziff-Davis with its ZDTV. Viewers call in technical questions to real-time live programs like "Call for Help" and "The Screen Savers," many of them using netcams—personal video cameras attached to their PC. People watching the program see a picture with primitive, jerky motion of the person calling in while casually dressed hosts talk and punch up demonstrations on the keyboard in front of them. All the while, the bottom of the TV screen has scrolling e-mail messages coming in from viewers who apparently find this learning method personal, as many messages simply say "Hi, Leo!" or "Hi, Kate!" to Leo Laporte and Kate Botello, cohosts of "The Screen Savers." The scrolling e-mail is a technique also used by MTV, the pioneer music video channel, where viewers send notes to VJs with requests and personal greetings. ZDTV's Web site encourages viewers to buy netcams and urges them to "join our community." Their community has no streets and no houses; it's a community of people with a shared interest—a virtual community.

Relationship providers can participate in the virtual community, finding customers and associates online. These life-altering technologies are not available to everyone; setting up a computer with all the gadgets is still expensive. We haven't reached a point where every home has a computer or every householder is ordering groceries over the Internet. The ubiquitous URLs (Web addresses) on every ad and billboard are still foreign lingo to some. The new gulf that separates people may be technology: those who have it and those who don't. Relationship providers will be dealing mainly with those who have it. They need to understand and use technology to keep ahead of their competitors and, in some cases, to compete more effectively with encounter providers.

Understanding technology can also become a business, as some people become "infomediaries," working with a provider to deliver information using search tools. Information is power in the brave new service business. It may become increasingly difficult for organizations to have within themselves all the technical skills required to operate in today's technical environment, opening the way for technical consultants.

As long ago as 1980, Peter Drucker saw how computers would change business. In *The Information Explosion,* he wrote:

> The critical problem will not be how to get or to process information but rather to define what information really is. This is a task that cannot be left to that mythical creature, the "information specialist." Information is the manager's main tool, indeed his "capital," and it is he who must decide what information he needs and how to use it.[25]

Thinking of technology as just a way to automate old processes can be fatal. Vaudeville could not survive radio, a technology that brought entertainment right into peoples' homes and for free. Don Peppers and Martha Rogers open *The One-to-One Future* by talking about the year the telegram died, killed by a technology it could not survive called a fax machine. The automobile, they say, was another discontinuity in American life. "Who could have imagined," they opine in the pages of their seminal book, "that a noisy, smelly, unreliable machine would eventually be responsible for the creation of the suburbs; the fractionalization of families; and the growth of supermarkets, malls, and the interstate highway system?"[26]

Who, indeed. Technology is the wild card in business. Something new can come along and destroy businesses that once worked perfectly. Efficiency doesn't guarantee survival and is hardly even important to many relationship businesses such as those that don't compete with encounter businesses but rely on customers looking for traditional service. Peter Drucker wrote in one of his books, "The last buggy whip factory was no doubt a model of efficiency."[27] Perhaps the last telegraph office was, too. Maybe the last video rental store will have a lightening fast procedure for renting you a movie, but there will be no customers left to appreciate it. They will all be home downloading movies through their cable system.

Technology tends to turn mature businesses into encounter businesses and make opportunities in new areas. George Lucas employs rooms full of computer animators but puts actors out of work. Like others displaced by automation, actors will find other outlets, such as training videos and the huge number of productions for cable TV.

Conclusion

Technology created the modern manufacturing plant with its automated processes, and it is transforming service as well. Technology has created the equivalent of blue collar jobs for encounter workers, but in relationship work, it tends to empower those who use it. The problem is many relationship providers don't keep pace, with development in technology.

Points to remember:

- Providers working in encounter jobs tend to rely on technology but not learn much about it.
- Providers working in relationships use technology in a more flexible and general way, and learn what they need to know to use hardware and software that helps them serve customers.

These differences are summarized in Table 8-2.

Table 8-2   Encounter/Relationship Use of Computers

Encounter Providers	*Relationship Providers*
• Use specialty software	• Use general purpose software
• Hardware/software provided by the organization	• Select their own hardware/software
• Job depends on technology	• Technology is an adjunct to the job

In the coming years, businesses that integrate technology into their operation and have the insight to see new ways to do something through new technology will have the best chance of success.

Notes

1. Thomas, Paulette. "Creators of Staples Are Now Aiming to Reinvent Dry-Cleaning Business," *Wall Street Journal*, April 27, 1999.
2. Winner, Langdon. "Silicon Valley Mystery Home," *Variations on a Theme Park* (New York: The Noonday Press, 1992).
3. "Computer Help Lines Fail to Click OK In Survey That Finds Array of Glitches," *Wall Street Journal*, August 26, 1997.
4. Cusack, Michael. *Online Customer Care: Applying Today's Technology to Achieve World-Class Customer Interaction* (Milwaukee, Wisc.: American Society for Quality (ASQ), 1998).
5. Personal communications with Ms. Tucker-Welch.
6. "Cyber Call Centers 1998: From Internet Enabled to Internet Architected Call Centers," *Internet Computing Strategies* series from The Yankee Group, 3:2 (February 1998).
7. Wallich, Paul. "The Best Things in Cyberspace Are Free," *Scientific American*, March 1999.
8. Hallberg, Garth. *All Consumers Are Not Created Equal* (New York: John Wiley and Sons, Inc., 1996).
9. Peppers, Don and Martha Rogers. *The One-to-One Future* (New York: Currency Doubleday, 1993).
10. "Special Report: Privacy," *Business Week*, April 5, 1999.
11. Ibid.
12. Babcock, Charles. "ISPs Debate the Pros and Cons of Data Mining," from ZDNet's "Interactive Week Online," December 14, 1998.
13. Hardin, Garret. "The Tragedy of the Commons," *Science*, 1968, Vol. 162.
14. "Babbage, Charles," *Microsoft Encarta Encyclopedia 99* (Microsoft Corporation, 1993–1998).
15. "A Computer Method of Psychotherapy: Preliminary Communication," *The Journal of Nervous and Mental Disease*, 142: 2 (1966), quoted in Barbara Garson, *The Electronic Sweatshop* (New York: Simon & Schuster, 1988).

16. Asimov, Isaac. "The Three Laws of Robotics," *I, Robot* (New York: Doubleday,1987; originally published by Smith & Street, 1942).
17. Dvorak, John C. "What Ever Happened to . . . Androbot?" *Computer Shopper,* July 1997.
18. "Robot," *Microsoft Encarta Encyclopedia 99* (Microsoft Corporation, 1993–1998).
19. Cesarean Fact Sheet (www.childbirth.org/section/CSFact.html).
20. White, Joseph B. "GM Sets Curbs in Health Plan For First Time, to Limit Costs," *Wall Street Journal,* March 8, 1999.
21. Ibid.
22. Maister, David. *True Professionalism* (New York: The Free Press, 1997).
23. Martin, James. *Cybercorp* (New York: AMACOM, 1998).
24. Ibid.
25. Drucker, Peter. *The Information Explosion* (New York: Times Book, 1985).
26. Peppers, Don and Martha Rogers. *The One-to-One Future* (New York: Currency Doubleday, 1993).
27. Beatty, Jack. *The World According to Peter Drucker* (New York: Broadway Books, 1998).

Chapter Nine
Service Within, Outside, and Between Organizations: Creating Ties That Bind

Service Within Business Organizations

We've been talking about businesses that serve the public, but astute business people realize that everyone has a customer, even people in jobs that do not serve the public. Each person's customers are those people who depend on her. Most companies have service units whose purpose is specifically to service the rest of the organization. Businesses also interact with other businesses in which they can be either the provider or the customer. This chapter looks at in-house service units and company-to-company service.

In-House Service Units

Some examples of departments that exist to serve the rest of the organization are computer support, medical unit, employee assistance, organizational development, travel office, building services, legal department, and human resources. These organizations within an organization are comprised of providers who have as customers everyone else in the company.

As with individuals, internal service units can offer service in either an encounter or in a relationship. Management may view support units as a financial drain, since such units generate no revenue, and operating them is expensive. Internal support groups, therefore, are often under pressure to cut costs. That usually drives support units toward encounter-type service. Because of this, the customers of these groups may wish for more service or better service than they get. Provider and customer roles are within the context of a company, with the company determining the level of service. Providers working inside an organization have the same dynamics as those who serve the general public, but they have more opportunities to get to know their customers, since their customers are limited to the people who work in that location (or for the company). That may lead customers to try to establish relationships with specific providers they feel give good service or are especially capable. This can lead to conflicts, as customers want relationships, but management wants to provide encounters.

Relationships

To structure service in a relationship, the business unit assigns each person working in a provider role to service specific customers. The University of Arizona's Human Resources (HR) group works this way. Each HR representative is assigned a specific college within the university and has an office there to serve the employees who work at that college. Such a unit could have been organized as encounters by keeping all the HR people in a central administration building and having customers call a central number and talk to whoever is free.

We can use the same C-O-P model to show how internal support operations can be structured. In an internal organization offering service in relationships, the support unit is the organization in the model, shown in Figure 9-1. The providers and the customers are employed by the same company. This creates tight O-P and C-P links.

Customers of an internal service unit may not have a choice of providers; in the case of the University of Arizona HR unit, a provider is assigned. However, when people deal with each other over time, they get to know each other's strengths and weaknesses in the same way as people who choose each other. The customer knows which tasks the provider does well and which she doesn't do well because of repeated interactions. Although it may seem that this format would work best for professional ser-

Figure 9-1   Relationship Service Within an Organization: Company Support Unit

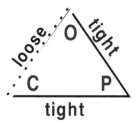

vices, it could apply even to the building handymen or janitors. People like to deal with the same person each time.

There are few drawbacks to a company setting up internal service in relationships. Providers usually cannot leave and "steal" customers since the customers are not free to choose outside providers. There is less need for expensive technology. Providers are more responsible for learning the needs of their customers and assessing whether they are satisfied with the service. There is less need for managers to define a service process. Each provider can communicate with his customers and work out methods of providing the service.

Relationships build trust, and that is valuable in company service in which customers often feel providers have a conflict between carrying out the goals of the company and providing useful service. Customers going to a company-provided counselor may wonder if what they say is really confidential. Computer users may feel support people operate more like "computer cops," enforcing company rules and restrictions on computer use more than helping customers get the tools they need. These conflicts can be real, but customers are more likely to trust providers when they work in relationships.

Encounters

More commonly, service within an organization is offered in encounters, as depicted in Figure 9-2. Customers come to the service unit's location or call when they need service and deal with whomever is available. The service unit could be a word processing pool, a graphic arts unit, building services, or computer support.

Figure 9-2 Encounter Service Within an Organization: Company Support Unit

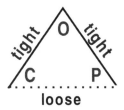

Because the provider always has information about the customer, and the customer will always be back, encounter service within an organization is always a pseudo-relationship, with the potential to be an enhanced encounter.

Internal support groups work for the same organization as their customers, so providers and customers can learn about each other if they want to. If they all work in the same building, they may see each other regularly. This can lead to customers trying to circumvent an encounter system by getting to know one of the providers and trying to deal with that person each time. A company that finds this happening should consider whether they could switch to a relationship format.

Encounter formats can make use of division of labor, having different people performing different parts of the work. For example, a human resources unit might have one person who does recruiting and another who handles insurance issues. A computer support unit might have one person for hardware problems, another person for software support, and someone else for network problems. This specialization may make it easier to hire service people. (How easy is it to find a computer support person expert in hardware, software, and networking?) Specialization makes it more difficult to offer service in relationships, although all providers could act as contact people for specific groups of customers, then refer work to each other. In larger organizations, a team of providers could service the same group of customers.

Managers who work in manufacturing companies and are put in charge of a service unit should consider the differences between managing people who build or assemble products and managing people who serve other people. In building a product, the worker just needs to get the motions right and put the product together correctly. Interacting with customers cannot be as easily reduced to a correct or standard set of actions.

It is important for managers to get buy-in for new work rules for service teams. When workers feel they are being treated unfairly, they are more likely to make their own unhappiness known to customers, especially when the providers and customers work for the same organization. Service units need to work together to establish procedures and working methods. Managers need to share information about budgets and goals so workers don't feel alienated.

Under cost pressures, management may try to limit use of a support service. For instance, a travel unit may offer services only in the afternoon, and a computer support group may require customers to come to a specific room or take only e-mail requests. The assumption in limiting services is that if the service were more available, customers would use too much of the service, and the cost would be too high. This can create antagonism between customers and the service unit, with implications for providers who have to face hostile customers.

Another source of anger for users is if ordinary employees have an encounter service but upper management has a relationship service. For example, in a large manufacturing company, most employees with a computer problem must call a help desk and wait their turn for service. But the same company has an elite support group that services vice presidents with ailing PCs who get immediate help. This is justified, of course, on the basis that the vice president's time is worth hundreds of dollars per hour, but that does not lessen the resentment of lower-level workers who can't get their work done when their PC dies and are expected to exercise patience waiting for the technician to show up at their desk. Most companies with elite service teams try to keep it quiet, but the jobs are plum positions for those who have them. These providers may attend many of the same meetings and training sessions as other providers who serve nonelite customers; naturally, the providers to the elite talk about their great assignment. Providers serving the elite can usually operate outside the rules. If a vice president wants non-standard software or the latest hardware gadget, he gets it. This kind of special treatment for some can make the customers cynical about the service they receive.

Managers who operate encounter services need some method of tracking the quality of service. Some establish a Service Level Agreement (SLA) with the units they serve or conduct focus groups or do surveys to find out if their customers are satisfied. They also rely on statistics that are compiled monthly and then compared to what was promised in the SLA. While some of this may be necessary and useful, their focus should be on supporting their staff so the staff can serve customers. And they should start thinking of their staff as their own "customer" because their staff needs leadership and the right tools to work effectively. Service managers who are viewed as bean counters by their workers are not likely to have as committed and loyal a workforce as those managers whose workers feel they are supporting them in their work.

Outsourcing

Many companies outsource an entire service unit as a way to save costs and obtain the services of a company with a lot of expertise in one area. Outsourcing is a popular way to obtain an ancillary service like computer support, designing and printing company literature, food service, or building maintenance. It can theoretically lower company costs, making a better impression on Wall Street for companies concerned with shareholder value. But managers sometimes forget that outside providers are not going to have much loyalty to the company they support. Call center vendors, who are more aware of the lack of incentives for good service, often put in place extreme measures for closely watching workers. This can lead to a circle of unhappy workers servicing unhappy customers.

Using an outsourcing vendor to provide help desk support is a growing trend. Gartner Group says over 40 percent of company help desks are at least partially outsourced.[1]

A number of cities that lack smokestack industries have gone after call centers as a way to provide jobs. The Southwest, especially Phoenix and Tucson, has many such operations as do

Omaha and Dallas. A November 1998 *National Geographic* article on Omaha called it "the nation's telemarketing capital" and informs us that "every evening about 30,000 of its citizens—more than 4 percent of the population—are dialing up their fellow Americans, trying to sell them anything from frozen steaks to CDs to the idea that they should switch phone companies."[2] Call centers gravitate to locations where residents speak English without an identifiable accent and where there are good telecommunciations facilities.

It is typical for these centers to pay low wages and closely supervise workers, allowing little flexibility for workers who may occasionally be late because of child care requirements or a car breaking down. Many are people without a lot of resources. When they arrive at work and put on their headset, most are kept busy with few breaks in the action. Art Quinn, manager of computer telephony integration for US West, quoted in *The Arizona Daily Star*, says "It's a high-stress, fast-paced job. They are handling one situation and move quickly on to the next."[3]

Providers who work in call centers servicing high tech companies command the highest pay and respect of call center workers because, theoretically, they have superior skills. Some companies may provide these technical support representatives with a month of training, and new hires may have a mentor for up to six months. It costs something to get and train better people, but it should result in a better experience for the customer.

To Outsource or Not to Outsource

If service customers prefer working in relationships with providers, can that still happen if the service is outsourced? It is an interesting question without a clear answer. A number of factors mitigate against relationships when the service is outsourced:

- The provider does not have an insider's understanding of the company culture.
- The outsourced unit may be in a different physical location where providers and customers would not see each other.

- The customers may feel the providers are outsiders who are not "good enough" to be company employees.
- The vendor company may not have any experience providing service in relationships.

Since outsourcing is supposed to save money, companies are usually looking for a situation in which the providers are paid less than company employees. That generally leads to breaking down tasks into components to make the work as simple as possible. Outsourced services almost always end up as encounter services. With high turnover and many providers serving many customers, the service may not even rise to the level of pseudo-relationship. Customers may experience it as a different provider each time, with no control over who they talk to and no way to report back when the service is not satisfactory.

Outsourcing does have its strengths. The vendor company has experience at what it does and may offer more opportunity for providers than it would have as employees of the company it serves. The company that hires an outsourced service does not have to provide any management of that service. While that saves time and money, it also creates a loss of control over the outsourced function.

Managing a Company Support Center

Let's take a look at one company's internal computer support operation. Imagine you are managing a computer help desk operation that services sixteen buildings full of employees and contractors for a major manufacturer. There are several different phone numbers, and each location has its own onsite technicians who respond to the calls. Generally, customers get an answering machine and leave a message, then a technician calls them back.

You have been told to bring down the cost of this operation. You decide to contract with a vendor to open a single-point-of-contact (SPOC) call center that would answer 40 percent of the problems over the phone. The other calls, those that require a site visit, would be referred to your onsite support people who would go to users' desks to fix their problems. This should enable you to operate with fewer skilled onsite support people, saving the cost of their salaries. Users will have the convenience of only one phone number to call and will always get a person on the line. Sounds good.

You make a deal with a well-known vender who sends you people to staff the call center. But it doesn't quite work out like you expected. The vendor sends you people who know next to nothing about the software and hardware they are supposed to support. Your customers start referring to your help line as "dial a dummy." The call center people close only 20 percent of the calls instead of 40 percent, and your onsite support people are as busy as ever. Users still stop them in the hallways and ask for help instead of calling the SPOC help line. Supervisors still ask for specific staff members whose skills they trust instead of accepting the next available technician. The call center people are frustrated and quit. In the first year, you have 100 percent turnover. Reducing your budget for the coming year seems out of the question, and customer complaints are piling up. What to do? More importantly, what went wrong?

The above scenario actually happened at the product development division of a major manufacturing company. The managers responsible for computer support ended up modifying their original plan. They sent their in-house people to work the phones with just a few people from the vendor. This way, their experienced people could teach the call center people (who did not do any work at customers' desks) and take the calls the vendor-supplied people couldn't answer. With this modified plan in place, the help desk finally achieved its goal of closing 40 percent of calls on the phone.

But the account manager involved in the pilot realized that closing 40 percent of the calls over the phone did not represent 40 percent of the work. The calls closed over the phone were the easy ones. With computer support, users' problems can get quite complicated, and some calls required a lot of a technician's time to fix. This led the account manager to another insight: They were measuring the wrong things. The vendor-supplied people had an incentive to close as many calls as possible because that is how their supervisors measured their productivity. So if someone called and hung up right away, they counted it as a closed call. If there were two parts to someone's questions, they counted it as two calls to make their numbers look better. The account manager came to believe that metrics could not tell the whole story of who was a valuable worker or indicate customer satisfaction. The technician who took on tough problems and took time to solve them properly did not look as good on paper as the person who had easy questions and quickly closed the calls. Some even closed calls before they were solved just to get better numbers.

There were many bumps along the way. The onsite support people balked at having to do phone duty, which they regarded as beneath their skill level. They didn't like working with the vendor, whose supervisory methods seemed draconian. The call center supervisor would stand by the door in the morning looking at his watch, noting anyone who was even a minute late and contacting that person's immediate superior about the tardiness. The vendor-supplied people were paid only six dollars an hour, which pretty much explained their lack of skills. The account manager, hoping to get better people, asked the vendor to supply resumes and allow his supervisors to interview call center applicants. He found the resumes often contained exaggerations. One candidate was said to have "service experience," but the interviewer found his experience consisted of serving ice cream cones at a dairy bar.

The arrangement also meant there were two sources of management—the company managers and the vendor managers, who had to work together. Their interests were not always the same, since the company's overriding concern was to provide good computer support for its engineering staff, and the vendor's main concern was to make a profit providing the service. The managers and supervisors who had formerly been in charge of the help desks now had people doing support who no longer reported to them. But there was a good side to this. For the account manager, that meant he could now concentrate on working with his customers, who were mainly product design engineers, to fine-tune and improve the service. He and his site managers established real relationships with customer managers and supervisors and continued to allow customers to work with a preferred technician where possible.

This company is still feeling its way, but clearly, having low-paid contractors working beside their own better-compensated employees is a situation sure to lead to low morale for everyone. Could this company provide computer support in relationships? They would have a much lower investment in the equipment and software needed to operate a call center but a bigger investment in people. Support calls often can't be solved by the person taking the call and some service requests must be referred to someone with different expertise. However, if one support person were assigned to a given number of customers, that person could serve as initial screener. Technicians would have to work together across customer groups or have access to a "second tier" support group to whom they could hand off those problems they couldn't solve. In smaller companies where everyone works on similar PCs, the relationship method might work well. The account manager noted that his customers typically want this, but their support model does not include personal representatives, instead treating all providers as interchangeable.

Company call centers staffed by low-paid unskilled people may not result in savings if internal customers don't get the help they need and end up paying for help elsewhere. Departments that are supposed to use the hotline might hire their own technician, or they might start using another service for which they pay a fee. If company policies prevent them from doing this, they might tie up a lot of someone's time with complaints or circumvent the process by going directly to the most competent technician and demanding service.

Assigning a specific technician to work with a group of customers lets the customer deal with someone she knows and who knows the customer's level of technical expertise. It provides some degree of comfort and gives the provider a sense of ownership of the problem. Assigning technicians to a specific customer group is going to involve paying the technician better. But the technician, who would have a more interesting and satisfying job, might stay longer. There might never be enough candidates who could just step into the role of relationship provider. Companies would have to offer apprenticeships or internships to bright people who could learn to do the work or start a training unit, as CDW has done. Although training is expensive, so is turnover. According to Jim Harris, author of *Finding and Keeping Great Employees,* it costs from two-and-a-half to five times the base salary of the job to replace a skilled employee.[4]

Companies need to decide whether it's better to operate their own service unit or outsource the entire service. The situation least likely to result in happy workers is a mixed group of in-house employees and low-paid contractors. How does a six-dollar-an-hour contract person feel about working next to someone making thirty dollars an hour? Resentment seems a fitting description. The higher-paid person resents it as well. The implication is that someone making a lot less money can do the job. This is not likely to inspire loyalty in either employee or contractor. If the service is kept in-house and operated as a relationship service using only company employees, it eliminates the problems of unequal pay and unequal skills. Creating conditions where providers like their work and want to stay is in the company's best interests. It saves money over the long run, and satisfied providers are likely to be servicing satisfied customers.

Leveraging Service Through Technology

Organizations are using the Internet to reach customers; internal organization can do the same, using their company Intranet. Support groups can use Web pages to explain their service, list their personnel, and use interactive Web-based software to take requests or suggestions. This use of technology eliminates some face-to-face and phone contact, but it also provides more information about the services available and, through effective design, can make customers feel welcome. It can allow some services to work asynchronously, reducing the need to have someone always on duty. Customers can get the information they need any time at their own convenience. If information is personal or confidential, passwords can be implemented.

A research service could take all requests online, acknowledge each request through e-mail, then deliver the requested material to the requester's desk through interoffice mail (or e-mail attachment, if the material exists electronically).

Companies can also make use of Usenet news groups and chat rooms to provide peer-to-peer help. News groups for specific areas of concern (in human resources, sharing information on medical providers, for example) can reduce the number of calls to a service unit. Chat rooms can provide real-time help as one person interacts with another to discuss something of mutual interest. These are especially helpful as add-ons to encounter-type service. They let customers help each other and provide some of the emotional support missing from encounter systems.

Companies cannot use technology effectively if they cannot attract and retain qualified people; and even when they do, their use of technology may not be effective if their computer development and support activity becomes isolated. Hal Rosenbluth has written an interesting book called *The Customer Comes Second and Other Secrets of Exceptional Service.*[5] Rosenbluth's company, Rosenbluth Travel, has an "employee first" policy that uses Schneider and Bowen's concept that happy and satisfied employees will result in happy customers.[6] In keeping with this policy, they have integrated their computer people into the rest of the company and try to let their employees choose their technology tools whenever possible. He says in his book, "We involve our technology associates in all aspects of our company and seek to have people throughout the company involved in technology." His company has avoided thinking of technology as a pure service provided by a separate group to the rest of the company.

When technology is part of everyone's work, it can help reduce the "us" against "them" mentality that sometimes develops. In the same manufacturing company discussed in the section above, a technically savvy customer who resented the help desk dictating his working conditions began calling in "nuisance" requests (like requesting that the clock on his UNIX workstation be reset when it was a few minutes off) just to annoy them and goad them into policy changes. This company was losing a lot of expertise and antagonizing valuable workers because it made technology an island.

Person-to-Person Service Within an Organization

Some jobs within an organization involve one person working as a personal assistant to another. Administrative assistants (who used to be called a "secretaries"), schedulers, production assistants, or anyone who essentially works for one person, doing whatever that person needs to have done, fit this category. These are relationship jobs within an organization, and the number of these kinds of jobs is shrinking as companies adopt encounter-format service.

While it may seem extravagant for someone to have a personal assistant, when you consider that relationships get more efficient with time, it often makes sense. Basically relationship providers with one client, personal assistants can get to know the other person very well and provide highly customized service that exactly meets the other person's needs. The weakness is the same as for other kinds of relationships. The provider cannot always be available, and if the workload increases, the provider must work extra hours. The cost of personal assistants leads companies to adopt encounter systems, which seem more efficient. By having a pool of providers, someone is always there to handle the work.

But this ignores the fact that the personal assistant knows the customer's needs and doesn't have to ask for instructions. He does his work based on his desire to win approval and be of value to his boss and also on knowing he must see her every working day. His boss gets to work with someone she knows and trusts rather than a stranger from the "pool" or a temp sent over for the day. These are advantages that don't show up on a balance sheet and are not reflected in service metrics.

Service Between Companies

Companies have as customers people who buy the product or service they provide, but companies also have other companies as customers. Service transactions between companies can be relationships or encounters.

Relationships

Relationships are common between people in two organizations that have working arrangements. When companies make partnering agreements or contract for work or services with other companies, the people in those companies who are assigned to work together on a regular basis form relationships. When one performs a service for the other, this becomes a service triangle, with the provider's company as the organization.

Consulting and Organizational Customers

Consultants are an example of relationship providers who almost always have companies for customers, whether those consultants are part of a large firm or work individually. Consultants will probably deal with one person or perhaps a few people at the customer organization. The provider technically is engaged to work for a company, but his work actually depends on his relationship with people at the client company with whom he works, who determine his purpose in being there (see Figure 9-3). His ability to get more work at that company depends on the relationships he builds. Maintaining those relationships may become more important to some professionals than their ties to their firm.

David Maister discusses the problem of professionals becoming cynical as their firms seem to pursue short-term gains rather than take any risks or look to long-term development of people. "Some professionals," he writes, "motivated by what they see as self-protection, are participating less in firm efforts and acting more as independent contractors or free agents."[7] Sometimes the client company will hire away the consultant, which may serve the interests of all concerned. The professional firm cannot provide opportunities for all their associates to move up in the firm, and having a former colleague at the customer company builds more ties between the two organizations. Maister notes that professional firms wanting to retain good people should give them the support they need to succeed. "Most professional firms," he writes, "are very good at demanding that people succeed, but are pathetically bad at helping them to do that." For professionals who work for such firms, their strong ties are to their clients, not to their own organization.

Many service providers prefer working for organizational customers rather than for individuals, since businesses have more money to spend, require more service, and usually pay their bills on time. An architect or landscaper, for example, might seek institutional work as he finds residential customers change their minds about what they want, or interfere too much with the process, or are not likely to have repeat work.

Figure 9-3 Consultant Working on Assignment

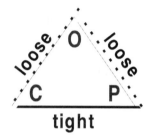

Companies that have both individuals and other companies for customers might make different arrangements for these different kinds of customers. They might offer business customers, who are more profitable, a higher level of service. A power company, for example, might offer personal representatives for their business customers but a call center for residential customers. An office supply chain might have a special desk for business customers and offer them free delivery, a service not offered to individual customers. These companies are looking at "share of customer," and business customers represent a larger pie than individual customers. Offering personal service to your best customers but encounter service to those who spend less is a way to concentrate resources where the return is greatest.

Some provider-customer company situations can be fairly unequal, where the provider depends on the company for most (all, in some cases) of the business. The company, however, could always get someone else. The provider has a powerful motivation to deliver the desired service. To the extent that the provider learns the customer's needs and customizes what is done to meet those needs, the provider is less likely to be replaced. An artist who knows the style the company wants and who has learned to work effectively with the inside people is unlikely to be dumped in favor of someone with no track record with the company. Her good working relationship with insiders is her job security.

A service provider with long-term or continuous assignments for a company builds a relationship with people inside the provider organization, and this tight link is what maintains his employment. The other links may be loose. The same is true for sporadic assignments for a specific provider. If the provider goes to a new company, he will continue calling the consultant whose work he knows and respects.

When Relationships Don't Work

When the provider and customer are both representing companies and not acting for themselves personally, it raises some problems that do not exist when individuals interact as provider and customer. Companies are an abstraction and can interact only through the people they employ. Organizations cannot have relationships. Only people can have relationships, so organizations interact through the people assigned to the *roles* of customer and provider.

The person in the role of customer may or may not be the same person who negotiated the contract with the provider. If the person acting as customer inside the organization is the same person who selects the provider, there can be some conflicts of interest. For the provider, having a relationship with that inside person can make the difference between getting the work or not getting the work. On the one end of the spectrum, this is the time-honored practice of "networking" that consists of the inside person using her contacts to find a qualified provider. At the other end, it is nepotism or just plain paying off a buddy with a fat contract. The person at the customer organization may convince himself he has chosen the provider based on some logical criterion, even though it was mainly the good times they had on the golf course. Or he may hire friends, former colleagues, fellow students, and family members for cushy consulting positions for which they are only marginally qualified, putting his personal interests ahead of his responsibility to the organization.

A provider may get a contract because of her great work or simply because of the common interests or backgrounds she has with the customer. Agents for a potential provider company may offer inducements to the persons inside the customer company, such as wining and dining the contact person, or inviting that person to sports events. Where those things seem like a bribe or are against company rules, the agent might substitute a lot of friendly personal contact. If the company person finds a lot in common with this person, he may be persuaded to go with the new provider, and that may not be what's best for the company. Like the story in Chapter Seven of the football player-turned-investment counselor who recruited other football players and then made poor investments, choosing providers based on common interests rather than professional competence can be disastrous.

In the worst scenario, the customer and provider can get together and simply agree to defraud the customer organization. The customer could agree to approve payment for the provider who would do little or no work. Since the customer and provider are not acting for themselves but on behalf of their company in roles designed by management, their interests will not always be the same as their company's interests.

Management needs to review the results of these service transactions from time to time to make sure they are meeting the company's objectives. Business relationships, like social relationships, take on a life of their own and tend to continue because the parties involved enjoy interacting or simply through inertia.

For some kinds of functions, it is clear that relationships have built-in dangers. If you need someone to do a financial audit, it is important that the audit be impartial, based on the best accounting practices, and that there be no appearance of dishonesty. Having someone with no personal ties to the company avoids any appearance of collusion. In this case, it is better to avoid establishing a relationship with an auditor.

Management should also not underestimate the advantages of continuing an already established relationship or the effect on morale of replacing a well-liked vendor. As with other relationships, ending an arrangement with a long-standing vendor is not as simple as canceling the contract. There are ripples within the company as people who have built relationships are told those relationships must end because managers decided it should be so. A lot of business literature treats the contract as a "relationship" between companies, but in fact it is the people in the companies who have the relationships. The contract is only a piece of paper.

When Quality Rules

In some kinds of work, a provider who did not deliver the quality would not be retained, even if he had a close relationship with an insider. Creative work is often like this. At Rhino Records, for example, in-house artists design CD covers and booklets that go with the boxed sets that are a Rhino specialty. The artists here work with representatives from large printing companies who print the final materials. Artists take pride in their creative efforts and expect printing firms to meet their standard for quality. Unlike other companies that issue CDs, Rhino compilations come with beautifully done liner notes that have a lot of information about the musician and his or her work. One Rhino artist who designed a boxed set that won a Grammy award says the printing vendor showed her many versions before they selected the final one. Although she noted that Rhino is cost-conscious, price is less important than quality. "Quality and service," she says, "are very important."[8] The work of an artist is personal, and that artist's interests are served by having finished pieces that she can proudly display. In this situation, an artist is not likely to hire a friend with no track record or give work out on the basis of a low bid.

Relationships Do Not Always Depend on Choice

Managers who choose a vendor but then do not work directly with that vendor might be more inclined to make their decision on who gets the contract mainly on price. For example, when a manager needs to establish a contract to repair the company's copy machines, he may talk to a number of companies and ultimately give the contract to the low bidder. The administrative assistants who actually deal with the copier repair person may think the service is poor, or they may think it's great and be unhappy when management contracts with a different company that puts in a lower bid. If administrative assistants are not consulted about such matters, the relationships they build with the repair persons do not help the copier repair company keep its contract.

Snack food delivery persons who stock the shelves of convenience stores, copier repair persons whose company has a contract with specific businesses, and the UPS driver who picks up packages on a route all get to know the customers they service, but both they and their customers work for organizations. The customers in these cases probably did not get to choose their specific provider, and the provider did not get to choose his customers. But the relationships these people establish will still become more efficient over time. As in other relationships, the provider may customize her service if she is asked to do so. For instance, the UPS driver may alter his schedule one day for a customer who needs a later pickup or an earlier delivery. The customer values these extra services he gets that result directly from people getting to know each other. Management has to be involved in these service arrangements, since they negotiate the terms for the provider and customer roles, but management should remember that these efficiencies are lost when they switch to another provider company.

Enhanced Encounters: Building Ties Through Technology

Relationships build tight links, but there are other ways provider companies can strengthen their ties to a customer organization. Giving customers access to inside information can build a competitive advantage. UPS does this through its Web site that lets any customer log on and track a package. UPS has invested in the technology needed to know where any package is at any time, and it makes this information available to its customers. Through electronic signatures and use of the UPS Global Tracking System, any package can be automatically located. This helps customers feel safe about trusting important packages to UPS and builds an enhanced encounter between customer and company.

Another example of a company that uses technology to build enhanced encounters is Cisco Systems, which manufactures much of the network routing equipment that makes the Internet possible. Cisco uses the Cisco Connection Online (CCO) to keep in touch with customers for both support and sales. Available around the clock, CCO gives customers access to much of the same information as Cisco employees have. Before CCO, customers had to call a hotline for technical support. Now through use of CCO, customers, who must register to use the site, can check the status of an order, get pricing and product data, review information on their contracts, register for seminars, and download software upgrades. Some of the functions in CCO simply add convenience, like letting customers print copies of their invoices. Once CCO came online, it handled almost 80 percent of the customer calls. The growth rate of incoming phone calls in 1998 was 6.5 percent, but the growth rate of accesses to the Web site was closer to 15 percent.

Handling support through a Web site hasn't only been helpful in reducing support costs, it has also been a huge money-maker. CCO has brought in an astounding $10 million a day in sales! Cisco uses other technology besides CCO to realize these tremendous sales figures. It uses "commerce agents" to guide customers through such functions as pricing, ordering, lead-time, and configuration; and its Quick Starts program provides hardware installation instructions for experienced users. Another way Cisco makes its profits is through its global presence. The company has servers located throughout the world, and the CCO Web pages are available in fourteen languages.[9]

Another example is Hewlett-Packard, which uses tracking software to build a database of corporate customers who call or e-mail for service. By retaining information about each customer's concerns, HP routes future requests to the agent with the most know-how to solve the problem. *Business Week* reported in March 1999 that HP's customer database strategy has resulted in $180 million in incremental sales.[10] Note that matching calls to the most-qualified agent means not regarding all providers as interchangeable but recognizing and (one would hope) rewarding individual competencies.

Partnering

Partnering is a little different from a customer-provider transaction. Partnering acknowledges a continuing association between companies and involves more than the people who actually work together at both companies. It requires a shift in thinking, away from an adversarial approach where company A tries to get the best deal with company B. Partnering, like the relationships it imitates, requires trust.

In the past decade of downsizing and reengineering, most medium-size to large companies acquired partners. In shedding some in-house functions, these companies often find it makes sense to partner with another company to provide that function. It may be the printing work that is now done at an outside organization. It may be prototyping that is now sent out. It could be software development or an entire IT effort, food service, or any number of functions. A manufacturer of car seats works with an auto manufacturer. A seafood distributor works with a restaurant chain. A computer training company works with a large bank. When the same people from each company interact on a regular basis, they are working in relationships. If different people interact each time, the arrangement is a pseudo-relationship and will be less effective in creating a strong bond between the companies.

Partnerships can also make companies more agile as they use each others' resources to fuel fast growth. James Martin explains that "virtual operations can allow a corporation to grow very fast in an exploding market because they enable the corporation to use resources owned by other organizations. It would cost too much or take too long to grow those resources in-house. The corporation may need to use highly skilled designers, or complex software development, or manufacturing capability from another company."[11] The emergence of the virtual office enables multicompany teams to work together across distances via e-mail and audio or video conferencing. These working arrangements facilitate relationships.

True partnering arrangements are not just vendor-client agreements but involve long-term stategic alliances vitally important to both companies. In partnering arrangements, people at both companies who interact with one another have access to higher management and are consulted on matters of importance. They gain an opportunity to talk to and educate upper manager about the day-to-day pressures that affect their work. These partnerships may result in jobs being upgraded, as former paper-pushers now get involved in broader tasks. Rosabeth Moss Kanter relates her observations of a situation at Digital Equipment Corp., which formed partnerships with suppliers. She quotes an official saying, "Our competitive edge has to come from new supplier relationships which make suppliers feel like a credible extension of Digital."

The supplier partnerships at Digital resulted in a change in the way jobs in purchasing were structured. Previously, there was an emphasis on meeting specifications, but that changed to "a need for more experienced people who can be involved in every aspect of a business process and handle complex negotiations. Instead of rewarding staff for never running out of parts, the department now emphasizes meeting broader time-to-market and profitability goals. Instead of using the purchasing staff as an opportunity to promote less sophisticated clerical personnel, the department seeks people who can effectively take more complete business responsibility for their decisions, represent the company in strategic discussions with partners, and even carry out such specialized professional tasks as writing contracts without using lawyers."[12] She also reports that the purchasing department lost jobs that involved "purely routine paperwork" due to new technology. This is a case where machines replaced the simple work, and the remaining jobs were upgraded because the partnering arrangement required people to work together in relationships.

In partnering arrangements vital to both companies, the organization part of the service triangle is really both companies, as shown in Figure 9-4. Workers at one company may still be the providers to workers at the other company, but their interests are closely intertwined.

Partnerships create tight links all the way around. The provider has a strong allegiance to her company, but she will also establish a close working relationship with people at the customer company. The customer likewise will have tight bonds with his organization, but also with people at the provider company. Eventually, a web of relationships lets the partnership become the Organization (O) for both.

Partnering arrangements, unlike mere vendor contracts that are usually pseudo-relationships, build bonds at all levels of each organization. This is a situation in which management will encourage workers to establish individual relationships to strengthen the partnership and make it work. The success of the partnering agreement will be based, not on the low price to the customer company, the number of calls made, or items built, but on the strength of the relationships between individuals in each company whose interactions will bring about the desired outcome.

**Figure 9-4
A Partnership
Between Two
Companies**

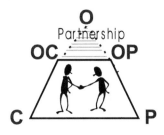

Rosabeth Moss Kanter studied a defense supplier that first began working with the U.S. Department of Defense (DOD) on a project requiring secrecy. Government and company people worked together over a long period of time and formed very close ties. "In terms of any measure except formal employer," she notes, "the contractor and customer form an organization with stronger internal ties than those either group has to its own official 'owner.' " The initial need for secrecy helped build these strong bonds with a legal contract governing the work, but, she adds, "a web of overlapping projects, joint planning, career incentives, and social relationships bind the parties more thoroughly."[13]

Encounters and Pseudo-Relationships

For services that are one-time or sporadic, organizations are more likely to put out bids and give the work to whoever has the lowest price. In these cases, service takes the form of an encounter between the two companies. If the customer chooses a vendor because she knows about the vendor through reputation or advertising and may need the service again in the future, the service may be considered a pseudo-relationship. In the pseudo-relationship, there may be continued contact, but the contact is between various people in each organization and does not build relationships.

The provider company must build awareness of its good service and low prices through the same mechanisms as other pseudo-relationships and enhanced encounters. It can do this by keeping information on their business customers and making it easy for customers to reorder, possibly offering around-the-clock service through an 800 phone line or a Web site. It can offer incentives for customers to continue doing business with the company through reward programs or discount schemes. Hotel chains offering frequent flyer miles or free rooms after so many dollars spent are examples.

The difference between these formats and the relationship format is that in these, there are no specific agents of each organization assigned to work with one another. In an encounter, there is no expectation of continued interactions. Businesses, like individuals, have occasional needs that do not warrant establishing long-term arrangements.

Conclusion

Service interactions can happen between individuals, between an individual and a company, between a service unit inside a company and the rest of the company, and between two companies.

Points for service units inside a company:

- Be aware of whether you are providing service in relationships or in encounters.
- If you are providing service in encounters, could you switch to relationships? Can you see advantages in doing so?
- What are the advantages of outsourcing the service? If outsourcing would mean service in encounters (and it almost always does), will that meet your company's needs?

Points for company-to-company service:

- Is your arrangement with another company a vendor-customer arrangement or a partnering arrangement?
- Does your arrangement encourage relationships between workers at the two companies? Do these relationships further the goals of the company, or can those in the roles of customer and provider act in their personal interests rather than in the interests of the company?
- If you have a vendor agreement, do you have a method of overseeing that agreement to make sure it continues meeting your needs?

Notes

1. "Outsourcing Vendor Evaluation and Selection Process," report from the Gartner Group, 1996.
2. Smith, Roff. "Nebraska, Standing Tall Again," *National Geographic*, November 1998.
3. Hogue, Ruth Ann. "Searching for quality: Good teleservice jobs, call for skilled workers," *Arizona Daily Star*, November 18, 1998
4. Harris, Jim. *Finding and Keeping Great Employees* (New York: AMACOM, 1998).
5. Rosenbluth, Hal F. and Diane McFerrin Peters. *The Customer Comes Second and Other Secrets of Exceptional Service* (New York: Quill-William Morrow, 1992).
6. Schneider, Benjamin and David E. Bowen. *Winning the Service Game* (Boston: Harvard Business School Press, 1995).
7. Maister, David. *True Professionalism* (New York: The Free Press, 1997).
8. Personal communication with Rachel J. Gutek, art director at Rhino Records.
9. "Cisco Reaps Huge Benefits From Superb Web site; Over $3 Billion in Revenue" report from the Gartner Group, 1998.
10. Stepanek, Marcia. "You'll Wanna Hold Their Hands," *Business Week*, March 22, 1999.
11. Martin, James. *Cybercorp: The New Business Revolution* (New York: AMACOM, 1996).
12. Kanter, Rosabeth Moss. *When Giants Learn to Dance* (New York: Simon & Schuster, 1989).
13. Ibid.

Chapter Ten

Brave New Service Strategy: Creating Satisfied Customers, Successful Organizations, and Effective Providers

Revisiting Dissatisfaction

We began by saying customers are unhappy with the service they receive. Surveys as well as anecdotal evidence suggests that people think personal service is disappearing and many say they want it back. We have looked at how the change from relationship service to encounter service, following the trend in manufacturing from hand-made to mass-produced, has contributed to this feeling that service is declining. But the picture we get is a bit fuzzy. Customers willingly trade the personal touch for lower prices at many chain operations. Some chains offer expertise (Home Depot, for example, hires experts and offers workshops for customers) and some emphasize quality (Starbucks charges *more* for a cup of coffee than a neighborhood coffee shop). The difference is not as simple as high quality, high price, personal service versus lower quality, lower price, impersonal service.

Customers are not always looking for relationships. Sometimes they want the lowest price and will put up with inconvenience to get it. As one customer of Dryclean Depot stated, as he waited in a line for his turn to pay in advance, "It's annoying but worth it—a matter of sheer economics."[1] This customer would probably agree that he is not getting personal service, but using a discount service is *his* choice.

What business owners need to do is look for opportunities to offer service using a different strategy. Are there customers using a cheap discount service who chafe under the lack of personal service, but don't have a relationship option? Or, are there customers paying high prices for a service that is more customized than they want or need? Or, are there industries using unsophisticated methods or inefficient service that could be restructured for greater reliability and lower cost for customers? These gaps are fertile ground for new businesses.

Technology plays a role, too. While people are resistant to new ways of doing things, show them a clear advantage to something new and they will eventually adopt it, as surely as the fax machine killed the telegram. Digitized sound is creating a discontinuity in the music industry, challenging traditional music distribution channels. When the winning format emerges and enough momentum develops, the music industry will be turned upside down, but consumers will have an incredible array of music choices and more chances to get to know the artists and even communicate with them. The convenience of downloading movies directly to a TV set will likely replace the neighborhood video store but not until everything is in place to make it work. That could happen soon as set-top boxes come on the market, replacing the old rental units from cable companies. Thanks to the Telecommunications Act of 1996 and rulings by the FCC, consumers can buy their own box and get the features they want, including on-demand movies.

Internet selling didn't take off until we had the bandwidth needed, and enough people had computers with fast modems or access to cable modems. The mail and phone order businesses as well as home shopping on cable TV served as models for Internet selling, giving customers the confidence to order products they couldn't touch from providers they couldn't see. When all the elements come together, new industries are born and old ones die. There are winners and losers.

The service economy is customer-driven. Even manufacturing companies are shifting their focus to think of themselves as consumer companies. Auto manufacturers, for instance, don't build cars; they provide "personal transportation products." Ford Chairman Alex Trotman told his employees in 1998:

> When you think about it, we're in an extremely interesting, challenging and exciting business. It's a time when literally everything is opening up and becoming more competitive—including the global economy, world trade, communications and capital markets. And the velocity of change is incredible. Those companies that really understand this change will be the winners in the 21st century—companies that look at the whole business the way the consumers do, drive their business by customer preferences, use the dynamics of change to drive the processes within the company to be much more attuned and connect with what the customers want . . . This is a revolution to turn the traditional engineering /manufacturing /sales-dominated companies into much more consumer-focused/market-oriented enterprises. It started with the global supplier consolidations, then the retail revolution began, then there were changes in the parts and services business all around the world, and then came the re-birth of brand strategy as the science or perhaps, "art of the science." Literally every aspect of our business is changing. All of our traditional paradigms are changing—and at a velocity that is unprecedented.[2]

One thing is certain. The service economy will keep going, providing old services in new ways and pioneering new services. The services change and the way they are delivered evolves, sometimes changing from relationship to encounter, sometimes riding on high tech advances, and sometimes using old-fashioned charm and skill in that oldest of all delivery systems, the relationship. Many commentators wondered if a service economy could provide enough jobs and create a good standard of living; some saw a service economy as a version of everyone doing each other's laundry. But that's not what it is. Just as efficient manufacturing processes resulted in a wave of prosperity in the twentieth century, so will applying intelligent, customer-driven processes to the delivery of service. A future dominated by service businesses is a future full of promise and prosperity for organizations, customers, and providers.

Service in the Twenty-First Century

As a nation, we've been though the industrialized economy with its emphasis on manufacturing and we've adapted well to the post modern era, which has given America an unprecedented streak of prosperity. What's next? It looks like there are some new wrinkles awaiting us.

The End of Mass Culture: The Special Interests Economy

Mass culture is dead, killed by technology that can deliver to each of us exactly what we like. Cable TV brings us hundreds of channels, many highly specialized. Internet radio is now bringing us extreme specialization in content, too. Interested in airplanes and love tango music? No problem. Watch the Discovery Wings channel (all airplanes, all the time) and the Tango Internet radio station (all tango, all the time) accessible from Shoutcast.com. Internet e-zines cater to all kinds of special interests, and newsgroups bring together people with diverse special interests, some who might be trying to match up pieces of sets of antique dinnerware, and others who want to know how to adopt a child. Even the software itself is getting more customized, as users change colors and fonts on their display and are greeted by name when they access their favorite portal site.

This extreme specialization creates opportunities for any area of interest not covered. Businesses don't have to be local, as they once were, but can reach people over large areas, potentially the entire globe. Communities can suffer when locally owned services are driven out by chain businesses, but when remote-ownership is applied to some specialty activity, it lets customers indulge their interest no matter where they live. Services delivered by cable TV or the Internet can reach enough people to support such special interests as garden lovers (the Garden Channel) or those interested in techno music (Internet music sites and Internet radio).

The dark side of extreme specialization is that some special interests are not in the best interests of society. The killings at Columbine High School in April 1999 brought a lot of publicity to hate Web sites and to the existence of information on making bombs. Racist sites and what has been the Internet's first and most successful type of commercial site, pornography, are offensive to many people. But the technology makes specialization easy and inevitable. It's there, and people can immerse themselves in whatever they like and lose touch with the majority culture. As a society, we must decide how to deal with it.

The end of mass culture is bound to have consequences. It may mean people have fewer common experiences that let us understand each other. We were once a nation where stores were empty during popular TV shows because everyone was home watching and water towers emptied as all the toilets were flushed at the same time, during the commercials on the Arthur Godfrey TV show. At one end of the spectrum we have conformity, everyone doing and thinking the same thing, at its peak in the 1950s, which spawned its opposite—censorship run amok with the McCarthy hearings and criticism of anyone who was different. At the other end is the chaos of so many diverse interests and points of view that we no longer can communicate with people outside our circle.

Real Feelings: The "Experience" Economy

Encounters are efficient but generally not very satisfying. Will a new form emerge? One theory is that the newest format is service as experience. Increasingly, customers will buy the ambiance and actions surrounding the service. Companies that make the service delivery unique in ways that involve senses and emotions will have an edge.

An example is a café that looks, sounds, and feels like a rain forest where guests are transported to a beautiful world of waterfalls and chirping birds while they lunch on chicken salad. Hard Rock Cafes offer guests an experience, which is even more important than their food. A beauty shop that uses a digital picture of each customer and lets them add different hairdos and makeup in a virtual environment lets their clients "try on" different looks. Customers enjoy the experience as much as they value getting their hair styled. Spas that pamper customers while giving facials and manicures are also in the experience business. Disney led the way years ago when it took an amusement park concept and expanded it into a total visitor experience, gradually adding theme hotels and even the Disney Institute where learning something new is also more than mere learning; it is an experience.

The Internet and satellite phone service provided a powerful experience for an audience that followed the arctic adventure of Paul Schurke and his team who recreated the 1909 journey of Robert Peary and Matthew Henson to the North Pole. Expedition members were connected via pager, cell phone, and satellite to the rest of the world. The contact with people back in civilization was an encouraging tonic to those on the expedition, but it was addictive to those following on the Internet. Updates including streaming audio were posted daily and attracted a wide following.

Doug Hall, an expedition member and founder of a company called Great Aspirations, said Internet followers were "bummed out" when it ended "because it was like an old time radio serial." He plans to offer other adventures online such as a Tom Sawyer-style riverboat journey.[3] Great Aspirations is geared to school children and has successfully raised both the aspirations and the confidence levels of kids who have participated in these real life events. Their formula of taking the learner along on a real time adventure could be a model for other businesses that want to cash in on the experience economy.

Another company tapping into people's desire to tune into

real life is Healthshop.com, an online vitamin and health food store that put up netcams to follow 29-year old "Dani" as she dieted and exercised her way into condition for an April 1999 wedding. Healthshop.com set up netcams in Dani's office, kitchen, and family room, and thousands of devoted followers watched and sent her encouraging e-mails. CEO Glenn Zweig says, "People were addicted to this thing."[4] Following a real person's efforts to live a healthier life is a better learning (and selling) tool for many people than reading articles.

The huge popularity of interactive role-playing games on the Internet is yet another example. Some people get hooked on these games and spend long hours pretending to be a knight or warrior doing battle with other unknown, but real, opponents.

Those businesses that offer experiences are mainly encounter businesses, in which sensing and feeling takes the place of a relationship. Like kids hooked on computer games, the customers of these businesses may become regulars. The main problem is keeping the experience fresh enough to continue being satisfying.

Reaching More People: The Internet Economy

The Internet grew into a huge economic engine in the 1990s, a new way to transact business. It gives consumers new power to compare prices and learn about products before they buy. Internet businesses are encounter businesses. They do not involve face-to-face transactions, although they can give customers more information about products they buy. And what the customer sees on the Web page can be customized based on what the organization knows of his interests.

Information services on the Internet give their users quick information and a sense of control. Finding the facts you want online is faster than going to the library and looking through books. Newspapers and news services from around the world are available to anyone with a connection. These services are anonymous. At the library, if you can't find what you're looking for, you can ask a librarian for help. With an online service, if you can't remember your password, or you lose the Web address, you're stuck. Like any encounter business, the customer does not know (and doesn't even see) the provider. But once someone masters the use of Internet services for research, he is not likely to go back to relying on the library.

The Internet economy is also an island. It has its own radio stations, its own video not seen on TV, its heroes, and villains. Interactive games on the Internet are making the old single-player games obsolete. Netcams bring a new kind of viewing experience, watching an actual person go about their life. In some of these areas, the Internet economy, the experience economy, and the special interests economy converge and give us a picture of what service in the future will look like.

Rediscovering Our Souls: The Nonrationalized Economy

Many people left corporate America in the last twenty years of the twentieth century and began their own small business, perhaps working from their home. Many new college graduates aspire to own a business, preferring it to working in corporate America. The people who own small businesses cater to customers who trust a person more than they trust a big corporation. Instead of going to a chain business, these customers seek out an individual provider or small business.

George Ritzer warned us about the dangers of McDonaldization[5] and some people have listened. They have decided not everything can be commodified, packaged up, and sold as a product, and they will patronize businesses that don't operate that way. Likewise, many dislike the phone trees that seem omnipresent when customers call a business. These customers complain that pressing buttons on the phone and listening to recordings is not like talking to a real person.

Businesses that are truly personal can use that as a selling point but not through big-budget advertising. They need to reach customers in a more personal way. Ben and Jerry's began small and had no system at all for dealing efficiently with the swarms of customers who had discovered their delicious ice cream confections or for figuring profits. Ritzer writes that two months after they opened their ice cream shop, Ben and Jerry hung a sign on the door that said, "We're closed today so we can figure out if we're making any money." They certainly needed to make money, but their customers saw that making great ice cream was their first priority and responded by coming in droves to buy it, even if the lines were long.

Businesses that offer an "alternative" product or service have a growing market. New Age bookstores are thriving as are stores selling vitamins and herbal remedies. People will spend money on services that can only be described as spiritual, an area that cannot be rationalized. From Feng Shui consulting to psychic readings to past life therapy, people are seeking out ways to enrich their lives and find meaning. A flip through a New Age newspaper, *PhenomeNews,* published in Michigan, shows ads from the following types of providers:

- Chinese acupuncturist offering "free Iridology—diagnosing of ears and eye" plus "free pulse and tongue diagnosing"
- Holistic veterinarian offering acupuncture and homeopathy for animals
- Psychic and hypnotherapist who will "resolve troubling issues in your life"
- Channeler who offers "detailed channeled readings on your soul mate"
- Consultant who will help you access "your other mind's eye"
- Success coach who will help you "create the life of your dreams"

These services appeal to people who want a relationship with their provider and are willing to pay for it. Interestingly, the services of these providers are often aimed at helping people have relationships. Perhaps our busy, encounter-heavy society has produced many people who doubt their ability to have and retain effective relationships. What once came naturally is now something those with enough money pay to learn.

Many providers of alternative services hold seminars as a way to make the price a little lower than a personal consultation. The seminars, of course, bring together people of like mind who can share their experiences and make friends with each other. For the provider, the seminars may bring them some customers who want personal consulting in a one-to-one relationship. For the attendees, the experience is an enhanced encounter. It offers a friendly, welcoming atmosphere and a chance to participate along with other supportive people. New Age practitioners know how to tap into what is perhaps a pent-up desire for personal services. Their customers want to do business with a person, not a faceless corporation. They are really yearning for relationships, making perfect opportunities for providers with a suitable service.

The Future for Customers

What will service be like for customers in the decades to come?

Customers always deal with a provider and usually deal with an organization. If they do business in a relationship, they will have a tight C-P link. But most of their service will be in encounters, where they are only loosely coupled to a provider. Enhanced encounters have a tight C-O link.

Fewer Relationships

Some customers will have few, if any, relationships. While companies are busy mining data to figure out which customers are valuable, some people who are not deemed valuable may go through life with few real relationships. University of Arizona studies found everyone in their surveys had some business relationships, but it would be possible for a person to get all the services she needs in encounters.[6] In the past, most people had a relationship with their doctor, but managed care is reducing the number of people who have personal doctors. Many consumers will buy insurance through an 800 number, book travel on the Internet, and buy stocks through a discount brokerage. Independent drug stores are disappearing, along with the personal pharmacist. Drugstore.com may reduce human-to-human contact even more.

What encounter businesses offer sounds like a good idea—

getting a lower price, using a standard service, or eliminating the middle man. It's part of the American way of life to look for a bargain. But customers who lack real relationships can get used to superficial interactions and lose the ability to sense genuine emotion. It could lead to a lack of empathy and sensitivity. Relationships allow people to have and to express genuine emotions and feelings, while encounters require a show of emotion that may not be real.

The decline of neighborhoods made it easier for people to go to giant big box stores like Wal-Mart and Home Depot, since they were used to driving rather than walking to shops. In suburban areas where people live in houses on large lots with no sidewalks and don't know their neighbors, it's easier to drive to Burger King than seek out an independently owned place.

But . . . Some Customers Still Have Many Relationships

Not everyone has gone to a "fast food" lifestyle. There are communities of upper-income people where everyone has a nanny for their children, a cook, a maid, a gardener, a fitness consultant, a tax consultant, an attorney, an investment consultant, an interior designer, a hairstylist and manicurist, personal doctors and medical specialists, a therapist, and, if they are so inclined, an astrologer and a spiritual healer. Each of these services is tailored to them and their needs. To such people, standing in line at McDonald's would be unthinkable. Wealthy people do not need to believe in egalitarianism, a hallmark of encounter businesses. They get services that are fast and efficient by training their providers in what they like and getting rid of providers who do not deliver. Price is not a problem; finding the right people is the problem.

Businesses catering to this market need to be very attentive and differentiate their personal service from the encounter businesses patronized by the masses. These customers are interested in luxury, not economy. Businesses need to avoid low class methods like glitzy advertising and discount coupons and instead build a classy and exclusive image for themselves. A provider offering to come to customers' homes and cook special dinners, for instance, might have an attractive invitation-type flyer mailed to potential customers. It would stress the personal and highly customized nature of the service. Entrepreneurs who can think up new ways to service wealthy customers can find a market if they use the strengths of relationships to build customer trust.

Encounter businesses serving the wealthy need to manage their process down to the smallest detail to meet the expectations of their customers. The *Wall Street Journal* ran an article about a "hotel spy" firm that checks out hotels belonging to the exclusive Preferred Hotels & Resorts Worldwide, a group of 120 independent luxury hotels that share a common reservations system. The firm's owner, David Richey, believes all areas of hotel service can be quantified. Like Frederick Taylor with his stop watch, Richey, who checks into the hotel under a pseudonym, keeps notes on how long it takes staff to perform various actions. For instance, the Preferred hotels require that a doorman greet a customer within thirty seconds after a taxi pulls to a stop. Waiters in the restaurant are expected to make eye contact, and the chef must accommodate orders for items not on the menu. The "hotel spy" (really a high class mystery shopper) tests the staff and jots down how they perform and later makes his report to management.

The requirements at these luxury hotels go beyond what most people expect from a hotel, but their customers are not most people. There is an emphasis on speed of service in things like delivering luggage to the room, preparing food and bringing it to the table, picking up and pressing a suit, and bringing coffee quickly after the guest is seated for breakfast. In other areas, the emphasis is on flexibility. If a guest asks a hotel employee to make airline reservations on short notice, the employee is expected to do it.

The typical guest at a luxury hotel has many relationship providers serving her when she is home. *Worth* magazine, in an article on the wealthiest communities in America, quoted the owner of a $1.8 million, 7,000 square-foot home, who said, "We have a pool-cleaning man and a mow and blow crew, a plant waterer, and a flower arranger and an outdoor-light man. We have a man for everything."[7] When such people travel, they are forced to deal with some strangers, but the attentive service at these hotels—still not a relationship, except where guests get to know long-time hotel employees—is an acceptable substitute.

There are other groups of people besides the wealthy who look for relationships. Disabled people, for example, need services tailored to meet their needs. This can lead to conflicts with insurance companies that don't distinguish between encounter and relationship services. Mike Utley, a former Detroit Lions football player who suffered a spinal cord injury, has fought with Liberty Mutual Insurance over the company's unwillingness to pay for his personal nurse to accompany him when he must travel. The company insisted that instead, he hire a nurse on a day rate at the destination location. Utley says, "I tried their way for almost a year. It was a disaster. I had people not show up, not know my own personal care, not know my bowel program—very uncool. Very, very degrading. That is very difficult for somebody to handle emotionally. I have to have people around me who believe in me and are going to give the support."[8]

The value to someone like Utley of having a relationship with a nurse who knows him cannot be reduced to a dollar amount. In-home caregivers to the elderly are another example of a service that works best when the customer can keep the same provider over time. Agencies that send "someone" over each day may offer a lower price, but anyone who can afford it will prefer finding a reliable and regular caregiver on their own. To the customer of personal care services, providers are not interchangeable. It is impossible to standardize care that really must be customized. The fact that good personal providers are difficult to find and are expensive opens the way for encounter services. When insurance companies are paying the bills, it is in their financial interests to insist an encounter service is the equivalent of a relationship service, but customers who live with the results will never believe it is so.

Encounter businesses are aimed at average customers and tend not to work well for those at either end of the spectrum. Whether customers are "different" because they are much wealthier than most, or because they are disabled, or for some other reason, they are likely to feel their needs are not met in encounter services. There is a real opportunity for entrepreneurs in this unmet need.

What Do Customers Want?

Will customers continue to complain that service is declining? Maybe not, if organizations stop pretending they offer a relationship when what they actually provide is an encounter. Customers can appreciate service that is quick, inexpensive, convenient, and reliable if that is what businesses say they are delivering. Recall the reaction of columnist Laura Berman to the letter she received from Northwest Airlines (her reply is in Chapter One). She was looking for an improvement in basic service, not to be told she had a "special relationship" that entitled her to gold luggage tags. Airline passengers are looking for the airlines to do what they say they will do and to do it with courtesy and respect for their customers. Other businesses that want to improve their image with customers should do the same.

There is a persistent belief in the Golden Age of service, which each decade seems to define as a different time in the past. People continue to hold to an image of service being delivered by someone they know, who cares about them and their community. But that just doesn't fit the facts of service in encounters. It doesn't even fit what people actually say they want in service transactions. Researchers Leonard Berry, A. Parasuraman, and Valerie A. Zeithaml conducted thirteen customer surveys and found in each survey respondents rated *reliability* as their most important indicator of service quality.[9] If reliability is what is most important, then it appears Ray Kroc was on to something when he insisted his franchisees make the hamburgers exactly according to his instructions. McDonald's delivers the same hamburger reliably.

The importance customers place on reliability, we think, relates to the fact that most service is in encounters. Exactly what is it customers want to be reliable? In a relationship business, the satisfaction for customer and provider comes from the shared understanding of what the customer wants as the provider learns the customer's needs over numerous transactions.

In the context of a relationship, service is customized for the customer, so it doesn't depend on uniformity. A relationship provider does not have a standardized process he uses every time, but that is the essence of encounter service. Reliability as a measure of service makes sense only if we're talking about encounter service. Customers want the service to be the same and to work according to the standard process each time. If an ATM is supposed to dispense cash, accept payments, and give a receipt (with ink dark enough to read), that means it always has cash to dispense, always accepts payments, and always spits out a readable receipt—twenty-four hours a day, seven days a week. The chain drugstore needs to have prescriptions ready when they say and be able to locate the customer's order quickly. This is accomplished by having processes that let clerks use more than one key for finding an order, not just doing a search by name which doesn't work when the customer's name is misspelled, but also by phone number or address. Each procedure needs a structure that builds in the reliability that customers value.

The number two quality, *responsiveness*, also applies uniquely to encounters. To maintain a relationship, service providers must be responsive. But encounter providers are interchangeable, doing a job that involves dealing with customers, all of whom are strangers. It is much more difficult for providers who don't expect to see a customer again to provide exactly the service the customer wants (i.e., be reliable) and to do exactly what the customer wants done when he wants it (i.e., be responsive).

Will customers continue to give service a low rating? Organizations could respond by starting a relationship service for customers with special needs, or there might be enough customers for a niche business. The key is that organizations should not promise more than they can deliver. Encounter businesses cannot service customers with nonstandard needs.

Berry, Parasuraman, and Zeithaml say in their commentary that "conformance to company specifications is not quality; conformance to the customer's specifications is."[10] However, encounter businesses are organized to deliver service in a standard way, according to company specifications. The uniformity of service is what creates the reliability customers say they want and that the organization expects the provider to deliver. Customers go back to the same organization because they expect to receive the same service they got before. While a relationship business can deliver service to the customer's specifications, an encounter business cannot.

Berry and associates may be really saying that providers should develop a customer orientation, which is a great idea, but organizations cannot guarantee their providers will care about customers, even when they ask those providers to deliver service with a smile. What they *can* do is set up procedures that ensure customers get what they expect. As long as organizations mislead customers into thinking a service is more personal than it is, they will receive low ratings. Organizations need to be clear with customers about exactly what they offer. The customer at Dryclean Depot is not getting personal service, but he knows that, and he knows he is standing in line because when his turn comes to pile his dirty clothes on the counter, he gets a lower price than he would get at the small shop offering personal service. When the provider makes clear what he is offering and the customer understands it, you don't get mismatches between expectations and results.

Relationships are more satisfying to customers, but people can get services through encounters and be satisfied too. Perhaps they say they want reliability because that is the one thing that is the strength of an encounter—it is always the same—and when there is some significant variation in what the customer expects, this is seen as a serious offense. In a relationship, customers who like their provider will forgive an off day or an inconvenience because they know that over all, their provider does a good job. In an encounter, customers have no way of knowing the provider is having a bad day or that the computer broke down. They just know the service was not what they expected.

Even when service in an encounter *is* what they expect, it may not be what they want. The customer eating a hamburger at McDonald's may wish he was eating sirloin at a steak house. He doesn't blame McDonald's for that. He just doesn't get excited about his hamburger. But using the researchers' definition, we could hardly say McDonald's didn't deliver quality because it didn't serve the customer a sirloin steak.

The Future for Service Organizations

Despite the criticism chain businesses will continue to receive, they are still the main purveyors of service in the industrialized world. Encounter businesses, including chains, can provide many of the services people need and do it in a manner that satisfies their customers.

Technology Matters

Technology that identifies customers and what they buy will continue to be important. Eventually, Americans will decide what kind of data gathering is acceptable. They will learn when mining data is helpful to both marketer and customer and when it is intrusive. On the other side, marketers will figure out when giant databases are useful and when powerful cross-referencing software is helping their bottom line. All of this will sort itself out and marketers who use technology wisely will be winners. *Wired* magazine tells us that Acxiom, the country's largest data mining company, will introduce an internet service offering data on 95 percent of the U.S. population, including income level, marital status, and buying habits. As we mentioned in Chapter Four, when Lotus Development Corporation tried to sell this kind of data in 1991, there were so many protests that Lotus withdrew the product. Perhaps people are getting used to the idea that their lives are transparent, or perhaps marketers are learning to use data more responsibly. *Wired* says "Data is a commodity. The true weapon is knowing how to use it." It remains to be seen which companies learn how to use it.[11]

Instead of one-to-one marketing, business owners may have to confront many-to-one marketing as customers use technology to get bids on the items they buy. Priceline.com, for instance, lets customers say what they want and what they'll pay for it. The Internet has given customers more power to initiate and control the purchasing process.

Technology doesn't have to lead a business, it can follow from the overall service plan. Relationship providers need to keep up with technology that affects their area of service so they can remain competitive with other relationship providers as well as the more numerous encounter services. Like CDW which trains its workers at its own training center, companies that work with customers in relationships can guide their employees to higher skills.

Federal Reserve Board Chairman Alan Greenspan credited large investments in computers and other high-tech products with increased productivity in 1999. Productivity increases, he said, allowed the economy to be strong without producing inflation.[12] Effective use of technology makes businesses efficient and creates prosperity.

Providers Need Satisfaction, Too

Encounter businesses don't have to use technology to deskill workers. They can try to keep their workers by giving them some leeway in dealing with customers and helping them to learn about the technology they use. Workers can be included in reengineering efforts and consulted about ways to improve the business.

Hal Rosenbluth of Rosenbluth Travel writes in his book about the necessity of happiness in the workplace: "Cries from corporate America lament a lack of motivation in the workplace, absenteeism, turnover, apathy, lethargy and a host of other evils . . . The origin of these maladies is lack of happiness in the workplace. Without it, the best-planned processes, the finest tools, and most marketable products go to waste. Without it, eventually all else breaks down."[13]

Companies should care about this because it matters to investors. Ernst & Young studied pension and mutual fund managers in 1999 and found that 35 to 40 percent of their portfolio allocation was influenced by nonfinancial factors such as how employees feel about the company and how well employees are trained and compensated, essentially morale issues. The managers who had the greatest accuracy in predicting value were those that relied the heaviest on these factors. This supports the view of those who say happy workers produce happy customers, and happy customers make for a healthy bottom line. Sears has demonstrated the link with statistics showing that for every 5 percent rise of employee satisfaction rating, they get a half percent rise in store revenue.[14] What John Willard Marriott knew intuitively, companies like Rosenbluth Travel and Sears are demonstrating. Pay attention to how you treat workers (all workers—surveying your "real" employees and ignoring your contract workers does not give you an accurate picture of your workplace), and find out how they feel about the company.

Relationship providers, too, need satisfaction to stay on the job. Taking away control over the work reduces worker satisfaction, whether that worker is a doctor or a clerk in a retail shop. There's a lot of evidence of dissatisfaction among doctors, but most are sticking with their profession. A story in The *Wall Street Journal*[15] told of professionals who traded their high-paying careers for more satisfying work as fitness trainers. That's right, fitness trainers! The people cited in the article were a dentist, a restaurant manager, a computer programmer, a lawyer, a teacher, and an accountant. All had abandoned their years of education to work in gyms, where they felt they got more appreciation from clients. Their customers were mainly educated people like themselves, and the relationship these providers established were close and satisfying. The dentist, who must have had control over his former practice, cited the fact that most people hated to see him when he was a dentist, but love to see him now that he is a fitness trainer. Having people really like and appreciate what he does mattered more to him than what he did as a dentist. Fitness training brings in only about $30,000 a year, so these people valued the personal satisfaction so much they were willing to give up much more lucrative work. The lawyer, when asked why he would turn his back on his years of education, replied, "Why throw good time after bad?" People giving up professional careers for fitness training clearly sends a message about the importance of having satisfying work.

Managers need to keep in mind the powerful human need for satisfaction in work. The more educated the worker, the more she will want and expect to have control over her working life. When an organization determines everything for its providers and gives them little control over what they do and how they do it, that organization can expect worker defections. When customers are really grateful for the service, which only happens in relationships, providers derive great satisfaction from their work. For many people, this overrides even low pay. This is something for businesses to think about as they face worker shortages.

Thinking About the Business in a New Way

The usual formula for starting an encounter business will keep on working, especially for people who can take a traditional relationship business and make it into an enhanced encounter. The Massage Bar has done a good job of providing a service most people do not usually get because of the cost and making it accessible and affordable. There is room for more of this kind of business that brings a luxury service to more people by making it into a convenient and inexpensive encounter.

Entrepreneurs should look for changes in any type of service work that has been primarily a relationship business. If whatever has made "chaining" the business unworkable changes, then an opportunity exists. For example, the development of new processes for dry cleaning has eliminated one of the obstacles to building a large chain of dry cleaners, just as the prescription release laws in optometry opened the way to chain eyewear businesses.

Sometimes the entrepreneur herself can bring about the change, as Ruth Owades did with Calyx & Corolla. She had to organize and train flower growers to make flower arrangements to her specifications and work with a standardized delivery process, which they had never done before. These growers had previously only shipped flowers in large orders to wholesalers, and they had never created products meant for the end customer. Ruth Owades built a successful mail order floral delivery business by seeing that she could provide fresher flowers by replacing both the wholesaler and the mom-and-pop flower shops with a well-planned process.

Services that people need but can't necessarily afford are

also ripe for turning into encounters. Medical care has gone this route because the deluxe version is just too expensive. Where the service can be provided by someone who will work for lower pay (nurse-practitioners, for example), there is a potential for retaining a relationship format within an organization. This is a good strategy for a service like medical care where having a relationship is important to customers—usually more important than the actual credentials of the provider. People want to get medical care and advice from someone they know and trust. Forcing people into basically pseudo-relationships with doctors who change with each rushed visit may be a worse strategy than letting people establish relationships with another professional like a registered nurse (RN).

Sometimes a market can open for relationship services among the nonwealthy because of changing conditions. Investment adviser Suze Orman spotted a need for help among ordinary people when she first went to work at Merrill Lynch. As fewer people have company pension plans, more are investing. *USA Today* says Suze saw her coworkers searching out the wealthiest clients, but she thought the people who needed her help were "waitresses, truck drivers, and small business owners." True to the best way to reach more people, Orman eventually put her advice into books and seminars that her target group could afford. Orman's followers trust her, and that's why they're willing to spend money at her seminars and buy her books. They do not think this woman who is "part Dr. Laura, part Dr. Ruth, and part Martha Stewart" would mislead them.[16]

Business owners need to look at where their type of service fits, and if it could be delivered in some other way that would give them a competitive advantage. This willingness to examine the process is what separates business professionals from unsophisticated operations, which tend to do what they've always done, even when it no longer makes sense.

Some types of medical treatments, for example, have been turned into consumer products. Operations to reverse nearsightedness, cosmetic surgery, and procedures/products to regrow hair are examples. Some of these are based on new technology, but all are based on a new way of thinking about the service. Like the eyewear business, some medical procedures can be sold as lifestyle products that improve the quality of life for buyers. Providers need to stress their experience and excellent record at what they do. Taking a cue from Shouldice Hospital, these kinds of services can align the customers' interests with their own by offering service in a pleasant environment and using the strategy of having customers help each other. These organizations may not provide a relationship, but the customer gets an enhanced encounter that meets his needs and brings a nice profit to the business.

Service Success

At the heart of what's been said in these pages is the need to understand that an encounter is not a relationship. This simple insight can change the way your business relates to its customers. Many organizations do not see the distinction between the organization and the actual provider. But that distinction is crucial if you want to have a successful service business. Your customer interacts with a provider; the organization is an abstraction. The organization can try to keep that customer's business over time by providing the service at a reasonable price and offering incentives to its best customers, but this is not a relationship. At its best, it is an enhanced encounter.

We think enhanced encounters can prosper if they respect the customer's privacy and use their customer data only to provide a service faster or in a more convenient way. Too many organizations chasing the same group of lucrative customers can result in those customers getting turned off and perhaps bringing about unwanted government restrictions on data gathering. In a tragedy of the commons, all marketers will find their customers increasingly hostile to any offers. Like columnist Berman, whose letter to Northwest Airlines appeared in Chapter One, customers may react very negatively to suggestions that they have a "relationship" with a company. It is not a relationship they are looking for, but the service they expected to receive. A bribe or a smile will not make the difference when the service itself is flawed. As Berman suggested that Northwest Airlines put its house in order by having its planes take off on time, service businesses need to make sure the customer gets what he thinks he's buying.

Companies should not say they are providing one-to-one service unless they are set up to offer relationships. If the customer always sees the same provider, that is a relationship and it can bring a marketing edge when you point it out. Successful service businesses that offer relationships *do* point it out. CDW, which has built its business by giving clients a personal representative, advertises this advantage in its catalogs. Telecommunications company Coast-to-Coast points it out in its radio commercials ("Larry, Larry, Larry—You always talk to Larry"). If you are in the insurance business and you provide a personal agent, or you sell computers to business and you provide a personal sales representative, or you operate a gym and provide a personal trainer, then you really are doing business one-to-one and need to point it out to potential customers.

If your customers do *not* have a personal representative but deal with whichever representative is free, you have an encounter format. You can turn it into in enhanced encounter in one of two ways:

1. Learn about your customers by retaining basic information about them that helps you serve them more efficiently, and track what they buy; use the data in a responsible way to encourage sales and reward frequent customers
2. Build an image for your company and make information available about what you offer; provide a high-quality service experience that is reliably the same with each customer visit

Relationships businesses need only a limited number of customers and get them mainly by recommendations, but encounter businesses need to find value-added ways to build their customer base. Reach customers by giving them something, not by harassing them.

It's hard to imagine anyone getting angry because a clerk

failed to smile or did not call them by their first name. But make someone wait in line or on hold for a long time, fail to deal with their complaint, make them explain their problem over and over to successive people and they will be angry. Give your providers the empowerment they need so they can deliver what you have promised and can fix it when anyone in the organization screws up or the process doesn't work.

Collect information once rather than making customers provide the same facts over and over. Have more than one key to data about a customer's order or prior transactions so providers can quickly find any customer "in the system." Build in redundancy to accommodate the mistakes that are bound to occur. Make it easy for the customer to access the service and give them options so they can use whatever method they prefer, whether it's a web site, a phone call, or in person. Don't force them to use the method *you* prefer. Train providers so they can answer customers' questions. If you have to put customers on hold or have them wait in line, have a way to let them know about how long it will be before they are served.

Encounters are supposed to be fast and efficient. Remember, customers who are already angry because they have been kept waiting too long are not going to be forgiving and cooperative. The next time they need service, they may go somewhere else if they have a choice. Customers may take out their displeasure on the service provider, which leads to unhappy providers and high turnover.

Following these guidelines will take your business a lot further toward building customer loyalty than false chumminess and forced smiles.

Because personal relationships are the pattern for every kind of service business, business relationships will always exist. They are as natural as a backyard conversation with a neighbor, or a lunch hour shared with a friend. In modern parlance, people get customers through networking—talking to people and meeting people through other people. While well-established chain businesses service millions of customers, much of business is still personal, between people who meet and talk and come to trust one another. When getting it right really matters, customers want to deal with someone they trust. Once upon a time, everyone got all their services in relationships because towns were small, and everyone knew everyone else. There was no need for creating brand images, or mass advertising, or having telemarketers call people with special offers. Our population and our cities are too big for that now, and most services have shifted into encounters because that is the most efficient way to reach a lot of people with a service. Relationships have become scarcer, but that makes them all the more valuable. Relationships can meet the customers' needs, whatever those needs are. At the same time, the relationship itself can be a source of enjoyment and satisfaction to both customer and provider. Like the fitness trainers whose customers love them, any relationship provider gets more than money for her service. Relationships add to the richness of life and help people keep in touch with genuine human emotions. It is a business strategy that will always work with the right provider and the right service.

Conclusion

If you wanted to know which format is right for your business, you should have gathered enough information now to answer the question yourself. Relationships work. Encounters work. Enhanced encounters work, too, but pseudo-relationships that offer only smiles and offers based on incomplete data can fail if you mistake them for a relationship. As a business owner, you may have a preference for one strategy over the other, but some types of service work better in relationships, and some services (fewer and fewer) aren't likely to make it as chain encounter businesses. In other cases, chaining is the whole reason for the business.

Services are making our country prosperous. Now take this new way of looking at service businesses, and use it to provide others with a worthwhile service. In so doing, you will get your share of the wealth.

Notes

1. "Discounters Put the Press On Area Dry Cleaners," *Washington Post*, February 19, 1999.

2. E-mail note to employees from Ford Chairman Alex Trotman, November 1998.
3. Boyle, Alan. "A Wired Trip to the Top of the World," MSNBC, May 5, 1999.
4. Ballon, Marc. "What Level Playing Field?" *Inc.*, May 1999.
5. Ritzer, George. *The McDonaldization of Society* (Pine Forge Press, 1996).
6. Gutek, B.A., A.D. Bhappu, M.A. Liao-Troth, and B. Cherry. "Distinguishing Between Service Relationships and Encounters," *Journal of Applied Psychology*, 1999.
7. Adamson, Loch. "Where the Money Is: Annual Ranking of America's Richest Towns and What It Takes to Buy Your Way In," *Worth*, June 1999.
8. Girard, Fred. "Frustrated Utley Battles for Benefits," *Detroit News*, May 16, 1999.
9. Berry, Leonard L., A. Parasuraman, and Valerie A. Zeithaml. "Improving Service Quality in America: Lessons Learned," *Academy of Management Executive*, 8:2 (1994).
10. Ibid.
11. "40 Companies Driving the New Economy," *Wired*, June 1999.
12. Associated Press, "Greenspan: Good News With Caution," as reported in *USA Today*, April 5, 1999.
13. Rosenbluth, Hal F. and Diane McFerrin Peters. *The Customer Comes Second and Other Secrets of Exceptional Service* (New York: Quill-William Morrow, 1992).
14. Molpus, David. Ernst & Young study and Sears statistics reported on "Morning Edition," National Public Radio, May 18, 1999.
15. "They Left Professions for a True Calling as Personal Trainers," *Wall Street Journal,* February 25, 1999.
16. "From Waitress to Wall Street: Bootstrap Success Lessons Lead Masses To Oracle of Orman," *USA Today*, May 24, 1999.

Index

About the Authors

Barbara A. Gutek is McClelland professor in the Department of Management and Policy in the Eller College of Business and Public Administration at the University of Arizona, where she was also department head from 1993 to 1999. Dr. Gutek has been a consultant to companies and government, and serves as an expert witness in cases involving employment issues. In 1994 she was awarded the American Psychological Association (APA) Committee on Women and Leadership award, the APA Division 35 Heritage Award, and the Academy of Management (Women in Management) Sage Research Award. She is the author or editor of 10 books.

Dr. Gutek is available as a speaker or consultant on service delivery and organizational effectiveness. Her original insights on the nature of service transactions form the basis of the concepts in *The Brave New Service Strategy.*

Theresa Welsh has worked in the business world as a writer and editor for over fifteen years. Through her own consulting company, Explainamation, she currently is editor of two internal customer support newsletters at Ford Motor Company. Working with managers, she has helped write business plans and service level agreements for organizations at Ford. She has also created many business presentations and taught classes in how to improve presentation visuals. She has many free-lance writing credits.

Ms. Welsh is available as a business and technical writer, for creating presentations, or for consultation on the ideas in

The Brave New Service Strategy. She lives in the Detroit, Michigan area with her husband, teenage daughter, and two cats. Her resume is online at www.explainamation.com.

Contact either author with your comments on *The Brave New Service Strategy* at www.explainamation.com/service or send e-mail to Theresa@explainamation.com.